Natural Wonders of
India & Nepal

NH
NEW
HOLLAND

TEXT BY BISWAJIT ROY CHOWDHURY,

Natural Wonders of
India & Nepal

BUROSHIVA DASGUPTA & INDIRA BHATTACHARYA

First published in 2002 by New Holland Publishers Ltd

London • Cape Town • Sydney • Auckland

86 Edgware Road	80 McKenzie Street	14 Aquatic Drive	218 Lake Road
London	Cape Town	Frenchs Forest	North Cote
W2 2EA	8001	NSW 2086	Auckland
United Kingdom	South Africa	Australia	New Zealand

www.newhollandpublishers.com

2 4 6 8 10 9 7 5 3 1

ISBN 1 85974 523 7

Distributed in India by
CBS PUBLISHERS & DISTRIBUTERS
4596 / 1-A, 11 Darya Ganj
New Delhi - 110 002 (India)

Commissioning Editor: Claudia dos Santos
Managing Editor: Simon Pooley
Editor: Mariëlle Renssen
Designer: Lyndall du Toit
Cartography: John Loubser, Carl Germishuys, Elaine Fick,
Ryan Africa and Nicole Engeler
Picture research: Karla Kik, Bronwyn Allies
Production: Myrna Collins
Consultant: Mandip Singh Soin (New Delhi)
Reproduction by Unifoto (Pty) Ltd
Printed and bound in Singapore by Tien Wah Press (Pte) Ltd

PUBLISHER'S NOTE

For ease of reference by the general reader, species are for the most part referred to by
their common, as opposed to scientific, names throughout this book. In some instances,
however, they have had to be used; in a number of others (where they are likely to
prove helpful) both the common and scientific names are given.
The maps published in the book are intended as 'locators' only; detailed,
large-scale maps should be consulted when planning a trip.
Although the publishers have made every effort to ensure that the information contained
in this book was correct at the time of going to press, they accept no responsibility for
any loss, injury or inconvenience sustained by any person using this book.

Page 1: The Dhaulagiri mountains in Nepal form part of the mighty Himalayan range.

Pages 2–3: Tourists on an elephant safari in Nepal's Chitwan National Park.

Right: Sambhar at Raj Bagh lake in Ranthambhore National Park, Rajasthan, with the
18th-century pavilion in the background.

Overleaf: *Rhododendron arboreum* is a flowering tree indigenous to India and common
in the Himalaya. Rhododendron species create spectacular displays on the
hillsides between March and May.

CONTENTS

FOREWORD 9

INTRODUCTION 11

Regional Map 18

WESTERN HIMALAYA 21

Dachigam National Park 23

Great Himalayan National Park 27

Corbett National Park and Tiger Reserve 31

Dudhwa National Park and Tiger Reserve 35

NORTHEASTERN HIMALAYA 39

Namdapha National Park
and Tiger Reserve 41

Manas National Park and Tiger Reserve 43

Kaziranga National Park 47

Keibul Lamjao National Park 51

Dampa Tiger Reserve 53

Balphakram National Park 55

Buxa National Park and Tiger Reserve 59

Gorumara National Park 61

Jaldapara Wildlife Sanctuary 63

GANGETIC INDIA 67

Simlipal National Park and
Tiger Reserve 69

Palamau Sanctuary and Tiger Reserve 73

CENTRAL INDIA 77

Tadoba National Park and Tiger Reserve 79

Melghat National Park and Tiger Reserve 83

Pench National Park and Tiger Reserve 85

Kanha National Park and Tiger Reserve 89

Bandhavgarh National Park
and Tiger Reserve 95

Madhav National Park 99

SEMI-DESERT INDIA 105

Ranthambhore National Park and
Tiger Reserve 107

Keoladeo Ghana National Park 111

Sariska National Park and Tiger Reserve 113

COASTAL INDIA 117

Sunderbans National Park and
Tiger Reserve 119

Chilika Lake 123

Middle Button Island National Park 127

Dhangadhra Wildlife Sanctuary 129

Gir National Park 131

Bhagwan Mahavir Wildlife Sanctuary
and Molem National Park 137

PENINSULAR INDIA 141

Ranganathittoo Waterbird Sanctuary 143

Nagarhole National Park and
Wildlife Sanctuary 145

Bandipur National Park and
Tiger Reserve 149

Mudumalai National Park and
Wildlife Sanctuary 151

Vedanthangal Waterbird Sanctuary 155

Mundanthurai-Kalakkad Wildlife
Sanctuary 157

Periyar National Park and Tiger Reserve 159

Nagarjunasagar Srisailam Tiger Reserve 163

NEPAL HIMALAYA 165

Royal Chitwan National Park 167

Sagarmatha (Everest) National Park 169

Useful Information and Addresses 172

Index 172

FOREWORD

India is one of the twelve countries in the world considered to reflect 'megadiversity', and it alone accounts for nearly seven per cent of the world's biodiversity, having as it does a broad range of ecosystems and species within its seven recognized biogeographic zones. Its flora comprises 15,000 flowering plants, some 13 per cent of which are endemic and represent six per cent of the world's total. India's faunal diversity is also high, with its 1178 bird species representing 14 per cent of the world's total. An amazing 75 per cent of all medicines in India are derived from plant species, many of them harvested in the wild. It is unfortunate, however, that as many as 3000 to 4000 plant and over 250 animal species are endangered and in need of immediate protection.

India is the second-largest most populated country in the world, with one billion people, and the survival of more than one-fifth of these people is linked to the forests. This, coupled with a very large livestock population, is regarded as the most important issue affecting conservation throughout the land. The frequent grazing of cattle on forest lands, the cutting of trees for firewood and timber, and the extracting of non-timber forest products necessary for the subsistence of the human population are widely practised. The local people, who often have limited, or no, rights have no alternatives or little incentive to find alternatives for sustenance. India is passing through a critical stage – and sustainable use of all its resources is the demand of the day. Conservation efforts are now under tremendous pressure as the development of infrastructure, rather, is given topmost priority and more land is the most immediate need. In spite of these pressures, we have been able to manage our key wildlife species like Tiger, Rhinoceros and Asiatic Elephant fairly well. The Tiger is subject to maximum conservation pressures because of international demand, and we are determined to save it from extinction. Our management practices cannot be compared with any other country because local sentiments and customs are involved in conservation issues – our traditions hold a special respect for wildlife and our laws do not allow the consumptive use of wild animals or any of their body parts.

This megadiversity of India's wildlife and the complexity of the conservation issues make it extremely difficult for anyone to write a comprehensive and up-to-date account of Indian fauna: the data keeps changing and although efforts have been made, in most cases the writings have focused on subjects in which the authors specialize, while books of a general nature are often outdated or incomplete. This book by the present authors has attempted a fair cross-section of Indian flora and fauna, covering significant national parks and wetland sanctuaries. I hope it will prove to be a useful record of India's (and Nepal's) valuable natural heritage.

P K Sen
Director, Tiger Conservation Project (TCP)
WWF India

INTRODUCTION

No region in the world can match the subcontinent of India in its variety in terms of culture, climate, vegetation, and wildlife. Although the country occupies two per cent of the earth's total land mass, five per cent of all known living organisms exist here: that is, over 15,000 plant species, 1200 bird species, and 500 species of mammal.

Culturally, India has always, over the centuries, taken a caring approach to its wildlife. Since the early days of Vedic civilization (ancient Indo-European settlers who lived around 3000–1500BC and are believed to be responsible for the traditions immortalized in the Vedas, the sacred writings of Hinduism) animals have served a role as vehicles for Indian gods and goddesses. India's spiritual heritage is closely linked to the *Aranyakas*, or the forest texts, so called because many of the incantations or mantras in the texts required the solitude of the forest for meditation. Two 'religions', or philosophies, that have their origins in India – Buddhism, founded in North India by Siddhartha, and Jainism, of ancient Hindu origin – promulgated teachings that speak of preserving animals. Civilizations of earlier times adopted the Tiger as the national animal, and it remains so today.

The destruction of wildlife is a more recent phenomenon. The hunting of animals began with the *mughals* in the 16th century when hunts on horseback or elephant-back became a sporting event. But the real killing began in the early 19th century; the *nawab* (wealthy Muslim princes or landowners) and maharajas were addicted to this as a sport. Most of the maharajas had their own reserved hunting areas into which general hunters were not allowed. The British who followed regarded Tiger hunting as a mark of bravery and valour. During the Victorian era, John Yule slew 400 tigers in the space of 25 years; 500 were killed by the Maharaja of Rewa, 433 by Maharaja Shamsur Jung and 300 by the prime minister of Nepal. Jim Corbett (of British descent but born in India) was famous for shooting the man-eating Tigers and Leopards in the Kumayun area of Uttaranchal and was worshipped by the villagers for saving their lives. Eventually, influenced by a forest officer, F W Champion, Corbett hung up his guns to become a pioneer for the conservation of India's wildlife.

With the modern concepts of conservation introduced after Independence (1950), these game parks set up by the early rulers were subsequently restyled as national parks and sanctuaries, and many of the maharajas' private hunting grounds were turned into protected tiger reserves. New parks were rapidly created, with the result that India today has over 300 national parks and sanctuaries falling under the comprehensive Wildlife (Protection) Act of 1972.

Left: A detail portraying the 10-armed goddess, Durga (wife of Siva), astride a tiger – she is believed to embody the tiger's natural feline power.

Opposite: From the Kankwari fort in the Sariska Tiger Reserve, Rajasthan, there are encompassing views across the dry deciduous vegetation of the valley.

Below: An 1899 photograph of a tiger shoot showing the Nizam (ruler) of Hyderabad surrounded by guards. Hyderabad was a princely state founded in the late 16th century.

Top to bottom: Animal species unique to the Indian subcontinent, thus unaffected by zoogeographical links from other continental masses, include the Sloth Bear, Blackbuck, Nilgai (Blue Bull) and Chausingha (Four-horned Antelope).

An exceptional diversity of fauna

The position of the Indian subcontinent has led to its unique biogeographical heritage (which concerns the link between living organisms and their environment), blessing India with an exceptional variety of wildlife. Three different continental faunas – Ethiopian, Palaearctic (a zoogeographical region encompassing Europe, Africa north of the Sahara, much of Asia and north Himalaya), and Indo-Chinese – have converged here, making India a haven for wildlife lovers and researchers.

Formation of the Himalayas

The Indian land mass has, during the course of its long history, undergone (at least) three great upheavals. It was German scientist Alfred Wagner, a meteorologist and geophysicist, who constructed the theory of a mega-continent named Pangaea existing about 300 million years ago during the Carboniferous period, and surrounded by what was the original ocean, Panthalossa. His hypothesis put forward that Pangaea broke up into two supercontinental masses, namely Gondwana, which comprised South America, Africa, Antarctica, India and Australia, and Laurasia (also known as Angaraland) comprising North America, Europe and Asia excluding the Indian subcontinent. These two supercontinents were separated by the Tethys Sea which over time received river-borne deposits originating from the land masses. These deposits gradually became compacted and stratified on the floor of the Tethys.

Around 55 million years ago, during the Tertiary period – the first period of the Cenozoic era which lasted for 69 million years – there was a northward advancement of the Gondwana land mass which was resisted by Laurasia's land mass and sedimentary rock from the floor of the Tethys was pushed up to form the present-day Himalayas. This formation is still ongoing today.

In this Tertiary period, peninsular India is thought to have been joined with Africa, and the massive Himalayan range was submerged by sea. India's Ethiopian, Palaearctic and Indo-Chinese links can be traced back to this prehistoric time and the ensuing land upheavals. The Ethiopian zoogeographical links (the relationship between animals and their environment) are represented by the Chinkara (Indian Gazelle), Striped Hyena and Ratel (honey badger); the Palaearctic by the Lynx, Wolf, Markhor (a member of the goat family) and Hangul, or Kashmir Stag; and the Indo-Chinese by the Red Panda and Musk Deer.

Links with fauna of Peninsular Malaysia (i.e. Malayan) are evident in the Indian Elephant, Hoolock Gibbon (an ape species), Mouse Deer, and several goat antelope species. Genera that are indigenous to India are the Sloth Bear, Blackbuck (Indian Antelope), a four-horned antelope known as Chausingha, and Nilgai (Blue Bull).

The distribution of Indian wildlife depends largely on migratory patterns and the varying climatic conditions throughout the country. Experts have established that the Indo-Chinese and Malayan fauna types occur in abundance in the eastern, or Assam Himalaya, regions while the Ethiopian types are more plentiful in the western regions. Statistics reveal that wildlife in western India and those in the northeastern state of Assam share only about 33 per cent of common species. The animals of these two regions differ greatly because of the different continental influences of their origins. In peninsular India, on the other hand, the migration of these two fauna types has been more equal.

Divergent Climatic Conditions

Differences in rainfall are largely responsible for greatly influencing the distribution of India's flora and fauna: for example, the meagre 100mm (4in) a year in the Thar deserts of Rajasthan State in the northwest compared with 5000mm (200in) in the Cheranpunji hills in Assam to the east. The vast Himalayan range stretches for 2400km (1500 miles) from the gorges of the river Indus in the northwest to the roaring Brahmaputra in the east. The mighty rivers of India play an important role in nurturing and sustaining life. Besides those rising in the Himalaya, the rivers of peninsular India, such as the Narmada, Godavari and Tapti, have their source in the central Vindhya and Satpura mountain ranges or the Western Ghats. The Indian subcontinent's massive drainage system carries about 1.7 million cubic metres (60 million cubic feet) of water a year.

The country's dry-air, high-altitude areas occur in the great Himalayan mountain heights which soar hundreds

Below: The formation of the massive Himalaya began roughly 55 million years ago during the meeting of the two supercontinents Gondwana and Laurasia, when buckling and folding of the earth's crust thrust up a series of craggy mountains.

Above and right: Two faces of the Thar desert, Rajasthan. The rising hot winds of the desert are the initial catalyst in the succession of winds that bring the monsoon from the Arabian Sea and Indian Ocean. Desert areas bordering on wetland become flooded during the onset of the rains (right).

of metres above the perpetual snow line, while the lower hills, or the 'terai' (meaning 'grassy foothills') region, consist of both tropical and temperate forests. The terai extends from Uttar Pradesh and Nepal to northern West Bengal and Assam. It supports 'seas' of tall Elephant Grass interspersed with tracts of dense forest. Large parts of it have now been cleared for cultivation. The true forest zone of the Himalaya extends from the northwestern Kashmir region to the central Asian kingdom of Bhutan in the northeast. The eastern Himalaya suffer the severest monsoons, contrasting greatly with the high-altitude deserts of Ladakh to the west.

The Indian Desert

India's desert region is an extension of the Thar desert which lies mostly in Pakistan and forms the arid plains of western Rajasthan State. West of the Aravalli mountain range this desert is known as Marwar ('place of death') yet it is the most densely populated of deserts throughout the world. This tract slopes away westward to the Indus valley in Pakistan and southward to the Rann of Kutch. It has three geomorphologic subdivisions, namely Marusthali, Bagar, and Rohi.

The Marusthali region to the west and along the Pakistan border is covered with longitudinal sandy dunes called *dhria*. There are no perennial streams although lakes, called *bhands*, are formed during the wet season and persist during the dry period. The Rajasthan Bagar is a belt of steppe lands stretching westwards from the foot of the Aravalli and merging into the Marusthali zone. The northern and central parts comprise the Rohi region which features large patches of more fertile tracts.

The rising hot winds of the desert, near Mount Abu, are the first of the complex chain of winds that finally bring the monsoon rains from the Arabian Sea and Indian Ocean sweeping across the Indian subcontinent.

The monsoons

These occur once a year in northern India (usually from June to September, although in the northeast they can arrive as early as April/May) and twice annually in parts of the south – once during the monsoon season of the north and again in winter (from October to February).

English astronomer Edmund Halley explains that the Asiatic monsoons occur because of the thermal contrasts of land and sea which determine the wind direction. The humid southwest monsoon winds blow from the Indian Ocean and Arabian Sea, first towards peninsular India, then gradually towards the Himalayan range, causing heavy rains particularly on the Gangetic plains and in the northeast. The 'retreating' monsoon rains, called the northeast monsoon, consist of dry, cooler land winds that blow seaward to the Bay of Bengal and cause rain over the coastal plains of the eastern peninsular regions and the Andaman and Nicobar islands. Most national parks in India close during the monsoon months.

Management of India's Natural Areas

The complex man/land/animal issue is constantly at the forefront of any matters concerning wildlife management in India – and it was only after India's independence (1947) that the subject garnered focused attention. In considering management of wildlife, the Indian Board for Wildlife set themselves the following challenges:

- to manage wildlife in such a way that it serves human recreational needs (these encompassed tourism, wildlife enthusiasts, nature lovers) without causing damage to the environment
- keeping the ecosystem in balance.

The latter, particularly, is fraught with problems such as an increasing human population, encroachment on wildlife territory and the consequent shrinking of their habitat, declining food resources, and a decrease in wild animals through poaching and disease introduced via domestic animals. This situation is exacerbated by:

- the plundering of the forests' natural resources for industry and advancing technology
- the felling of timber, plants and shrubs for fodder, firewood and domestic construction work
- Land clearing for human settlement, agriculture, mining, road-building, the creation of dams and reservoirs
- Competition between domestic animals and wildlife for food.

In an effort to analyze the value of wildlife to Indian society, the future management of wildlife was determined according to the following values: ethical, cultural, ecological, scientific, aesthetic and recreational, commercial and economic, and wildlife preservation.

The establishment of protected areas

The broad term protected area is applied to the establishment of game reserves, sanctuaries, national parks and biosphere reserves with the intention of protecting wildlife and its habitat.

The Wildlife Protection Act of 1972 opened the way for the creation of these protected areas: the state governments may constitute national parks and sanctuaries while central government has more powers in terms of forests and wildlife. The aim when proclaiming protected areas was firstly, to try to ensure adequate representation of all biogeographic regions of the country, and secondly, to try to provide corridors between major protected areas.

By mid-1987, 372 sanctuaries and 54 national parks combined formed 3.3 per cent of the total geographical area of the country. In 1984 a report by the Wildlife Institute of India recorded that efforts would be made to increase the protected areas in India to 4.6 per cent of the country's geographical area (i.e. national parks 1.5 per cent and sanctuaries 3.1 per cent).

Wildlife sanctuaries

Sanctuaries can be constituted (by state government) for the following reasons: faunal, floral, ecological, zoological or geomorphological (structure, origin and topography of earth's crust), for the purpose of protecting, propagating or developing the environment or the wildlife therein.

Once an area is considered for sanctuary status, investigation is undertaken into the rights of any persons inhabiting the land being demarcated. The following conditions then apply to the sanctuary:

- Once the rights have been determined and settled, no person is permitted to move freely within the sanctuary unless given permission by the relevant authority.
- Permanent residents are permitted to remain within specific settlements, but are legally bound to help in the event of fires, report injured or dying animals, inform the authority if offences are detected and help to apprehend the offenders.
- The Chief Wildlife Warden may authorize any person to enter the sanctuary for study, research, or tourism free of charge or for a prescribed fee.
- Carrying weapons or explosives is not permitted unless permission has been granted by the relevant authority.
- Lighting of fires is not permitted unless permission has been granted.

Above: India's wildlife habitat is being encroached on by a burgeoning human population and the felling of forest timber to fulfil daily needs is a constant threat.

Left: This park sign is testament to increased efforts in recent years towards wildlife conservation; as a result the cat population in India has increased from 1700 to 4000.

Above: The brilliant plumage of this pheasant species, the Satyr Tragopan (*Tragopan satyra*), makes it difficult to miss in the forest understorey.

Below: It is not an unlikely event for tourists to encounter Tiger on the main route in Ranthambhore National Park.

- Grazing and fishing may be regulated by the relevant authority in order to conserve wildlife and its habitat.
- No felling of a commercial nature is permitted within sanctuary boundaries.

National parks

A national park can be constituted within or without a sanctuary, and the same values used to determine the establishment of sanctuaries apply here.

Once an area is constituted a national park, the following is not permitted within its boundaries:

- exploitation, destruction or removal of wildlife habitat or forest resources, any harming or killing of wild animals plus byproducts such as skins, horns, or trophies.
- digging, blasting or quarrying operations.
- carrying firearms and explosives within the park.
- forest villages are required to be shifted to areas out of the boundaries; no permanent residents are permissible in a national park.
- any grazing of cattle.
- the Chief Wildlife Warden may issue special permission for the capture of animals for scientific study/research.

In addition to the above, a special order may be issued by the Chief Wildlife Warden to prevent humans from entering specific parts of the national park, for example, what is known as the core area where no interference whatsoever is permitted.

Biosphere reserves

These are protected areas in terrestrial, coastal and marine environments that have been internationally recognized for their conservation value and potential to further scientific knowledge and human skills, thus supporting sustainable development. Once potential biosphere reserves have been selected and demarcated, both the central and the relevant state government are required to take the legal process further. To date, out of the number of biosphere reserves that have been created by central government, only a few have been legally notified by the relevant state government.

Project Tiger and conservation efforts

Special conservation programmes have been established in certain sanctuaries and national parks to protect a particular animal species, the most important of which is Project Tiger. Because the number of Tigers had fallen so dramatically by 1972, Project Tiger was launched by the central government of India, aided by the World Wildlife Fund (WWF). These special reserves set up within sanctuaries and national parks to protect this feline species are funded by central government. This project has seen relative success over the years.

At the turn of the 20th century, it was estimated that there were 30,000 to 40,000 Tiger in India. Thereafter, due to urbanization, the destruction of habitat and ruthless poaching, the Tiger population started to decline. In 1972, a Tiger census was conducted throughout India and conservationists were startled to discover that the total count had dwindled to just over 1700; the World Wildlife Fund in the USA stepped forward with funds and Project Tiger was launched by the government of India in 1973, initially with nine national parks and sanctuaries. The main objective of Project Tiger was to save this cat from extinction. Today 27 national parks and sanctuaries fall under Project Tiger, which achieved considerable success up till 1990 when the total number of Tiger had steadily increased to 5000. However, the demand for Tiger bones (ground and used in wine, believed to have special healing properties) in China, Taiwan, Korea and other South Asian countries led to rampant poaching, causing the population to drop to about 3000. Because of strict measures being reinforced in recent years, the population has again risen to nearly 4000.

There are other conservation moves in India such as Project Elephant and Project Rhino as well as certain nongovernmental organizations like the Ranthambore Foundation, WWF-India, and the Nature Environment and Wildlife Society who are active in organizing programmes to preserve the country's natural treasures – although these efforts are far from adequate.

This book is an attempt to outline the wealth of India's wildlife, but with the full awareness that it is far from complete since it is impossible to dwell, for example, upon its 20,000 species of insect, 2000 species of butterfly, 142 frog species, and over 700 fish species.

Visiting the parks

India is a hot and humid country except for the Himalayan regions. It would seem, therefore, preferable to visit India in winter. However, in the states of Uttar Pradesh (this has recently been split into two, the new state being Uttaranchal), Madhya Pradesh, Bihar (also recently split into two, with the new state officially named Jharkand) and Rajasthan, the best time to visit is peak summer (March to May) when water sources have dried and only a few waterholes remain, thus attracting the wildlife. And with the drying of the grasslands, visibility, too, improves. In the northeastern states, however, the monsoon arrives in April so it is advisable to visit these areas in winter (November to mid-March). The Himalayan region during winter is gripped by an icy cold, so here, summer is best. In some places of eastern India, like the Sundarbans marshland where rivers are the only mode of conveyance, the water becomes turbulent from March to May so it is not advisable to visit in the summer; the winter months of November through February are good. Southern India experiences two monsoons and it is best to visit these parks from March to June and September to October.

Permits and entry fees

Generally, most of the national parks and sanctuaries require no special permit. To visit the northeastern states of Arunachal, Mizoram, Nagaland, Manipur and Sikkim, however, permission needs to be sought, in advance, from the Ministry of Home Affairs in New Delhi or the nearest Indian embassy or high commission. Securing permits is an uncomplicated procedure.

Entry fees to India's parks and sanctuaries are collected at the gates. Generally for foreigners, fees per person vary between 50 and 200 rupees, while entry fees for vehicles vary between 100 and 500 rupees (fees change from time to time but the increase is negligible). Many parks allow self-driven petrol vehicles, but in most parks visitors need to be accompanied by a local guide.

Private hotels are located near most of the parks, although in the much more remote northeastern region, there is seldom any private accommodation. Here, forest rest houses are the only places to stay.

Left: Domesticated Indian (Asian) Elephants are used as a form of transport through the parks.

Below: An air of mystique permeates many of India's parks – embalmed in the ruined palaces and hunting lodges of the early wealthy maharajas who would hunt in the land's fertile forests.

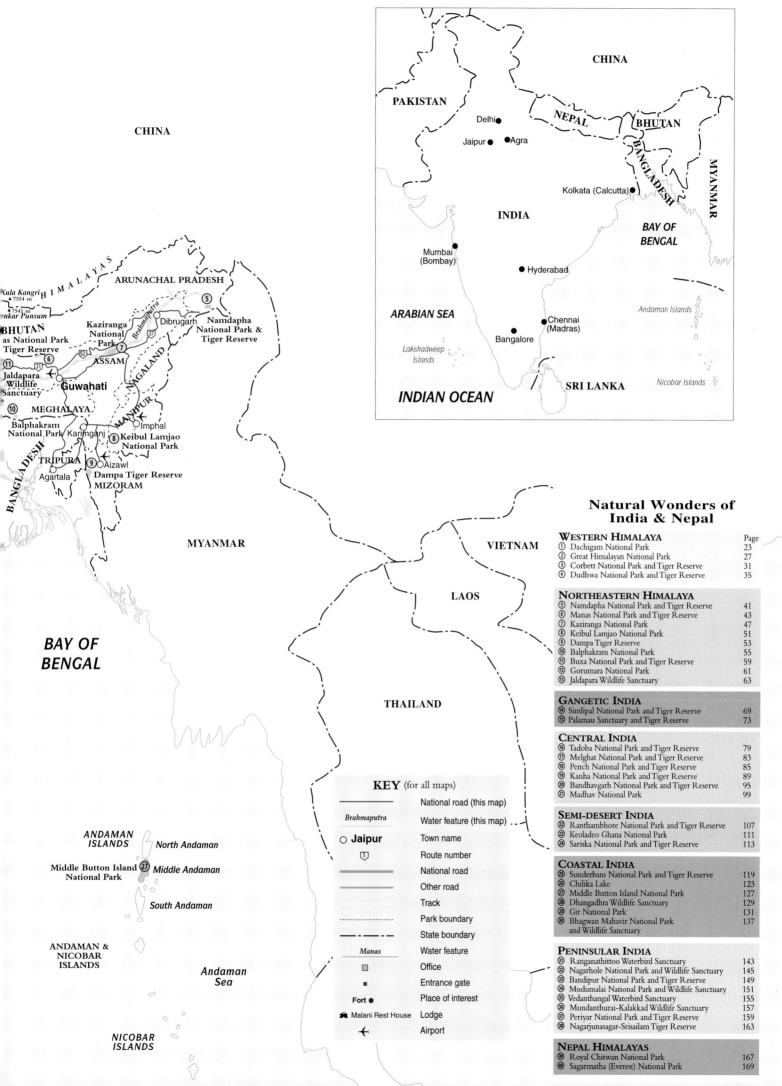

Natural Wonders of India & Nepal

WESTERN HIMALAYA — Page
1. Dachigam National Park — 23
2. Great Himalayan National Park — 27
3. Corbett National Park and Tiger Reserve — 31
4. Dudhwa National Park and Tiger Reserve — 35

NORTHEASTERN HIMALAYA
5. Namdapha National Park and Tiger Reserve — 41
6. Manas National Park and Tiger Reserve — 43
7. Kaziranga National Park — 47
8. Keibul Lamjao National Park — 51
9. Dampa Tiger Reserve — 53
10. Balphakram National Park — 55
11. Buxa National Park and Tiger Reserve — 59
12. Gorumara National Park — 61
13. Jaldapara Wildlife Sanctuary — 63

GANGETIC INDIA
14. Simlipal National Park and Tiger Reserve — 69
15. Palamau Sanctuary and Tiger Reserve — 73

CENTRAL INDIA
16. Tadoba National Park and Tiger Reserve — 79
17. Melghat National Park and Tiger Reserve — 83
18. Pench National Park and Tiger Reserve — 85
19. Kanha National Park and Tiger Reserve — 89
20. Bandhavgarh National Park and Tiger Reserve — 95
21. Madhav National Park — 99

SEMI-DESERT INDIA
22. Ranthambhore National Park and Tiger Reserve — 107
23. Keoladeo Ghana National Park — 111
24. Sariska National Park and Tiger Reserve — 113

COASTAL INDIA
25. Sunderbans National Park and Tiger Reserve — 119
26. Chilika Lake — 123
27. Middle Button Island National Park — 127
28. Dhangadhra Wildlife Sanctuary — 129
29. Gir National Park — 131
30. Bhagwan Mahavir National Park and Wildlife Sanctuary — 137

PENINSULAR INDIA
31. Ranganathittoo Waterbird Sanctuary — 143
32. Nagarhole National Park and Wildlife Sanctuary — 145
33. Bandipur National Park and Tiger Reserve — 149
34. Mudumalai National Park and Wildlife Sanctuary — 151
35. Vedanthangal Waterbird Sanctuary — 155
36. Mundanthurai-Kalakkad Wildlife Sanctuary — 157
37. Periyar National Park and Tiger Reserve — 159
38. Nagarjunasagar-Srisailam Tiger Reserve — 163

NEPAL HIMALAYAS
39. Royal Chitwan National Park — 167
40. Sagarmatha (Everest) National Park — 169

KEY (for all maps)

——	National road (this map)
Brahmaputra	Water feature (this map)
○ **Jaipur**	Town name
⑤	Route number
——	National road
——	Other road
——	Track
·········	Park boundary
—·—·—	State boundary
Manas	Water feature
▪	Office
▪	Entrance gate
Fort ●	Place of interest
🏠 Malani Rest House	Lodge
✈	Airport

WESTERN HIMALAYA

India's northern boundary has been created by the mighty Himalayan mountain range. The mountains falling within the Indian border are divided into two zoogeographical regions: Western and North-eastern Himalaya. States falling into the western region are Jammu and Kashmir, Himachal Pradesh and the new state of Uttaranchal. The lowest elevation is 400 metres (1300 feet), rising to an altitude of more than 7600 metres (25,000 feet) on the higher ridges. Notable high peaks here are Nanda Devi, Trishul, Panchachulli, and Nanda Ghunti, while major rivers include the Indus, Ganges, Yamuna, Kosi, Beas, Sutlej and Jhelum.

Flora is naturally influenced by altitude and climate. On the foothills of the Western Himalayas the area is known as Patlidun ('patli' literally translates as 'slender' and 'dun' a Himalayan 'valley', combining to denote 'foothills' – in other words, smaller in size). It comprises tracts of terai (several forest tree/shrub species typical of the lower foothills) and bhabar (forest species typical of the upper foothills). Cooler temperatures due to increasing altitude give rise to coniferous trees – various pine species, junipers, and Silver Fir. The alpine region of the higher altitudes consists mostly of trees such as Chir Pine (*Pinus roxburghi*), willow and birch. Here, the minimum temperature often drops below freezing, and some of these areas remain snow-bound all year round. In summer maximum temperatures reach 35°C (95°F) while winter lows are generally 3°C (37°F). Summer (April to June) is therefore preferable for visitors to a park such as Dachigam, which lies within the snow line.

Fauna also varies according to altitude. The Patlidun area is inhabited by more traditional species such as Indian Elephant, Indian Bison (Gaur) and Sloth Bear, but on the higher mountain ridges, more exotic animals can be seen such as the Serow and Grey Goral of the goat-antelope family; mountain-inhabiting sheep; and two wild Himalayan goat species, Markhor and Himalayan Tahr.

Significant preserves of the Western Himalaya include Kashmir's Dachigam National Park, Himachal Pradesh's Great Himalayan National Park, Corbett National Park in Uttaranchal and Dudhwa National Park in Uttar Pradesh.

Above right: Red Lace-wing Butterfly (*Cethosia biblis*).

Left: Treks on the western side of Nanda Devi include the famous Valley of Flowers.

DACHIGAM NATIONAL PARK

Sanctuary to the rare Hangul

The scenic splendour of Kashmir has always drawn tourists, naturalists and trekkers from all over the world to the region. Conifers such as Blue Pine, Chinar and junipers, and oaks, willows, poplars and birch create vibrant colours that change with the seasons. Autumn (fall) arrives with brilliant russet shades. The gold and crimson-red of the Chinar's foliage, in particular, and the sunlight filtering through the leaves of these forest trees while crystal-clear streams gush down from upper ridges create a magnificent vista.

Srinagar, a city in north India and the gateway to many major trekking routes in the Himalaya, is the capital of the state of Kashmir and Jammu. Dal lake, situated in the northeast of Srinagar, is fed by Dachigam's Daghwan River.

The national park is roughly rectangular in shape. With a length of 23 kilometres (14 miles) and a width of 8 kilometres (5 miles), its total area is 142 square kilometres (55 square miles). Dachigam was proclaimed a sanctuary in 1951, and it was upgraded to national park status in 1981.

The park consists of two sectors: Upper Dachigam, which lies in the higher reaches on the eastern side and makes up two-thirds of the entire area, and Lower Dachigam in the west. The beautiful Daghwan River flows across Lower Dachigam through a shrub-covered rocky ravine. Mulberry trees, willows and oaks are predominant in Dachigam's lower reaches, an area of thick undergrowth, while Blue Pine, juniper and birch and thinning undergrowth exist in the upper region. Several fire lines exist, and these are cleared every March, helping increase visibility of wildlife in the park.

Where the Hangul roam

Dachigam harbours the last, rare herds of the Kashmir Stag, known locally as Hangul. Related to the Red Deer of Europe, the Hangul's name is derived from the local chestnut, called *han* in Kashmir. Hangul are characterized by their branched antlers and the white patch on their rump. When autumn is behind them, the Hangul deer leave Upper Dachigam (they migrate here every summer to graze). Returning to the Lower Dachigam forest in winter for their rutting season, the calls of the males reverberate through the area. Their calls serve to reinforce the male hierarchy, and the stags can often be seen confronting one another. It has been established that the larger males gather and mate with the females before moving on to the slightly higher slopes to rest and feed.

Sighting the Hangul herds is best during the onset of winter when they range in the Lower Dachigam in the more protected valleys, sheltering from the cold, snowy upper reaches. It is also a time when Leopard move down to the lower zones to prey on the deer. Feral dogs, too, pose a great threat to the Hangul.

Above right: The still-developing antlers of this Hangul (Kashmir Stag) indicate its immaturity. Full-grown males sport branched antlers.

Opposite: In Dachigam forested tracts of leafy trees set the stage for splendid autumnal foliage in the cooler seasons.

Map labels: to Srinagar · Hoksar · Delhi · Mumbai · Dachigam National Park · Lower Dachigam · Daghwan · Waskhar Rest House · Lake Marsar · Draphama Rest House · Daghwan · Upper Dachigam · N · Pahlipora · Sangar Gulu · Naga Beran · Gratnar

Location: In the valleys of Kashmir, Western Himalayas. Park is relatively close to Srinagar (the nearest airport), 22km (14 miles) away. Jammu (200km; 125 miles) is the nearest railhead.

Climate: In Upper Dachigam, minimum winter temperatures are -10°C (14°F), bringing snowfall; winter maximum is 4°C (39°F). Lower Dachigam experiences winter lows of 10°C (50°F) and summer highs of 20°C (68°F).

When to go: Best time to visit Upper Dachigam is April to June (summer), Lower Dachigam between September and December (autumn/winter).

Getting there: Bus services very irregular; visitors should hire a car in Srinagar and take the metalled (asphalt) road from Srinagar into Lower Dachigam. Upper Dachigam is best explored on foot, via several good trekking trails.

Facilities: Srinagar has many good houseboats on the Dal and Nagin lakes. Deluxe hotels include Grand Palace Intercontinental, Broadway, Green View, Mount View, New White House and Shah Abbas. No camping huts along Upper Dachigam's trekking routes; it is advisable to carry a portable tent.

Wildlife: Kashmir Stag (winter), Leopard, Himalayan Black Bear, Brown Bear, Serow, and Musk Deer. Extremely varied birdlife.

Precautions: Blankets and woollen clothes essential in winter.

Permits and reservations: For permits: contact Chief Wildlife Warden in Srinagar. For accommodation: The Tourist Officer, Tourist Office of Jammu and Kashmir, Tourist Reception Centre, Srinagar–190001.

Special precautions: In recent years political militancy has spread through Kashmir and it is advisable to seek local advice before visiting.

Right and below right: As winter takes hold and covers the earth and trees with a mantle of snow, the Hangul deer return to the less exposed river valleys of the park for their rutting season.

Below: A tiny Himalayan Marmot; this creature occurs in large colonies in Dachigam. During winter, they excavate deep burrows in which to hibernate.

During spring, male Kashmir Stags can be spotted returning to the upper reaches, after which they are rarely seen. They drop their thinned antlers, and soon the new, velvety growth on their head begins. The female Hangul give birth to their fawns in May and June. Thereafter, they are also nowhere to be seen in Lower Dachigam as they join the males in the upper tracts for the summer.

No official record exists of the exact number of Hangul; unofficially, nearly 2000 of these animals survived in 1947. However, subsequent years marked a sharp decline in the count, and in 1954 it revealed that there were only 300 deer remaining in the park. Despite the national park theoretically providing protection for the deer, nonimplementation of effective conservation methods subsequently brought the count down to 180 within a decade. Effective measures have since been implemented to protect this species, and these have led to a consequent rise in population.

Himalayan goats and bears

Dachigam sustains 20 species of mammal and 150 species of bird. Brown Bear have made the Upper Dachigam their habitat, although sightings of these animals are very rare. They are occasionally reported by graziers who pass through these areas in summer, bringing thousands of sheep and goats to feed on the lush green pastures which border the course of the Daghwan River, flowing down from the Marsar lake. The graziers are presently causing a thinning of the pine forests, as they use these trees to build their shelters.

The Himalayan Black Bear is also a resident of the area; when the acorns ripen in autumn during the month of September, these bears can be seen wandering in the park. Along with the wild Himalayan goat species Markhor and the rare Musk Deer, another visible species is the Himalayan Marmot, a member of the squirrel family which has its burrows in the pristine flower pastures of the higher elevations (4000 to 5500 metres; 13,000 to 18,000 feet). Before their long winter hibernation, the marmots' loud screeching sound can clearly be heard echoing across the valleys.

The sole predator in this Himalayan paradise is the Leopard (Panther). There was a single report by Holloway in the 1970s that its cousin, the pale, elusive Snow Leopard, had been spotted, but since then there have been no further sightings, and the report has been discounted. The Hangul carcasses left by Leopard are devoured by the park's scavengers – Himalayan Black Bear, Indian Wild Boar, Jackal and foxes – while the park's herbivores, the grey-coated Common Langur, scamper about in happy groups.

Lower Dachigam is an ornithologist's paradise: among its many recorded species are colourful pheasants such as the Crimson Tragopan, the iridescent

Monal, and the Blood and Koklass Pheasant. Gliding overhead are Golden Eagle and Lammergeier (or Bearded Vulture) while Western Yellow-billed Blue Magpie, White-cheeked Bulbul, Paradise and Red-breasted Flycatcher, and Kashmir White-browed Rose Finch join Kashmir Black Redstart, Kashmir House Sparrow, starlings, and wrens in the dense treetops.

Above left and right: Both Himalayan Brown Bear and Indian Wild Boar scavenge on Hangul carcasses discarded by Leopard in the park, although boars also forage for subterranean roots and tubers.

Left: Arguably more beautiful than the peacock, the jewel-hued Monal Pheasant (*Lophophorus imperjanius*) makes a colourful addition to the Himalayan slopes of Dachigam park.

GREAT HIMALAYAN NATIONAL PARK

Snowcapped ridges and watered valleys

Amidst the snowy mountains of the Western Himalaya lies one of the finest wildlife reserves in India, the Great Himalayan National Park. In the state of Himachal Pradesh, this emerald-green park with its alpine vegetation falls within the Seraj Forest Division of the Kullu district. In 1984, the northern part of a protected area, the Tirthan Wildlife Sanctuary (originally formed in 1976) was incorporated into the Great Himalayan National Park, and adjoins its southern boundary. The park and sanctuary in turn form part of a much larger protected area which includes Rupi Bhaba Sanctuary and Pin Valley National Park, creating an area of roughly 162,000 hectares (400,000 acres). The management of this increased area was formulated in July 1987, including plans to develop it into a tourist zone. Renamed the Jawaharlal Nehru Great Himalayan National Park in 1989, it is still commonly known as the Great Himalayan National Park.

Forests and snow-sculpted peaks

Except for the western flank, all other borders of the national park are bounded by high mountain ridges. About 53,000 hectares (130,000 acres) of land within the park make up forest reserve while the remaining portion is a snow-covered, pastoral, and agriculturally cultivated land. The eastern part of the Great Himalayan park remains permanently under snow and ice.

The park comprises the upper catchment areas of the rivers Jiwa, Sainj and Tirthan, all of which flow west into the Beas River. The valleys of the Tirthan and Sainj are narrow and steep throughout their length, and show few signs of glaciation. The upper section of the Sainj valley shares a common boundary with the upper Parvati valley to the north, while the upper Tirthan forms part of the watershed that separates the catchment of the Beas and Sutlej to the southwest.

Identical, dense vegetation is a feature of the Sainj and Tirthan valleys, with Blue Pine the predominant species below altitudes of 2000 metres (6560 feet). Between the little villages of Bandal and Rolla, the Tirthan valley supports small areas of *Quercus* oak species (Ban, Kharsu and Moru). The higher, moderately sloping ridges are dominated by broad-leaved deciduous forest, while Silver Fir occurs in the steeper areas. Above the tree line, wide meadows characterize the landscape, and contain herbaceous plants like Primula, Gagea and Iris.

Above right: The Bharal, or Blue Sheep (*Pseudois nayaur*), has similar characteristics to both the sheep and the goat.

Opposite: Nun Peak from the Svru Valley in the Ladakh region, across which the Great Himalaya mountains lie.

Location: Lies at a distance of 60km (37 miles) southeast of Kullu town in Himachal Pradesh. The park's altitude ranges from 1500–5800m (4900–19,000ft). Nearest airport is Bhuntar (50km; 30 miles) away, with flight connections to Delhi and Shimla.

Climate: Receives good rainfall during summer (maximum temperature 20°C, or 68°F). Snowfall in winter (average minimum temperatures of 5°C, or 41°F) is less in comparison to Upper Beas valley.

When to go: Between February and May (summer months); September to early November is also good.

Getting there: The only way to visit the park is by jeep; these can be hired in Kullu.

Facilities: There are 13 rest houses in the park and seven rest houses on the outskirts of the reserve, although the influx of tourists is low. Cooking facilities and utensils are provided in the rest houses; visitors must supply own provisions.

Wildlife: Trekking within the park is advisable to better appreciate the wildlife. Typical Himalayan species – Goral (goat-antelope), Bharal (Blue Sheep), Himalayan Tahr, as well as Black and Brown Bear.

Landscapes: Beautiful scenery; the park lies in narrow, steep-sided valleys drained by several rivers, while some segments of the park reach the snow line.

Reservations: Permission to visit the park must be obtained from: The Director, Great Himalayan National Park, Shamshi–175125, Kullu District, Himachal Pradesh; or The Range Officer, Tirthan Wildlife Range, Banjar–175123, Kullu District, Himachal Pradesh.

Right and below: Muntjac (*Muntiacus muntjac*) – the fawn (inset) is a dark form of the species. Male Muntjacs (below) develop a small set of antlers extending from a short unbranched beam that originates on the brow; females do not carry antlers.

On the park's south-facing slopes, the grass- and shrub-clad hillsides are interspersed with Blue Pine and cedar (*Cedrus deodara*) together with plantations of Kharsu oak. Much of the park's northern slopes contain a dense understorey of bamboo (*Arunidaria spathiflora*), which forms impenetrable thickets in some places, particularly at heights of 2200 to 2800 metres (7200 to 9200 feet). At lower altitudes, within the vicinity of the hamlets, the forests feature an understorey made up of a profusion of shrubs.

Animals of the Himalayas

There is a unique biodiversity in this Himalayan region. Mammals include Barking Deer (Muntjac), Musk Deer, Blue Sheep (Bharal), and India's largest population of Himalayan Tahr. This wild goat, generally deep reddish-brown in colour, has a heavy body, long robust limbs and narrow erect ears. It stands about 1m (3ft) high. The Bharal on the other hand, both in physical appearance and in its habits, is a cross between a goat and a sheep.

Similiar in height to the Tahr, it is brownish-grey, and has smooth, rounded horns that curve backwards. Unlike the Tahr, though, Bharal rams are not bearded.

Leopard, Himalayan Black and Brown Bear, Rhesus Macaque, and Common Langur (or Hanuman Monkey) also occur. The presence of Ibex is not confirmed.

The Upper Beas valley harbours a rich variety of avifauna. Nearly 117 species of birds have been recorded, of which 68 are resident birds and 49 are summer visitors. The park is notable for its pheasant population; it is one of the two most significant parks in India that support the Western Tragopan (which inhabits the Upper Beas River valley). The Chir Pheasant's habitat is the Bandal area, and both the Koklass and Monal Pheasant are numerous throughout. The Kalij Pheasant is uncommon here.

Below: The Musk Deer (*Moschus moschiferus*) is so-named for its musk gland, located in the epidermis of the male's abdomen; the gland's secretions, when dried, are used in the production of musk perfume. The removing of this gland is illegal, yet carried out by poachers succumbing to the demand of the perfume industry.

Plants of medicinal value

Within the Great Himalayan National Park are natural sacred spots that have religious significance for the local people. Located at the hot springs at Khirganga and Hans Kund are the temples of Lord Surya (god of the sun) and Siva who is both creator and destroyer, since destruction ultimately leads to rebirth and renewal.

These hot springs are also the source of the Tirthan River. In the Sainj area, there are four small hamlets, namely Sakti, Maror, Kunder and Manjhan. The local villagers still possess the right to cross the boundaries of the national parks; the original inhabitants of the area, the Gaddis, are issued with permits. They enter the forest to graze their livestock, collect fodder and wood for fuel, and gather the fruits of the forest.

During spring, throngs of villagers visit the forests of the Tirthan valley and the alpine meadows of the Sainj valley to collect plants, many of which have medicinal properties. These include Yellow Jasmine (Pitmuli), Aswagandha (Indian Cheese-maker) and Saussurea species.

Above: The locals are still licensed to graze their livestock and collect wood for fuel within the park boundaries.

CORBETT NATIONAL PARK & TIGER RESERVE

Jewel of the Himalayas

The ink-blue Shivalik ranges of the Himalayan foothills rising in the distance are touched by the mist and the golden rays of the sun. The first shafts of sunlight descend obliquely to a shimmering copper rivulet below, where there is a constant hiss of frothing and gushing water within the silence of the wild. This is Corbett National Park, once a 'hunter's paradise' but today perhaps one of the most fascinating of India's wild heritage areas. The country's first national park to be established (1936), it was originally named the Hailey National Park. By 1958 – at which time it featured unique, lush green tracts of terai (lower forest tract) and bhabar (upper forest tract) on the Himalayan foothills, and at this time it was decided to rename the park in honour of the onetime hunter turned conservationist, Jim Corbett (in its earlier days, this tract was better known for its man-eating tigers). Jim Corbett had been inspired by the area to write about his earlier hunting days in immortal works such as *Man-eaters of Kumaon* and *Jungle Lore*, which he wrote in his later, more conservation-minded years.

Tracts of Himalayan jungle

Corbett was the first national park to be incorporated in the Project Tiger scheme, in 1973. Today Corbett National Park and Tiger Reserve sprawls over an area of 1318 square kilometres (510

square miles) of undulating Sal (*Shorea robusta*) forest between the districts of Nainital and Pauri Garhwal in Uttar Pradesh, in northern India. In October 1991, a buffer zone was added to the park's area, consisting of just over 300 square kilometres (117 square miles). The additional expanses of natural land used to form part of the Kalagarh Forest Division, the Sonanadi Wildlife Sanctuary (part of the Ramnagarh Forest Division), and the Terai Forest Division. The newly created park with its adjoining verdant acres today make up the sole surviving jungles of the Garhwal Himalaya.

The Ramganga River gushes from the Upper Himalaya, flowing for about 40 kilometres (25 miles) through the northern part of the forest-covered hills, creating some of nature's most dramatic landscapes. Visitors can catch glimpses of fast-moving shoals of Indian Salmon and 'Freshwater Sharks' (the Mahseer) over the pebbled riverbed of the clear but turbulent waters of the Ramganga.

A dam has been constructed at Kalagarh, and the reserve encloses part of this reservoir. It attracts numerous water birds like pintails,

Above right: A gentle-paced elephant safari in Corbett.

Opposite: The Ramganga River flowing through Corbett's northern reaches contributes to the park's scenic beauty.

Location: Situated at an altitude of between 120 and 400m (400 and 1250ft). Nearest railhead is at Ramnagar, approximately 19km (12 miles) southeast of the park. Nearest airport is at Pantnagar 50km (30 miles) away.

Climate: Summer temperatures soar to 40°C (104°F), while on winter mornings the temperature dips to 10°C (50°F).

When to go: Best period is between November and May; visibility of wildlife is better in the drier summer. Park remains closed in wet monsoon season from July to October.

Getting there: The Delhi-Moradabad National Highway connects the Kashipur-Ramnagar-Dhikala network of towns. Project Tiger headquarters are at Ramnagar, mandatory entry point for the park. Bus services operate regularly along the Nainital-Kathgodam-Ramnagar-Dhikala route.

Facilities: Basic facilities at Dhikala (forest rest houses and log huts), which has a canteen and shop selling provisions. Forest rest houses at Sarapduli, Gairal and Bijrani, all within the park. More upmarket hotels in nearby Ramnagar: Corbett Infinity Resort (Tiger Tops), Corbett Claridges Hideaway and Corbett River Side Resort.

Wildlife: The Indian Elephant population in Corbett is significant. A number of highly trained elephants are available to take visitors into the forest at dawn and dusk. January is best for birdwatching.

Reservations: Contact Chief Conservator Forests, 1, Rana Pratap Marg, Lucknow–226001; or The Field Director, Project Tiger, Corbett Tiger Reserve, Post Office: Ramnagar, Nainital District, Uttaranchal.

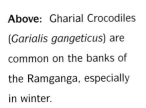

Northern Shoveller, Garganey, the Cotton and Lesser Whistling Teal, Wigeon, and many others. The reservoir serves as a waterhole for fauna during the hot and sultry summer days, and on winter mornings, Common Indian Crocodile (*Crocodilus palustris*) – also known as Marsh Crocodile – and the thin-snouted Gharial (*Garialis gangeticus*) can be spotted on the banks of the Ramganga, basking in the gentler sun. They feed on fish in the dam, and are only dangerous to humans if approached closely.

Above: Gharial Crocodiles (*Garialis gangeticus*) are common on the banks of the Ramganga, especially in winter.

Typical of terai-bhabar vegetation tracts, Sal is the dominant tree species. This thick Sal forest is interspersed with Shisam (*Dalbergia sissoo*), Jamun (Blackberry, or *Syzygium cuminii*), Khair (*Acacia catechu*), Ber (Indian Jujube), Mahua (Mowra Butter Tree), Rohini, and Haritaki. Further down the valley, clumps of spectacular rhododendron bloom in spring. The flowers of the Simal (Silk Cotton tree), Kachanar (*Bauhinia acuminata*), Palash (Flame of the Forest) and Amaltas (Indian Laburnum) bloom in abundance, creating a sylvan environment. Other floral species include the pink-flowered Foxtail Orchid, the Sariva orchid, Malajhan and ferns such as Hansaraj.

Great faunal variety

The most distinct feature of this terai forest is the expanse of tall Elephant Grass which provides an ideal home for the larger carnivores. The park has *chauds* – vast, wild grasslands of the terai region that serve as grazing grounds for the herbivores, and are excellent places for viewing wildlife. The most prominent *chaud* is at Dhikala (the park's main base offering accommodation, but also acting as a good viewing site), which extends for an area of roughly 11 by 5 kilometres (7 by 3 miles). Other major *chauds* are Phulai, Khinanauli, Paterpani, Mohanpani, Bhadahi and Bijrani.

The park has a great variety of wildlife. Cats include Tiger, Leopard (Panther), and Jungle and Leopard Cat. Corbett's population of 137 Tiger are notorious for avoiding human contact. Despite the fact that both Tiger and Leopard generally remain well-camouflaged within the dappled depths of India's forests, visitors with considerable patience do have the opportunity to see them. Those visitors spending at least three days in Corbett National Park are likely to come across a Tiger.

An imposing denizen of the park is the Indian Elephant, large herds of which can be sighted at

Below: In many cases, female Indian Elephants (*Elephas maximus*) do not carry tusks, and if they do, tusks are small – these are known as *tushes*.

Left: With the Himalaya as a backdrop, these tall grassland plains are particularly favoured by the park's great pachyderms, hence their name 'Elephant Grass'.

Centre: Once easy prey for hunters, the Tiger – sometimes also referred to as Royal Bengal Tiger – is fiercely protected in Corbett.

Of the smaller wildlife, the Common Langur – recognizable by its black face, silvery coat and long tail – and the Rhesus Macaque, which has a reddish face, can be spotted in the trees, while the Ratel (Honey Badger) and Indian Porcupine inhabit the dense undergrowth.

Reptile species such as the Barred Monitor Lizard, the deadly King Cobra – identifiable by the horizontal bands on its upper body – and the Indian Rock Python, a large, thick-bodied snake, inhabit the Corbett reserve. Otters delight in frolicking in the Ramganga River, which is also a breeding ground for fish such as the migratory Mahseer (a local freshwater shark) and Goonch (*Bagarius bagarius*). Nature lovers have petitioned the Uttaranchal government to declare the Ramganga belt a Mahseer sanctuary, in an effort to save the fish, which is presently endangered due to overfishing.

dawn and dusk during the summer season in the vast savannah of the Patlidun (valley), where the Ramganga valley has broadened out. A large population of Himalayan Black Bear and nearly 35 of the generally nocturnal Sloth Bear also find sanctuary in the park.

Besides its reputation for its prolific wildlife, Corbett National Park is equally famous for sheltering Asia's largest deer numbers within its forests, and visitors are likely to come upon extensive herds of deer; a single herd can comprise hundreds of Chital (Spotted Deer). Other deer species to look out for are Sambhar, Barking Deer (Muntjac), and Hog Deer – a piglike deer of the grasslands and open forest. The coat of a Hog Deer is brown tinged with yellowish and reddish tints. At shoulder height, it stands 60 centimetres (24 inches) high, and has the habit of running with its head lowered, like its namesake the hog. These deer live on grass and leaves.

A magnet for ornithologists

Corbett is popular among ornithologists and birdwatchers as 600 avian species have been recorded here. Some of the notable ones are Kalij Pheasant, Peafowl (Peacock), Red Jungle Fowl, White-crested and Black Gorgetted Laughing Thrush, Mistle's Thrush, Indian Pitta, Paradise Flycatcher, and the White-capped and Plumbeous Redstart. Of interest is the arrival of the Black-crested Cuckoo, which heralds the impending monsoon – the rains inevitably sweep through a week later. Corbett counts an extensive number of raptors among its bird species, Blyth's Baza, Red-headed Merlin, ospreys, Crested Serpent Eagle, Scavenger Vulture, and the Hen and Marsh Harrier being only a handful. Wading birds include snipes, egrets and herons.

Below: The Red Jungle Fowl (*Gallus gallus*) is from the pheasant family and is believed to be the ancestor of the domestic fowl.

DUDHWA NATIONAL PARK AND TIGER RESERVE

An impressive deer sanctuary

Not far from the Himalayan foothills nestles the Dudhwa National Park and Tiger Reserve; the park has only recently come under the umbrella of Project Tiger, with the addition of the Kishanpur Sanctuary's 200 square kilometres (78 square miles). The moist deciduous vegetation comprises virgin stretches of Sal forest which are contiguous with the terai, or lower forest tracts, of the Nepalese Himalayas.

Formerly, this region comprised a forest reserve belonging to the North Kheri division of the Lakhimpur-Kheri district of Uttar Pradesh State. The forest was declared a sanctuary in 1968 and subsequently upgraded to the status of national park in 1977. A metre-gauge railway line runs across the park, joining the towns of Gouri Phanta in Nepal and Bareilly in India.

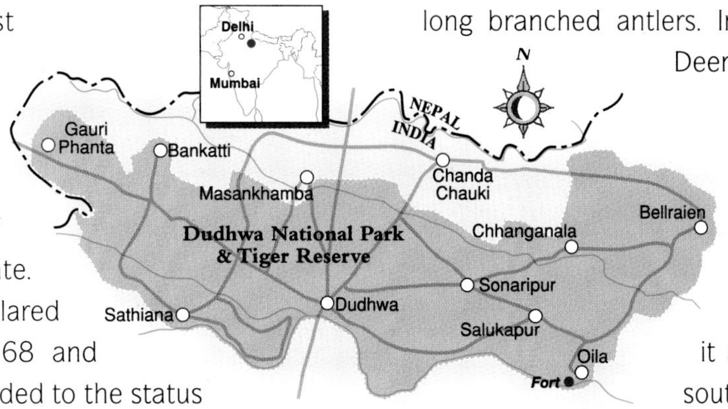

The park is synonymous with the name of 'Billy' Arjan Singh, a famous Indian conservationist whose singlehanded efforts turned Dudhwa into the notable tiger reserve it is today. In 1976 he was awarded a gold medal for conservation by the World Wide Fund for Nature International.

The vast 815 square kilometres (315 square miles) of terai vegetation comprise savannah grasslands interspersed with forests consisting of tree species such as Jamun (Blackberry), Shisam, Simal (Silk Cotton tree), Khair (*Acacia catechu*), Sirsa (*Albizza procera*), Haldu (*Adina cordifolia*), and Toon (*Cedrela toona*).

Two major rivers, the Suheli and Neora, converge in the park, becoming the Suheli in the southern flank. The Mohana flows between the northern part of the park and the Nepal border.

Barasingha, pride of the park

The prime mammal species of the park is the elegant Barasingha, or Swamp Deer. Yellowish-brown in colour, these deer feed on grasses and swamp vegetation, breeding in the summer. Stags carry long branched antlers. In Dudhwa the Swamp Deer is known as *gond*; this animal was pivotal to influencing conservationists to lay the foundations to protect the area and thus declare it a national park. In the southern part of the park, in the Sathiana and the south-east-lying Chakraha forest blocks, the marshlands of two of the park's rivers provide a perfect habitat for this deer, which is also referred to in India as Softground Barasingha.

Of late their population is facing an alarming decline – poaching has been recorded in the Ghola and Gajrola areas of the park, and in 1998 their count totalled about 500. Barasingha are coveted for their meat, skins and antlers.

Above right: Hog Deer (*Axis porcinus*) is an elusive species.

Opposite: A herd of Softground Barasingha (*Cervus duvauceli*) in the less-preferred drier grasslands.

Location: In the terai belt of Uttar Pradesh, close to the Nepalese Himalayas, which are about 30km (20 miles) distant.

Climate: Winter is bitingly cold and can drop to 4°C (39°F) while the summer months are quite hot (35°C; 95°F) although humidity is relatively low. The rains occur June to September.

When to go: The period between February and June is probably the best time to visit the park. April through June is very hot and dry, but good for viewing wildlife.

Getting there: The nearest small town is Palia; the nearest airport is at Lucknow. It is advisable to reach Dudhwa by hired car or bus from Lucknow railway station, which is 260km (160 miles) from the park.

Facilities: Forest rest houses and log huts in Dudhwa, located at Sathiana, Bankatti and Sonaripur, have cooking and catering facilities; provisions need to be supplied by visitors. Dudhwa has a full canteen.

Wildlife: Dudhwa is a deer haven, sustaining the largest number of Softground Barasingha (Swamp Deer) in India. Birdlife is one of the park's major attractions. Elephant rides on offer through the park at dawn and dusk.

Landscapes: Beautiful vistas across to the Himalayan foothills. Fine stands of Sal dominate the forest, and Jamun (Blackberry) lines the river banks.

Reservations: The Field Director, Dudhwa National Park, Lakhimpur, Kheri, Uttar Pradesh; or The Chief Wildlife Warden, 17, Rana Pratap Marg, Lucknow, Uttar Pradesh.

(Map labels: Delhi, Mumbai, NEPAL, INDIA, Gauri Phanta, Bankatti, Masankhamba, Chanda Chauki, Chhanganala, Bellraien, Dudhwa National Park & Tiger Reserve, Sathiana, Dudhwa, Sonaripur, Salukapur, Oila, Fort)

Rich in wildlife species

The greatest attraction of the Dudhwa reserve is the majestic Tiger, which occurs throughout the park and is seen regularly by visitors. As Dudhwa has no forested buffer zone along its park boundary to the south, incidents of the park's Tiger inhabitants attacking humans were at one time common. Dudhwa is presently one of India's best-managed parks and such incidents have not been reported in recent times. Tiger and Leopard are the park's major predators, and there is constant competition between the two cat species. Leopard numbers, though, are far less than those of the Tiger.

Increasing rhino numbers

An attempt was made in 1985 to introduce the Great Indian One-horned Rhinoceros into Dudhwa under the auspices of the rhino re-introduction programme, but they did not adapt well to their new habitat and some animals migrated to Sukla Phanta. Today, however, 'Gainda-Darshan', or 'rhino viewing' on elephantback has become a regular feature for tourists. The count of rhinos has reached 18; they occur mainly in the Kakraha block of the South Sonaripur range.

Another highly endangered animal whose numbers have reduced alarmingly is the elusive grassland dweller, the Hispid Hare. Predation and their dwindling habitat have been the main causes.

Indian Elephant, on the other hand, are not scarce, and herds of these pachyderms migrate throughout the year across the corridor between Nepal's Sukla Phanta and Royal Bardia wildlife sanctuaries and Dudhwa National Park and Tiger Reserve.

Among the park's carnivores are Sloth Bear (which prey on the kills of other predators to complement their diet of white ants, Mahua fruits, blackberries and roots), Jackal, Red Fox, the Fishing, Jungle and Leopard Cat, and Honey Badger. In winter, visitors can spy on basking snub-nosed crocodiles known locally as Muggar (Marsh Crocodile) on the banks of the Suheli and Neora rivers. In terms of the herbivores, five species of deer co-exist in Dudhwa: Chital, Sambhar, Muntjac (Barking Deer), Barasingha and Hog Deer.

Dudhwa's reptile life is abundant. Of the snake species, the Indian Rock Python, Indian Spectacled and Indian Monocled Cobra, and Common Krait – a venomous blue-black nocturnal snake with thin white bands on its body – are some of the more deadly types. Monitor Lizard, skinks and chameleons are all common in the forests. Visitors could disturb a snake at any time, and they should remain constantly vigilant for the highly poisonous krait and cobra species.

Rare birdlife

Dudhwa has 350 species of birds and enjoys the distinction of being the only region in Uttar Pradesh that contains such large numbers of bustards. Between 40 and 50 in number, they live in close proximity with the Swamp Deer in the grasslands. The Bengal Florican, a sub-Himalayan species, is perhaps the rarest bustard in the world, with a global population of 600. Also rare are the Lesser Florican, or Leekh, which flock to the park's

grassland areas. In the upper grasslands, Swamp Partridge are transitional, while Black and Grey Partridge, Red Junglefowl and Peafowl are plentiful.

A great number of migratory birds converge at Banketal ('tal' meaning 'lake') in south Sonaripur and at Jhadital in Kishanpur. Among the species are White-eyed, Red-chested and Common Pochard, Pintail Duck, Common Teal and mallards.

Particularly special in Dudhwa are the prolific owls and raptors. Great Indian Horned, Dusky Horned, Brown Fish, Forest Eagle and Scops Owl as well as the Spotted and Barred Owlet are just some of the owl species. Notable birds of prey are Sparrow Hawk, the Pale and Hen Harrier, the Crested Serpent and Spotted Eagle, Honey Buzzard and Shikra.

Above: Both the leaves and blooms of the *Schleichera oleosa* species are resplendent in the autumn months.

Left: During mating season, the Peacock (*Pavo cristatus*) displays its gorgeous plumage in an elaborate ritual to attract the female.

NORTHEASTERN HIMALAYA

The Northeastern Himalayan region includes, from the west, the states of Sikkim, the northern part of West Bengal, Assam, Meghalaya, Tripura, Mizoram, Manipur, and Arunachal Pradesh. China forms northeastern India's northern boundary, while Myanmar (Burma) forms the eastern border. The region is extremely wet and humid and experiences an early monsoon, which arrives in April. Mahasingram, in the Garo hills of Meghalaya State, receives the highest rainfall in India – 13,200 millimetres (520 inches) annually. On average, the annual rainfall of the northeast is 2030 millimetres (80 inches). Summer and winter in the foothills are mild, while the topmost ridges of Arunachal Pradesh, in the extreme northeast of India, experience snowfall all year round.

The mighty Brahmaputra River flows through the Assam valley and has created extremely fertile soils over the years which have given rise to a rich and dense evergreen forest. The top tier canopy of these forests projects upwards for more than 3 metres (10 feet), while the lowest tier harbours innumerable orchids, shrubs and climbers. The lower regions of the Assam valley and the northern part of West Bengal feature dense stands of Sal (*Shorea robusta*), constituting the moist deciduous forest type, with thick undergrowth.

Animal species endemic to the Northeastern Himalaya include Water Buffalo, Red Panda, and a great many primates. In terms of avian diversity, the rare Lesser and Bengal Florican, and Adjutant Stork are abundant here.

The major preserves are Kaziranga National Park and Manas Tiger Reserve and National Park in Assam, and Namdapha – a national park, biosphere and tiger reserve – in Arunachal Pradesh. Others are Kaibul Lamjao National Park in Manipur, Dampa Tiger Reserve in Mizoram and Balphakram National Park in Meghalaya. The government has in the past imposed restrictions on the movement of foreign travellers in the region because of political instability. However, the situation has eased; the problem posed by local insurgents fighting for greater independence has not affected foreigners. Visitors whose travel papers are in order will, in general, readily get permission to enter the region.

Above: *Pleione Praecox*, one of the prolific orchid species in the Meinam forest, south Sikkim.

Opposite: Kaziranga's wetlands act as a crucial water source in sustaining park wildlife.

NAMDAPHA NATIONAL PARK & TIGER RESERVE

Mountain retreat of secretive cats

Tucked away at the border of the Changlang district of Arunachal Pradesh State, Namdapha's evergreen forests with their occasional winter backdrop of snow-capped mountains are the home of tribes who are still abiding by their age-old customs.

Retaining an air of mystery, the sprawling valley of virgin tropical rainforest in the midst of misty, sombre blue hills is traversed by the turbulent Noa Dihing River, a tributary of the Brahmaputra. The forest was declared a national park in 1972 and covers an area of nearly 2000 square kilometres (770 square miles) including a buffer zone of about 177 square kilometres (68 square miles) to the north. The park stretches up to the point where Changlang meets the Lohit and Tirap districts; to the south lies the town of Miao's forest reserve on the Indo-Myanmar (Burma) border. Namdapha was declared a tiger reserve in 1983, and is the only one in Arunachal Pradesh.

Namdapha is bounded to the east by the Gandhigram settlement area and India's boundary with Myanmar, while to the west it is bounded by the Deban River, M'pen *nala* (stream) and unprotected forests. The park's altitude ranges from 200 to 4500 metres (650 to 14,800 feet) above sea level and includes the highlands of the Daphabum ridge belonging to the Patkai Himalaya, with its occasional snow and the Tushar valley just below. These alpine and subalpine zones merge into tropical rainforest around the Noa Dihing River valley. The river is one of several that drain the forest area.

Others are the Diyun, Namchick, Namdapha and Deban. The terrain is rugged with deep, wide valleys as well as narrow gorges, watered by streams, rivulets and falls, and clothed in deep dense forest. The region is well-known for its prolonged monsoon and torrential rains which flood the rivers.

Namdapha holds a tribal population of varied origin. Chakmas (refugees from Bangladesh) live on the fringes of the forest near the Deban valley. One of the park's most interesting tribes is the Lishu. Its members are of Burmese descent and used to live in the trees. They presently live in Bijay Nagar, a small fringe town near the border with Myanmar (Burma). The main group in the area is the Singpho tribe.

A region of amazing biodiversity

Namdapha National Park and Reserve is a highly productive ecosystem which has an enormous biodiversity. For several decades, scientists from the Smithsonian Institute in Washington DC (USA), the Zoological and Botanical Survey of India, and the Bombay Natural History Society explored the verdant terrain. Climatic and altitudinal variation as well as ample rainfall have

Above, right: The rare Snow Leopard (*Panthera uncia*).

Opposite: A trek through Namdapha's virgin evergreen forest is a truly memorable experience for visitors.

Location: In Changlang district of Arunachal Pradesh. Nearest township, Miao, lies 20km (20 miles) away. Airport at Dibrugarh (140km; 90 miles) has connections with Calcutta and Guwahati. Most convenient railhead is Margherita, 70km (40 miles) from Namdapha.

Climate: Prolonged monsoon from April till end September. Winter nights bitterly cold, mornings sunny (3°C; 35°F). Mild summers (maximum of 32°C, or 90°F).

When to go: Best time to visit is between November and March.

Getting there: Vehicles for hire at Dibrugarh airport. Miao accessible by helicopter from airport; also daily bus service to Miao. Taxis available from town of Dibrugarh.

Facilities: Self-catering forest rest house at Deban centre (has four rooms overlooking confluence of Deban and Noa Dihing rivers and snowcapped peaks of Daphabum). Deban has canteen facilities.

Visitor activities: Trekking only way to explore the forest; permission to undertake week-long treks can be obtained in the park. Advisable to carry portable tents. Visitors can rest in temporary bamboo structures made for forest guards. The farthest point, Gandhigram, 102km (60 miles) from Deban, is a paradise for birdwatchers and ornithologists.

Wildlife: The Snow Leopard is so elusive that some believe it may no longer exist here.

Permits and Reservations: Indians require an Inner Line Permit, foreigners a Restricted Area Permit, from Ministry of External Affairs in the state capital, Itanagar, or any major city. For reservations in Deban forest rest house, contact: The Field Director, Namdapha Tiger Reserve, Miao, Changlang District, Arunachal Pradesh.

Map labels: Delhi, Mumbai, Happy Valley, N'Pen, Bulbulia, Hornbill Point, Ranijheel, Firm base, Deban, N'Dong, Camera Point, Chakma Camp, High Land, Lake View, Tushar Valley, **Namdapha National Park & Tiger Reserve**, N, Gandhigram

to yellowish-brown with, on its flanks, dark blotches separated by paler areas to form a 'clouded' pattern, while the face is marked with the stripes common in smaller cats. This leopard, which hunts by night, is limited to the forests of the northeast Himalaya only. The Snow Leopard, similar in length to the Clouded species, is distinctive in the shortness of its muzzle, its high forehead and vertical chin. Its soft grey coat pales to pure white on the underside, while unbroken spots occur on the head, nape and lower limbs. It lives above the tree line around 4300 to 6000 metres (14,000 to 20,000 feet).

The only member of India's ape family to be found in the park is the Hoolock, or White-browed, Gibbon. These noisy gibbons live in small families, and throng together at dawn and dusk, scampering from the branches of tall trees using their long arms. Monkey species include the endangered Slow Loris and the Assamese Macaque, and among the smaller forest creatures are Malayan, Hoary-bellied and Flying Squirrel. Indian Elephant, Sambhar, Muntjac (Barking Deer), Red Panda, and Binturong (Bear Cat) complete the circle of Namdapha's wealth of forest wildlife. The Binturong is a nocturnal, arboreal animal living on small birds, eggs and insects. It has no predators, and very little is known of its breeding habits.

Namdapha's birdlife spans many-hued species like Niltava, Mrs Gould's Sunbird, Yellow-backed Sunbird, Himalayan Roller, Black Bulbul, Prinia, Red-breasted Falconet, Red-headed Merlin, and three varieties of hornbill. Of the laughing thrush species are the Black Gorgetted, White-crested and Striated species. The most vulnerable duck species, the White-winged Wood Duck – which has fallen prey to poaching – is a resident bird of the marshes and ponds of Namdapha.

endowed the undulating valley slopes with forests ranging from tropical evergreen to moist deciduous, as well as tracts of Hollock bamboo (*Terminalia myriocarpa*) and shrubs. In the lower reaches of the reserve, the vegetation is also varied, with thick and virtually impenetrable undergrowth. Extensive stretches are covered with palms, bamboo and woody brakes of cane. Namdapha's unique three-storeyed forest is composed of tall trees like wild Mango, Banana, and Chickoo (which bears edible, juicy fruit), Bandardima (Monkeybread tree), Makai (*Zizyphus* sp.), Jutuli, Agarwood, and the flowering tree Kadamba (*Adina cordifolia*). Some commonly occurring fern species include *Pteris*, *Drypteris*, *Asplenia*, *Onychium*, *Aisophila*, and *Gleichenia*. There is also a variety of colourful wild orchids such as Lady's Slipper, Dendrobium, blue and orange Vanda, and Foxtail.

Tourists should be aware that the wet, tropical vegetation has spawned over 22 species of leeches, including the Tiger Leech; they need to be adequately prepared.

Prolific wild cats

What sets Namdapha apart is that the park supports eight members of India's wild cat family. They are Tiger, Leopard (Panther), Clouded and Snow Leopard (disputed), and Marbled, Jungle, Leopard, and Fishing Cat. Pug marks on the sandy riverbeds indicate their existence in the forest.

The tail of the Clouded Leopard is almost as long as its body; from head to tail this cat measures 1.95 metres (6 feet 5 inches). Its colouring varies from earthy-

MANAS NATIONAL PARK AND TIGER RESERVE

Lair for endangered species

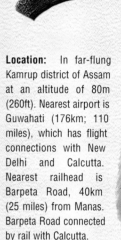

With the Himalayan foothills not too far distant, Manas in the northeastern state of Assam, which also borders on Bhutan, occupies the most prominent mountain-dominated position of all the sanctuaries in northeast India. A forest tract here extending over 2837 square kilometres (1095 square miles) was declared a sanctuary in 1928, and for decades Manas played a pivotal role in conserving the wildlife of India. In 1973, the sanctuary was brought under the wing of Project Tiger, at which time the core area comprised 390 square kilometres (152 square miles) forming the Manas Tiger Reserve. This unique ecosystem was declared a World Heritage Site by UNESCO in 1986 for its glorious pristine qualities. Today Manas is also a national park.

It was unfortunate that in 1988 political Bodo rebels shattered the tranquillity of this wild paradise, paving the way for chaos and conflict as they used the region to shelter from the Indian authorities. Conservation efforts inside the reserve were hampered by the ongoing political agitation, and the reserve remained closed to visitors for several years. In 1997, Manas National Park and Tiger Reserve was reopened to tourists.

Sub-Himalayan forests

A remarkable diversity of forest vegetation exists within the confines of the park. It is flanked by the sub-Himalayan mixed deciduous forests and Assam valley evergreen forests to the north and a combination of rich bhabar Sal, eastern wet alluvial grassland around the

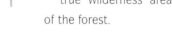

Benki and Hekua rivers and alluvial savannah woodlands to the south. Manas is a treasure-house of plants and trees – 550 species – which include some rather rare varieties of wild orchid. Shisham, Badam (Indian Nut), Lali, Chalta (*Dillenia* sp.), Amla, Bauhinia, Flame of the Forest and fruit trees such as Mulberry and Guava dot the true wilderness area of the forest.

Wet and wild monsoons

The park experiences a relatively long monsoon period beginning in May and lasting till September. Torrential rains give rise to countless seasonal rivers and *nalahs* (narrow tributary streams). Monsoon rains contribute to the swelling of Himalayan streams, turning them into carriers of stones, pebbles, silts and plant materials. Where these streams enter the plains and deposit their waterborne materials, the area develops certain distinct physical characteristics – this is how the terai landscape comes about.

In the upper foothill areas, where heavy materials like rocks and coarse sand are the first to be deposited, the uneven ground surface becomes porous and eventually loses its capacity to hold water; as a result, there is a drop in the water table. This belt is the bhabar tract. It supports excellent patches of Sal, a tree species associated with moist deciduous semi-evergreen and evergreen forests. Even though water may not be plentiful throughout the seasons, the forest cover of the bhabar vegetation belt is profuse.

Above right: Golden Langur (*Presbytis geei*).

Location: In far-flung Kamrup district of Assam at an altitude of 80m (260ft). Nearest airport is Guwahati (176km; 110 miles), which has flight connections with New Delhi and Calcutta. Nearest railhead is Barpeta Road, 40km (25 miles) from Manas. Barpeta Road connected by rail with Calcutta.

Climate: Between May and September is monsoon season. Winter nights are chilly (can drop to 7°C, or 45°F) while days are pleasant (24°C; 75°F). Summer is mild, reaching highs of 35°C (95°F).

When to go: Best time to visit is between November and March.

Getting there: One can reach the park via bus or hired car from Barpeta Road. No motorable roads in the park, but trained elephants at Mathanguri (the entry point) take visitors through the forest.

Facilities: The tourist lodge is located at Mathanguri, which offers a panoramic view across Manas. Provisions need to be supplied by visitors, but good facilities are provided in the lodge (cooking utensils, cutlery, fuel).

Wildlife: Visitors ride on elephant-back into the park's forests, home to some highly endangered species (Golden Langur, Pygmy Hog); excellent birdwatching along Benki and Hakua rivers, and at Mathanguri.

Landscapes: Spectacular mountain views with their green, forested mantle; rare wild orchids.

Permits and reservations: Permission to visit the park, bookings and any special permits may be obtained from: The Field Director, Manas Tiger Reserve, Barpeta Road, Assam.

In contrast, the terai tract contains plenty of ground water all year round, which helps to maintain perennial water sources. The tall grasslands of the terai belt support an ecosystem that sustains an extensive number of wild animals, and harbours some rare and endemic species. Manas is home to 60 mammals, of which 41 have been listed in the IUCN's (International Union of Conservation of Natural Resources) Indian Wildlife Protection Act of 1972. They include Tiger, Leopard, Clouded Leopard, and of the smaller cats, the Marbled, Leopard, Golden and Fishing species. Other mammals are Great Indian One-horned Rhinoceros, Indian Elephant, Indian Wild Buffalo, Red Panda (or Cat Bear), and Capped Langur (Leaf Monkey).

Pygmy Hog and Golden Langur

The most endangered animals in the reserve are Golden Langur, Pygmy Hog and Hispid Hare. Today, Pygmy Hog and Golden Langur survive only in this park.

The latter is the smallest known member of the pig family, and according to IUCN, is one of the 12 most endangered animals in the world. It was rediscovered, together with the Golden Langur, in the Manas forests in 1971. The Pygmy Hog is nocturnal by nature and lives in herds of five to 20; its habits are similar to those of the Indian Wild Boar. Predation is the cause of this animal's dwindling numbers.

The existence of a new species of monkey – eventually named Golden Langur – was established by a Mr E P Gee, and it was given the Latin name *Presbytis geei*. Small troupes of about nine consisting of one adult male, one or more females and several sub-adults exist in localized zones of evergreen forest between the Sankosh River in the west and the Manas in the east. During winter, this species' coat is a golden chestnut colour, which becomes paler with the advent of summer. Golden Langur feed on fruits, flowers and leaves.

Manas' varied habitat is ideal for countless types of birds. Species of interest are Assamese Myna, Indian Lorikeet, Rufous-bellied Niltava, Rubycheek, Crossbill, Malkoha, Kalij Pheasant, Orange-bellied Blue Magpie, Blue-headed Flycatcher, Great Indian Hornbill, Indian Hobby, and Blyth's Baza. Huge populations of migratory waders and water birds such as large cormorants, Grey Heron, Yellow Bittern, Lesser Whistling Teal and Comb Duck make the Manas River and its tributaries, the Benki and Hakua, their temporary home.

Opposite top left: The Golden Langur, characterized by its dark, mask-like face framed by a golden halo of hair, was first seen and recorded in the mid-20th century.

Opposite top right: The diminutive Pygmy Hog (*Sus salvinius*) is rated a highly endangered species – not only in its native country India but also in the world.

Opposite bottom: To cross the Manas River from India to the other side, which belongs to the kingdom of Bhutan in the eastern Himalaya, visitors require no permits.

Above: A view across the lower foothills which are clothed in extensive grassland, referred to in India as the terai tract; beyond the terai stretches the upper reaches, referred to as bhabar.

Right: The Cat Bear, also known as Red Panda (*Ailurus fulgens*) partly due to its russet colouring, lives in the temperate forests of the central and eastern Himalaya at elevations of up to 1500 metres (4900 feet). It is a nocturnal creature, spending much of its day sleeping in the topmost branches of the trees.

KAZIRANGA NATIONAL PARK

Conserving the rare rhino

Kaziranga's sprawling valley of 430 square kilometres (166 square miles) with its stretches of untamed landscape is situated in the state of Assam. An expanse of forest contiguous with the Mikir hills to the south and the turbulent Brahmaputra River to its north, it was accorded the status of a forest reserve as early as 1908. At this time, a law was imposed to restrict the ruthless shooting of rhinoceros, but by 1926 it was noted that the population had been further drastically reduced. Kaziranga was closed to visitors from 1930 to the end of 1937, and in 1940 it was upgraded to a wildlife sanctuary. Eventually, in 1974, Kaziranga was declared a national park.

Kaziranga's forests are known for their great biodiversity, comprising as they do mixed savannah grassland together with evergreen, moist deciduous and swamp forest.

Rhino, a threatened species

The park has recently become one of the last strongholds of the exotic Great Indian One-Horned Rhinoceros, which during the mid-1950s was facing such an alarming decline of the species that numbers had dropped to about 12 animals. These vulnerable, short-sighted mammals are an easy target for poachers, who value their horns (which are, in fact, not of bone and keratin but rather composed of tightly compressed hairs) and which are used in powdered form for medicinal purposes in the Far East. In both India and Nepal, much of the rhino anatomy has some significance,

whether aphrodisiac, medicinal or spiritual. Intense conservation efforts have increased the rhino population to approximately 1500 today. Rhinos are generally solitary animals, but can often be seen grazing on grass and leaves in the open grasslands. They enjoy muddy swamps, in which they submerge themselves. These animals have no predators, although Tiger and Leopard can become a threat to newborn calves.

Herds of Indian Elephant migrate between Kaziranga, the Darang district and the southern Mikir hills. Watching enormous families of elephant bathing in the rivers Diflu, Mora, Bhalukjhuri and Barjuri is an exhilarating experience for visitors. The total population is believed to be nearly 650.

It is unfortunate that due to the destruction of the corridors as a result of local tea cultivation, today the animals are being driven to seek out new habitats.

Above right: In the past, the Great Indian One-horned Rhinoceros (*Rhinocerus unicornis*) existed in many parts of India. As a result of extensive poaching, it's occurrence today is limited to a handful of protected areas.

Opposite top: The vast swampy grasslands of Kaziranga are favoured by rhino, which wallow in the muddy waters.

Opposite bottom: Excursions into the park on elephant-back are leisurely and slow, but have their advantages: besides their elevated vantage point, visitors are also likely to get much closer to the wildlife.

Location: Tucked in Golaghat district of Assam, the park lies along the main highway between Jorhat and Guwahati. Hamlet of Bokakhat lies to the east, 23km (14 miles) from Kaziranga. The park is flanked by the Bodo hills to the west.

Climate: Summer months are moderate (35°C; 95°F) while winter nights are chilly (minimum of 7°C; 45°F). Very heavy monsoon rainfall in summer (2300mm; 90in).

When to go: A favourable time for travellers is from November to March. Closed during monsoon season, mid-April to mid-October.

Getting there: Daily flights to Guwahati combined with drive to Kaziranga make this a good option. Flights to Jorhat only twice a week. Bus services from Bokakhat to the park; car hire also available.

Facilities: Tourist information centre in Kaziranga. Jeeps are available within the park for drives at dusk. Early morning elephant rides can also be booked in the park. Accommodation in Kaziranga in forest rest houses and a tourist lodge owned by ITDC; canteen facilities. Comfortable accommodation at Wild Grass Resorts in Kohora.

Wildlife: Unique species such as Great Indian One-horned Rhinoceros, Asiatic Wild Buffalo, Mouse Deer and Barasingha. Elephant rides through park bring visitors much closer to wildlife, although great distances aren't covered.

Permits and Reservations: Permit required from the Ministry of Home Affairs. For reservations, write to: The Deputy Director, Tourism, PO-Kaziranga Sanctuary, Shibsagar District, Assam; or Director, Kaziranga National Park, PO-Bokakhat, Shibsagar District, Assam–785109.

Seasonal flooding of the Brahmaputra

Although the Brahmaputra River acts as a lifeline to civ-ilization in the northeast Indian states, it causes great distress to Kaziranga's wild fauna when it floods its banks and submerges the forest floor. These annual floods inflict an enormous loss on deer, as well as smaller and and also larger mammals. Many of the park animals seek refuge in the Mikir hills of the Darang district, but unfor-tunately a large number are hit by heavy vehicles while attempting to cross the highways. After the flood waters subside, the soil is rich from the alluvial deposits and the forest floor is gradually transformed into an emerald-green expanse with the sprouting of new shoots which give rise to new plants, climbers and shrubs.

Above: A watchtower near Kohra offers expansive views of the open grasslands.

Above right: The park guards make use of boats to patrol the park.

Right: The Indian Elephant (*Elephas maximus*) is smaller than its African counterpart, seldom exceeding a height of 3 metres (10 feet). What also sets it apart is its small ears, domed forehead and trunk ending in a single protrusion – in contrast to the African elephant's two protrusions.

Prolific birdlife

Kaziranga National Park protects as many as 325 avian species. Often the solitude of the forest is interrupted by the musical notes of the Hill Myna in the distant valleys and hills. Resident birds include Bengal Florican and the Adjutant Stork, while other prominent species are the Fishing and Crested Eagle, Sultan Tit, Collared Bush Chat, White-capped Redstart, Yellow and Pied Wagtail, Indian Lorikeet, Red-breasted Parakeet, Spotted Forktail and Blue Rock Thrush. Among the many waterbirds are large Cormorant, Lesser Whistling Teal, Bar-headed Goose, Merganser and Comb Duck.

Haven for herbivores

Kaziranga is a vast wildlife refuge, and sustains large numbers of herbivores. One species is the Asiatic Wild Buffalo, or Water Buffalo (*Bubalus bubalis*), which breeds with domestic buffalo thus producing a hybrid race. The latter species is quite temperamental and often charges, unprovoked. The Manas National Park and Tiger Reserve is also home to this subspecies of buffalo. There are around 40 Indian Bison and many species of the deer family, including Hog Deer, Sambhar and Chital (Spotted Deer). The Softground Barasingha is one of Kaziranga's most highly endangered deer species (it is also present in Dudhwa National Park) and the park's monsoon-fed, waterlogged terrain provides a most suitable habitat since its hooves are specially adapted to this environment. The elusive Mouse Deer is also a threatened species. The smallest of India's deer, standing 25 to 30 centimetres (10 to 13 inches) high, it is recognizable by greyish horizontal stripes on its back. A characteristic of the deer family is its cloven hooves – but the Indian Chevrotain has four well-developed toes on each foot, where the bones of the petty, or side, toes are completely formed. Antlers on the male are not developed.

Populations of Jungle, Leopard and Fishing Cat thrive, as do Wild Boar, Sloth Bear, Himalayan Civet, porcupines, pangolins, the Common Indian Hare, Common Indian Mongoose and Jackal. An animal that is striking in appearance is the Hoolock, or White-browed, Gibbon but these apes are not easily spotted in the hilly evergreen forests. They live as separate families of parents and young, forming groups of no more than six. Their diet is comprised of spiders, insects, fruits, and leaves from which they sip the dew.

Finally, nearly 50 Bengal Tiger and a reasonable population of Leopard (Panther) survive in Kaziranga's jungles. Visitors who are patient are sure to have a chance at seeing Tiger in the forests.

Top right: Located at different points in the forest, these guard posts help park officials keep a watch on poachers.

Right: Although the Sloth Bear (*Melursus ursinus*) is docile in appearance, it becomes an extremely ferocious animal if agitated, more so than the Tiger.

Below: The Mouse Deer, or Indian Chevrotain (*Tragulus meminna*), is the smallest member of India's deer family.

KEIBUL LAMJAO NATIONAL PARK

Manipur's floating park

Lying in the state of Manipur, this is one of the most unique wildlife reserves in India. Contiguous with three hills – Pabot, Toya and Chingjao – it is a vast wetland area of floating islands covering almost 40 square kilometres (15 square miles) and adjoining the southeastern extremity of Lake Logtak, the largest freshwater lake in the northeast. The floating island mass consists of organic matter, called *phum* or *phumdi*, which is composed of decayed vegetation and varies in thickness from 30 centimetres to 1 metre (1 to 4 feet). The park is also the last stronghold of the Thamin, or Brow-antlered Deer – so-named for its gracefully curved horns – which is endemic to the region.

The water level of the lake fluctuates from season to season. During the drier months of February and March, the *phumdi* along the swamp edges rests on stable ground. With the coming of the monsoon, Lake Logtak becomes flooded, and the deer seek refuge in the higher regions of the surrounding hills, where they graze and breed. Within a week of this seasonal flooding, the *phumdi* that has established itself at the lake edges is freed and floats once more on the surface of the water. As more vegetation is added to the existing *phumdi* each year, it becomes thicker and heavier, and accumulates at the edges of the lake again, hardening as the dry season continues. If there is no heavy flooding for two or three consecutive years, this compacted *phumdi* forms solid layers of humus. In this way, the area of floating organic matter is reduced.

Logtak Lake has been declared a Ramsar site (this refers to conservation efforts established in Ramsar city, Iran, in 1971 in a move to preserve important wetland habitats of the world). Locally, Thamin are known as *sangai* or 'dancing deer' of Manipur because of the manner in which they negotiate their way over the lake's islands, which become their floating habitat. A unique grass, *Zizania latifolia*, with the local name of *ishing kombong*, forms the deers' diet.

The three hills rising above the wetlands form a good observation point from which to view these deer.

Until 1950, the Brow-antlered Deer was considered extinct due to relentless hunting by local tribespeople and soldiers during World War II. After India's independence, the deer was rediscovered by renowned conservationist E P Gee.

There are three subspecies of Brow-antlered Deer in the world: the *Cervus eldi eldi* occurs in Manipur, *Cervus eldi thamin* in Burma and *Cervus eldi siamensis* in Thailand. Of these three, Manipur's subspecies is the most vulnerable. An aerial survey conducted in 1977 revealed only 14 *sangai*. A subsequent survey conducted in 1979 confirmed that there were 30 of these deer surviving in Keibul Lamjao, of which nine were stags, 13 hinds and eight fawns. Intense conservation efforts since 1980 have seen a steady rise in *sangai* numbers. Today the count stands at about 150.

Map labels:
Thonga Hill
Marsh (flooded from July to February)
Keibul Ching
Keibul Lamjao
Delhi
Mumbai
Checkpoint
Checkpoint
Ching Joo
Thangbrel Checkpoint
Keibul Lamjao National Park
Offices & Staff Quarters
Sangoonkher Checkpoint
= MARSH
= SWAMP
Checkpoint
Settlement
Checkpoint
Settlement
Checkpoint
Settlement
Kumbi
Khungo
Manipur
N

Above right: The *Cervus eldi eldi* species of Brow-antlered Deer occurs only in India, in the state of Manipur.

Opposite: Locals negotiating the *phumdi* (floating marsh).

Location: At the southeastern point of Logtak Lake. The nearest airport is at Imphal, 32km (20 miles) from the park, while Dimapur is the nearest railhead, 229km (140 miles) away.

Climate: Summer months are warm (41°C; 106°F); in winter, nights are cold (minimum temperature 10°C, or 50°F).

When to go: Visitors should visit the park between the months of October and March.

Getting there: Tourist taxis and buses to the park are available from Imphal; buses run from Dimapur to the town. By car (which can be hired in Imphal), the park is a 40km (25-mile) drive.

Facilities: Although the national park is equipped with two rest houses, it is advisable and safer for visitors to drive from Imphal at dawn and return at dusk. Visitors are advised to carry their own food for the day. Imphal offers accommodation at the Tourist Lodge and Government Rest House.

Wildlife: The park is the only area in India to support the endemic Brow-antlered Deer (Thamin).

Permits and Reservations: Permit required from Ministry of Home Affairs. Further information from: The Chief Wildlife Warden of Manipur, Manipur Forest Department, Imphal, Manipur.

DAMPA TIGER RESERVE

Magic of the Blue Mountains

Mizoram is one of the most picturesque states of India's northeastern Himalayan region. Bangladesh lies to the west and Myanmar borders the south and east of the state, while in the northeast lie the beautiful Blue Mountains, with the highest peak at 2500 metres (8203 feet). About 65 per cent of the total state area is covered with forest. Up until 1950, the forested area fell under the control of one village chief and the land was used for shifting cultivation, known locally as *jhum* cultivation. In 1974, 600 square kilometres (230 square miles) of the moist deciduous forest was declared a sanctuary, and villages were shifted outside the forest area. The Dampa Wildlife Sanctuary was upgraded in 1994 to a tiger reserve of 500 square kilometres (190 square miles).

With undulating, medium to high hills running in a north-south direction, the reserve receives a very high precipitation. The lower reaches contain deep valleys with extensive flat land along the rivers Keisalam, Seling and Aivapui, which all finally drain into the Khawthlagtuipui River. The entire region, except for the upper reaches of the valley, is crossed by numerous small perennial streams. During the drier seasons, waterholes and salt licks are created at different locations for the wild animals.

Bamboo and evergreen forests

Dampa, like many of the other northeastern parks of India, has a rich biodiversity and a productive ecosystem. In its lower reaches are moist deciduous and thick evergreen bamboo forests, while in the upper reaches semi-evergreen forest with natural grasslands are prevalent. Trees consist of a mixture of different species like Simal (Silk Cotton), *Mesua ferrea*, White Cedar, Tun (*Cedrela toona*), Agarwood, Indian Rubber tree and several species of bamboo and cane grasses as well as orchids. Some parts of the forest are very dense and inaccessible. Embarking on the forest's trekking trails (both one-day and several-day treks) to view this unique and diverse ecosystem is a wonderful experience.

Besides its small Tiger population (the latest 1996 census reflects only five), Dampa supports Leopard, Clouded Leopard, Jungle Cat and Wild Dog. These predators depend mostly on the park's two deer species, Sambhar and Muntjac (Barking Deer), as well as Serow (a goat antelope), Indian Wild Boar, porcupines, and Malayan Squirrel for their diet. The forests harbour many primates, among them Hoolock (White-browed) Gibbon, Common and Capped Langur (Leaf Monkey), Stump-tailed and Rhesus Macaque, and Slow Loris. The latter primate belongs to the lemur family. It reaches around 40 centimetres (16 inches) in height and has particularly large round eyes set in a

Above right: The markings of the Clouded Leopard (*Neofelis nebulosa*) enable it to merge with the dappled forest light.

Opposite: The way the light filters through the distant shimmering haze − a combination of dust and heat − gives the Blue Mountains their name.

Location: In the district of Aizawl, Mizoram. The nearest airport is Tuirial; note that air services are not regular. It is advisable to arrive via Silchar airport, which is 290km (180 miles) from the tiger reserve. The nearest town, Feileng, is 10km (6 miles) from the gate. The nearest railhead is at Silchar.

Climate: Summer is mild while winter is quite chilly (minimum of 9°C, or 48°F).

When to go: November to March are the best months to visit.

Getting there: Park is accessible from the town of Aizawl, 128km (80 miles) away. Car hire available at Silchar airport. Feileng sells provisions for self-catering in the park.

Facilities: Two rest houses with cooking facilities are located within the forest premises. It is necessary to carry one's own provisions.

Wildlife: Tiger, Leopard, and Clouded Leopard present, although rarely seen. Many primate species, including Hoolock Gibbon and Stump-tailed Macaque.

Precautions: Anti-malarial prophylactics should be taken by visitors before arriving in the park.

Permits and Reservations: Permits required; obtained from the Ministry of External Affairs. For reservations, contact The Field Director, Dampa Tiger Reserve, Aizawl, Mizoram.

The map shows:
New Chikha, Dampa Tlang, Range Office, Andasmanik, Lallen, **Dampa Tiger Reserve**, Mualvawm, Saithah, = BUFFER ZONE, Range Office, Talhtum, Hnahva, BANGLADESH, INDIA, Delhi, Mumbai, N

Above: A Slow Loris (*Nycticebus coucang*) gazes balefully out of characteristic large dark-framed eyes.

round head. Soft greyish-brown, the Slow Loris has no tail. It eats small birds and eggs, but also enjoys fruit. Although its movements are very slow, the loris is very swift in catching prey.

Gaur (Indian Bison) and Sloth Bear are also inhabitants of Dampa Tiger Reserve, and the rivers are full of Smooth Indian Otter. Dampa's reptiles include the Monitor Lizard, and the Monocled, Spectacled and King Cobra species as well as Indian Rock Python.

To date, 124 species of birds have been recorded in the reserve. Himalayan and sub-Himalayan forest species are the Racket-tailed and Hair-crested Drongo, Mrs Gould's, Black-breasted and Yellow-backed Sunbird, Black-capped Sibia, Collared Bush Chat, Pale Blue and Red-breasted Flycatcher, Pied Indian Hornbill, Chestnut-bellied Nuthatch, Spotted Forktail, and Little Spider-hunter. Warblers include the Spotted Longtail Wren, Pallas's Leaf and Yellow-faced Leaf species.

BALPHAKRAM NATIONAL PARK

Where the wind blows continuously

The state of Meghalaya (meaning 'abode of clouds') has been carved out of the former Assam State and is part of what are regarded as northeast India's 'seven sister states'. Balphakram National Park lies in the southern part of Meghalaya, to the west of the Garo hills below the ancient granite Balphakram plateau. This fertile virgin land, which covers an area of 220 square kilometres (86 square miles), was proclaimed a park in 1988 and spreads from the foothills up to the plateau edge. Here, steep-sided cliffs rise up to 2000 metres (6560 feet).

In the local Garo dialect, Balphakram transcribes as 'the wind blows continuously', and Garo legend has it that Balphakram is the land of the disembodied spirit. Innumerable rivers and streams drain the park, the main ones being Rangra, Maheskhola and Mahadeokhola (the word 'khola' meaning 'river' or 'stream'), all of which eventually flow into the Brahmaputra River system.

Environmental threats

Past deforestation has already caused a great deal of destabilization on the Garo hills, and at present a plan by a cement company to set up limestone mining imposes a threat to the vital corridor that passes through the Siju Rekwak Sanctuary in these hills. In addition, a proposal to mine uranium at Domiasiat could multiply the effects of environmental degradation, and in particular raise the possibility of radiation which would affect the tribes and the wildlife of Meghalaya. The Garo hills are also being ravaged by timber smugglers who are armed as a result of working closely with militant insurgents. In terms of geological heritage, on the other hand, the belts of limestone and coal deposits in the Balphakram valley, together with rock layers of fossilized seashell, are as yet unexplored and offer immense scope for geological and archaeological studies.

The Balphakram National Park provides a habitat for rare, indigenous flora that is facing the threat of extinction and which is seldom discovered outside the sanctuary. Forest types in the park consist of tropical wet evergreen, thickets of cane and bamboo, semi-evergreen, and moist deciduous (predominantly Sal) trees, as well as moist Sal savannah and Khasi Pine (a species occurring on the Khasi hills). In the forests are Shisham (*Dalbergia sissoo*), Gamar (*Trewia nudiflora*), and wild Banana and Orange trees. Flowering shrubs include Bauhinia, Azelia and Lantana. Michelia (*Michelia champaca*) is a climber that eventually strangles its large host trees and at present is a problem in the forests.

Babblers and forest raptors

Birdlife features the Laughing and Blue Rock Thrush, Blackbird, and starlings. The only Chestnut-fronted Shrike Babbler recorded on the Indian subcontinent is a

Above right: The flowers of the Lantana bush; this plant species also produces shiny black berries.

Location: In Meghalaya State; the Balphakram plateau lies 13km (8 miles) away, on the border with Bangladesh, to the south of the park. The nearest airport and railhead are at Guwahati, 350km (217 miles) from the park. The nearby town of Tura (165km, or 100 miles, away) lies below Nokrek peak, 1457m (4780ft) above sea level, and serves as a good centre for exploring the surrounding forest-clad hills.

Climate: The state of Meghalaya experiences its monsoon season from June to September and because of its altitude, experiences a cool climate all year round.

When to go: The best time to visit is from December to March.

Getting there: Tura is reached by road from Guwahati. There are no motorable roads within Balphakram; trekking is the only option.

Facilities: The park itself has no rest houses. Visitors intending to visit the park can stay in a rest house in Tura managed by the forest department. There is a tourist lodge, Mahadeo, managed by Meghalaya Tourism at the edge of the Balphakram plateau. In September, February and March, woollens and rain gear will be required.

Wildlife: Significant species are Indian Elephant, Wild Buffalo, Tiger, Leopard and Hoolock Gibbon.

Permits and reservations: Permits to visit the park and reservation details to be obtained from: Divisional Forest Officer, Wildlife, Tura, Meghalaya.

specimen from the Garo hills. The park provides a good habitat for forest raptors such as Jerdon's and Black Baza, Crested Goshawk and Rufous bellied Eagle.

Balphakram is also the source for rare and valuable medicinal herbs, such as the *dikge muni*, which is difficult to find. It is known to produce a soporific effect when ingested and is presided over by vultures nesting on the rocks at higher levels.

Balphakram's faunal residents are Indian Elephant, Bengal Tiger, Leopard, Clouded Leopard, Wild Buffalo, Gaur (Indian Bison), and Muntjac (Barking Deer). Of the primates, Hoolock (White-browed) Gibbon, Assamese Macaque, Pig-tailed Macaque, Capped Langur (Leaf Monkey), and Slow Loris inhabit the treetops. The Pig-tailed Macaque, which stands about .6 of a metre (2 feet) high, resembles the Assamese species. It is differentiated from the Rhesus Macaque in that the orange-red hue on its rump and loin is absent. Its tail is distinctly arched, giving it its name.

Accurate information on the zoological aspects of the park has only recently been ascertained. The relatively unexplored Balphakram National Park will undoubtedly attract future scientists interested in undertaking in-depth studies of rare flora and fauna.

Left and above: Although the Assamese Macaque (*Macaca assamensis*) [left] and the Pig-tailed Macaque (*Macaca nemestrina*) [above] belong to the same family, they are quite distinguishable in appearance. The Pig-tailed Macaque, which lives in the Naga hills, carries its tail in a similar manner to the pig – erect and arched – hence the derivation of its name.

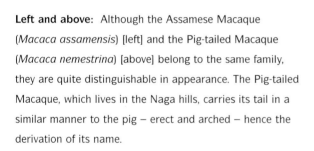

Top right: The orchid known as Lady's Slipper (*Papilio-pidilum viccosum*) flourishes in the northeastern states of Meghalaya, Mizoram and Nagaland. It flowers during April and May.

Above right: Raptors, including the Long-billed Vulture (*Gyps indicus*), are prolific in the high rocky cliff terrain of Balphakram National Park.

Right: *Calotropis procera* is an African plant species that has been used to stabilize sand dunes. Byproducts derived from this plant are a fibrous material that resembles kapok and latex.

BUXA NATIONAL PARK AND TIGER RESERVE

A corridor for elephant

In the Alipurduar subdivision of the Jalpaiguri district in the northeastern arm of West Bengal State lies a forest tract which acts as a significant corridor for Indian Elephant migrating between Manas National Park and Tiger Reserve to the east and the forests of Bhutan to the north. Buxa's forest covers an area of 700 square kilometres (270 square miles), of which 386 square kilometres (150 square miles) today forms the core area. The forest came under the protection of Project Tiger in 1982, and according to the last census, there are 23 Tigers living within its boundaries.

The forest is drained by many rivers, the major ones being the Rydak, Sankosh, Bala, Dima, Pana, Jayanti and Gabu. The Sankosh River, flowing along the eastern extent of Buxa, also forms the western boundary of the Manas reserve in neighbouring Assam. Almost every monsoon season the banks of the Rydak, which runs from north to south in the park, burst, flooding the surrounding areas, wreaking destruction.

In the winter months of December, January and February the banks of the Rydak and Sankosh rivers are the focus of some impressive migratory bird species. Ibisbill, Merganser, Golden Eye, Baer's Pochard, and Eastern Golden Plover are among the exotic birds that gather there. Over the last few years, with the arrival of winter, a pair of Black-necked Crane has visited the cultivated lands of the local populace living within the park boundaries. This is a rare phenomenon, as records of Black-necked Crane in such low altitudes are scarce. It is probable that the birds come down to this area from the higher altitudes of Bhutan.

Tropical shade-bearing trees

Buxa is composed mainly of tropical moist deciduous Sal forest lying in the (upper) bhabar and (lower) terai forest tracts of the sub-Himalayan foothills. A large portion of the lower-lying foothills and plains are also covered in Sal forest. Other predominant trees of the park are Sedha (*Lagerstroemia perviflora*), *Cedrela toona*, Lali (*Amoor wallichii*), and Bahera (*Terminalia bellerica*). On the banks of the river, a feature of the Silk Cotton tree, Sirish, or Rain Tree (*Mimosa sirissa*), Shisham, and Katha (*Acacia catechu*) is their large, spreading canopies. The upper ridges of the national park are dotted with a profusion of trees such as Katus (*Castanopsis*), Kimbu (*Carya arborea*) and Gokul (*Ailanthus grandis*).

In some parts of Buxa, dense patches of virgin forest with thick undergrowth still exist, while in other areas, there are old Teak (*Tectona grandis*) plantations.

Several members of the cat family live in Buxa – Tiger, Leopard, and Fishing, Jungle and Leopard Cat. In 1995, a Clouded Leopard was captured by the forest department in the nearby town of Alipurduar; it was ultimately released in Buxa. Pregnant female Leopards often stray into the adjacent tea estates to give birth to their cubs.

Above right: The White-rumped Shama (*Copsychus malabaricus*) can be seen in the Himalayan foothills.

Opposite: Elephant are water-loving animals and are often seen playfully spraying themselves and lolling in rivers.

Location: In the *dooars* (meaning 'door' or 'gateway') of the lower Himalayan foothills of northeastern West Bengal. Although nearest airport (which lies south of Buxa) is at Cooch Behar, it is advisable to go via Siliguri airport, 152km (94 miles) west of the park; road conditions from Siliguri are poor in some places, however. The nearest town and railway station is Alipurduar, 27km (17 miles) from Buxa.

Climate: Winter is cold (minimum 8°C; 46°F), while summer is moderately hot (maximum 32°C; 90°F).

When to go: A favourable time is from November to April. Park closed 15 June to 30 September.

Getting there: Cars for hire at Alipurduar and Siliguri to drive to Buxa. Buses from Siliguri.

Facilities: Several rest houses available in different areas of the forest: Rajabhatkhawa rest house at entry point of reserve; Jayanti rest house atop the gorge of the Jayanti River; Bhutanghat near the mighty Rydak riverbed; Raimatang rest house overlooking a gushing stream strewn with pebbles and boulders; and finally, Buxaduar rest house, nestles in beautiful lush-green forest and requires a 4km (2.5-mile) trek. All the houses supply cooking facilities including crockery and utensils. Provisions to be supplied by visitors.

Wildlife: Tiger (rarely seen), Leopard, Elephant, Indian Bison, Sambhar, Barking Deer, and Serow. Watchtowers located in different parts of the park.

Permits and reservations: Entry to park restricted to 06:30–15:00. No night driving. Permit and reservations required from Field Director, Buxa Tiger Reserve, Alipurduar, Jalpaiguri District, West Bengal.

Right: This serene view of the Rydak, a major river in the park, belies its destructive nature in the monsoon season when it overflows, immersing the area with its floodwaters.

Below centre: The Leopard Cat (*Felis bengalensis*) resembles the domestic cat in size but has longer legs. Its markings and colouring are similar to those of a Leopard.

Below right: The Serow, a goat-antelope, has a whistling scream. Its rutting season is the end of October, whereafter the young are born in May and June.

Other carnivores of the forest are Sloth Bear, Jackal and Civet. The large forest herbivores, such as Elephant and Indian Bison, are quite common, and during the migrating season (October to December), large herds of Elephant are often spotted in the Panbari forest range of the Himalayan foothills. They generally breed deep within the forest, and it is very rare to come across a mating pair.

Besides Indian Wild Boar, Barking Deer (Muntjac), Chital (Spotted Deer) and Sambhar, Buxa holds a viable population (no census has been done) of the goat antelope, Serow. Living on the upper ridges, this animal has a large head with donkey-like ears, a thick neck and short limbs, and feeds at dawn and dusk on grasses across the hilly slopes. Serow are distributed across an area stretching from Kashmir to the Mishmi hills.

Malayan Giant Squirrel can often be seen perching on the tall trees along the Bala riverbed. Endangered animals such as the Chinese and Indian Pangolin occur in the park, but because they are nocturnal creatures, they are seldom spotted during daylight. Reptile life includes Indian Rock Python and King Cobra. Mahseer (Freshwater Shark) can be spotted in the Rydak River.

Because of its wealth of forests, birdlife in Buxa is interesting. The park reverberates with the sweet notes of the Hill Myna at dawn in winter as they come down from the higher ridges. Other songbirds are the Hair-crested and Racket-tailed Drongo, Shama and Magpie Robin. Birds of the forest include Indian Pied and Great Indian

Hornbill, Yellow-backed and Mrs. Gould's Sunbird, Parrotbill, Indian Lorikeet, Blue Rock Thrush and Peafowl (Peacock). Among the raptors are Blyth's Baza, Pale Harrier, and Grey-headed Fishing Eagle.

GORUMARA NATIONAL PARK

A park of the flood plains

Verdant patches of terai forest still cover a vast expanse of the Jalpaiguri district of northern West Bengal. Of this forest, 9 square kilometres (3 square miles) of the total area were declared as a game reserve in 1842, making Gorumara one of the oldest in India. The game reserve was officially declared the Gorumara Wildlife Sanctuary in 1976, and in recent years, additional pockets of the Jalpaiguri forest division have been incorporated into Gorumara. It was eventually given national park status in 1994, with a total area of 80 square kilometres (30 square miles) inclusive of its buffer zone.

Riverine forest and indigenous trees

Most of the park falls within the flood plains of the Murti and Jaldhaka rivers. Jaldhaka forms the park's eastern boundary, while the Murti River divides the park into two sections – north and south. A third river, the Indong, also flows through Gorumara. The principal forest species is Sal (*Shorea robusta*), but Chilaur, Odla, Katus (*Castanopsis* sp.), Lali (*Amoor wallichii*), Bahera (*Terminalia* sp.), and Jamun (Blackberry) also make up the forest. The lower parts of Gorumara consist of riverine forest: Simal (Silk Cotton), Sirish (Rain Tree) and Katha (*Acacia* sp.) are interspersed with tall grasslands of mostly Elephant Grass and Typha (a marsh species). The forests are the abode of vibrantly hued birds. Species worth mentioning are Blossom-headed and

Red-breasted Parakeet, Peafowl, Collared Bush Chat, Maroon Oriole, Shama, Emerald Dove, Indian Pied Hornbill, and Imperial, Yellow-legged and Thick-billed Pigeon. During winter, Merganser, Ruddy Shelduck and Black Stork can be found on the Murti River.

Haven of the rare rhino

In the early years, Gorumara was declared a reserve to protect the Great Indian One-horned Rhinoceros, and other than Jaldapara in West Bengal and Kaziranga in Assam is one of the few last havens of rhino today. There are 19 in Gorumara. These animals sometimes bathe in a group of 10 or 12 in the waters of the Murti River.

Other major herbivores of Gorumara are the Indian Elephant and Indian Bison. Wild Boar, Muntjac, Sambhar, Jackal, civets and porcupines also find refuge in the forests; Leopard is present, but is very rarely seen.

Watchtowers for wildlife viewing

A few watchtowers are located at strategic points in the national park and are ideal for viewing the wildlife. Garati watchtower has facilities to stay overnight while Jatraprasad watchtower is only 1 kilometre (half a mile) away from the forest rest house. The latter was named after the most well-trained and obedient elephant of

Above right: The Emerald Dove (*Chalcophaps indica*) is extremely swift in flight, aided by its broad wing span.

Location: In the terai belt of the Himalayan foothills in the Jalpaiguri district of West Bengal. The nearest airport is Siliguri, 78km (48 miles) west of the park; buses from here to Jalpaiguri, the most conveniently located town after Gorumara. Chalsa, 14km (9 miles) from Gorumara, is the nearest railhead.

Climate: Winters are bitterly cold (minimum 7°C; 45°F), while summer is moderately hot (35°C; 95°F).

When to go: Best time to visit the park is from November to April.

Getting there: Cars for hire are available from Siliguri, Chalsa and Jalpaiguri.

Facilities: A well-equipped (good cooking facilities) forest rest house lies in the park and provides excellent facilities for wildlife viewing. Watchtower located here, and another at Garati with overnight facilities. It is advisable to carry provisions from Chalsa, 10km (6 miles) away. Elephant rides can be organized in the park (prior permission is necessary).

Wildlife: Major mammal species are the Great Indian One-horned Rhinocerus, Indian Elephant, Indian Bison, Sambhar, and Jackal.

Landscapes: Panoramic views from Gorumara onto some of the Himalaya's majestic peaks, among them the famed Kangchenjunga.

Reservations: Prior permission has to be obtained from the forest department for elephant rides. For accommodation reservations, contact: Divisional Forest Officer, Wildlife Division II, Siliguri, Darjeeling District, West Bengal.

The map shows: Delhi, Mumbai, to Siliguri, Chapramari Wildlife Sanctuary, Chalsa, Rest House, Murti, Watchtower, Rest House, Neora, Indong, Gorumara National Park, Jaldhaka, Jalpaiguri Forest, to Jalpaiguri, BHUTAN, INDIA

Below: The male of the Great Indian One-horned Rhinoceros (*Rhinoceros unicornis*) stands 1.8 metres (6 feet) at the shoulders; it is smaller than the African White Rhinocerus but larger than the Black species.

Gorumara's forest department, which died after serving the department for 60 years. These trained elephants can be hired by visitors for trips in the park. A third watchtower stands in front of the forest rest house, allowing an aerial view of the forest; Tondu is the fourth tower. There is a nature interpretation and ecotourism centre adjacent to the forest range of Ataguri.

Bordering onto Gorumara is the minuscule Chapramari Wildlife Sanctuary, with an area of 10 square kilometres (4 square miles). The Murti River flows along the western flank of this forest. Chapramari's vegetation consists of Bahera, Sindur, Tatari, Kanchan (*Bauhunia acuminata*) and Chalta (*Dillenia* sp.). Wildlife to be seen here are Indian Bison, Elephant, Leopard, Sambhar, Barking Deer, and the Malayan Giant Squirrel. The Giant Squirrel's tail, at 60 centimetres (24 inches) exceeds the length of this animal's body, which is deep brown (almost black) in colour, with buff-coloured underparts. The squirrel's favoured food is fruit. Birdlife in the Chapramari sanctuary is very similar to that of Gorumara.

Bottom left: The Murti is a haven for aquatic birdlife.

Bottom right: A Common, or Golden, Jackal (*Canis aurens*) with its recently killed prey of a Langur monkey.

Below: Most of the national park falls within flood plains fed by two major rivers, creating the perfect habitat for a large variety of amphibians, among them the Indian Common Toad (*Buto melanostictus*).

JALDAPARA WILDLIFE SANCTUARY

Land of the one-horned rhino

Nestling in the lap of the majestic Himalaya, the vast grasslands of Jaldapara face the lofty snowcapped peaks, offering magnificent vistas. This wildlife sanctuary, with its great variety of wild flora and fauna, ranks after Kaziranga National Park in Assam as the second largest natural habitat in India of the Great Indian One-horned Rhinoceros. Jaldapara is shaped like a pair of trousers, with each leg about 18 kilometres long and the waist 4 kilometres (2.5 miles) wide, with a total area of 115 square kilometres (44 square miles).

Changing face of the rivers

The western arm of the sanctuary is drained by the Torsa River, and the eastern arm by the Malangi River. These two principal rivers and their streams flow down to the plains from the mighty Himalaya. The rivers frequently change their appearance during the heavy monsoon floods, which give birth to myriad pools, swamps and marshes, rendering the forest an ideal home for large herbivores such as rhino, Indian Elephant, and Gaur (Indian Bison).

When the monsoon strikes heavily in Jaldapara, it causes great devastation. Most of the areas become inundated, and forest tracts are washed away from the massive onslaught of the floods. Enormous quantities of silt are deposited, damaging vegetation and inflicting losses on wildlife. But Nature recovers itself. Once the water has subsided, the entire area is transformed into a green palette of tall Elephant Grasses, presenting a feast for the sanctuary's herbivores.

As part of the eastern terai, Jaldapara's vegetation bears all the characteristics of typical terai forest. Mostly riverine, tall deciduous trees are interspersed with dense high grassland and crisscrossed by watercourses. Trees like Sal, *Cedrela toona*, Lali (*Amoor wallichii*), Katus (*Castanopsis*), Bauhinia and stands of bamboo predominate.

Protecting an endangered species

Jaldapara was proclaimed a wildlife sanctuary in 1941 to protect the Great Indian One-horned Rhinoceros, mainly due to the concerted efforts and keen interest of E O Shebbeare, the one-time head of the Bengal Forest Service. During the 1930s, the rhino was on the verge of extinction in West Bengal. It was killed – with little justification – for theoretically causing damage to cultivated areas, and rampant poaching was undertaken for its horn. The belief in rhino horn for its strong medicinal value continues unabated. Because of the large-scale poaching in Kaziranga's forest, it was assumed that the forests of North Bengal would become the next target for ruthless poachers and it was therefore highly essential to impose and enforce regulatory protective measures. In 1932, the Bengal Rhinoceros Preservation Act was enforced and later, in 1959, the name Jaldapara Game Sanctuary was officially changed to Jaldapara Wildlife Sanctuary. Finally, in 1976, the sanctuary was accorded the legal status of a rhino reserve.

Above right: Indian Roller (*Coracias bengalensis*); the name derives from the bird's habit of tumbling while in flight.

Location: Eastern Himalayan foothills in the Jalpaiguri district of northern West Bengal. Sanctuary lies at an altitude of about 50–70m (165–230ft) above sea level and is about 12km (7 miles) south of the Bhutan border. Sanctuary in the terai region of West Bengal, popularly known as *dooar* ('gateway'). Nearest airport is at Bagdogra (160km; 100 miles); Madarihat (1km; .5 mile) is nearest railhead.

Climate: The sanctuary enjoys a subtropical climate. During winter (November to February), the mercury dips to 5°C (41°F) while the hot and humid summer heat (lasting from April to June) soars to 38°C (100°F). The rainy season spans July to September; during the southwest monsoon, the wettest months are July and August.

When to go: Jaldapara is best visited between November and March.

Getting there: Madarihat is the gateway to Jaldapara. One can hire a car from Siliguri to drive to the sanctuary. Tourists taking a bus from Siliguri need to disembark at Madarihat.

Facilities: Accommodation is available at Madarihat Tourist Lodge, Hollong Rest House in the Hollong forest range, Baradabri Forest Rest House and Youth Hostel – all on the outskirts of Madarihat. Rest houses are self-catering; no cooking facilities provided.

Wildlife: Indian Elephant, Great Indian One-horned Rhino, Indian Bison and deer species.

Reservations: No permit required. For bookings, contact: The Tourist Bureau, Government of West Bengal, 3/2 BBD Bagh, Calcutta–700001; or Divisional Forest Officer, Cooch Behar, West Bengal.

The present distribution of the Great Indian One-horned Rhinoceros – from the Brahmaputra valley (Kaziranga) in Assam, the Gorumara and Jaldapara sanctuaries of northern West Bengal and the Chitwan range in Nepal – is today an isolated pocket of a former range that used to extend across the Indo-Gangetic plain and the foothills of the Himalaya. There is substantial evidence that all three species of Asian rhinoceros (the Great Indian, Sumatran and Javan) used to occur in India. In recent years, due to keen conservation efforts, there has been a steady rise in the rhino population (the count stands at between 1600 and 1800). Good sightings of these animals during the day are a regular occurrence.

Jaldapara also provides a habitat for Indian Elephant and Gaur (Indian Bison). Both these species migrate beyond the sanctuary boundaries from October to December. Sometimes, Elephant line the forest corridor adjoining Bhutan to the northeast. Representing the deer family are Sambhar, Chital (Spotted Deer), Muntjac (Barking Deer) and Hog Deer; populations of the latter two are greater than Sambhar and Chital. Wild Boar are also inhabitants here. Unlike the occasional Tiger and Leopard, Rhesus Macaque often make an appearance, and Sloth Bear are seen frequently. The waters of the Torsa and Malangi rivers may offer a chance encounter with the secretive Clawless Otter.

Due to its close proximity to the Himalayan ranges, Jaldapara sustains a large variety of sub-Himalayan birds such as Hair-crested and Lesser Racket-tailed Drongo, Red-breasted Parakeet, Himalayan Roller, Emerald Dove, and Yellow-legged, Green and Thick-billed Pigeon. Grassland birds include Grey Partridge, Bush Quail, Red Jungle Fowl, Meadow Pipit, and Dusky Leaf and Streaked Warbler. The sanctuary's most endangered bird is the Bengal Florican.

Right: Vibrant orange and yellow-gold neck feathers characterize the male Red Jungle Fowl (*Gallus gallus*).

Below right: The claws of this creature, as its name Small-clawed Otter indicates, are rudimentary – not much more than small straight spikes that do not extend beyond the toe pads.

Below: On the Wild Boar, thicker hair running from the head along the spine creates a mild form of a mane.

Opposite: Terai forest typifies the vegetation in Jaldapara.

GANGETIC INDIA

The Gangetic plain is one of the most fertile zoogeo-graphical regions of India, due mainly to the mighty Ganges River. It rises in the Himalaya in north India, and flows southeast across the country before running east through central Bangladesh, where the immense deltas of the Brahmaputra and Ganges meet to empty into the Bay of Bengal. The vast Gangetic plain extends from the state of Punjab in the north to West Bengal in the east. States falling into this zoogeographical area are eastern Punjab, central Uttar Pradesh, south Bihar (which has recently been declared a new state named Jharkand), northeast Madhya Pradesh, Orissa, and the south of West Bengal.

The plain can be divided into two biotic zones, which are clothed in tropical and riverine forests: the first, the Upper Gangetic Zone, originates in Punjab and extends to Allahabad where the Ganges meets the Jumna River; the Lower Gangetic Zone stretches from Allahabad across to West Bengal. The upper zone is comparatively drier, with sparse vegetation, as a result of a shorter monsoon period which yields an annual rainfall of more or less 1000 millimetres (39 inches). The minimum winter temperature is 2°C (36°F), while the maximum in summer is 45°C (113°F). The lower zone enjoys a longer monsoon period with an annual rainfall of between 1800 and 2500 millimetres (70 and 90 inches). Temperatures here are moderate, with an average minimum winter temperature of 13°C (55°F) and a maximum summer temperature of 35°C (55°F).

A feature of the Lower Gangetic Zone is the forested upland plateau known as Chota Nagpur, on which nestles the Palamau Sanctuary; and to the south, in the hilly tracts of Orissa State, lies the Simlipal Tiger Reserve and National Park. Political chaos in one-time Bihar has affected the wildlife of the region and depletion of the forest wealth is perhaps at its worst here. This situation may improve with the recent creation of the new states Jharkhand (south Bihar) and Chattisgarh (south of Madhya Pradesh), which encompass mainly the forests.

Left: Despite their size, Gaur often ascend to elevations of 1800 metres (5900 feet).

Top right: A Peacock, common symbol of India, displays its resplendent crown.

SIMLIPAL NATIONAL PARK AND TIGER RESERVE

An evergreen landscape

This little mountain kingdom, tucked in the Eastern Ghats which run down India's east coast, lies in the forest zone of northern Orissa State. It was once the royal hunting ground of the maharajas who ruled the princely state of Mayurbhanj. Simlipal was the first wildlife sanctuary in Orissa, lying south of Bihar with its east coast on the Bay of Bengal, to be incorporated as part of Project Tiger. Simlipal derives its exotic name from the prolific growth of Simal (Silk Cotton) trees in the park. In Oriya, the language of Orissa State, the word 'salmali' refers to the 'evergreen landscape', also contributing to the park's name.

Simlipal is steeped in history; its remote jungle provided an ideal hideout for rulers who escaped from the Maratha invasions in the 17th century, and consequently the dominance of the British. The Marathas originally were chariot drivers ('rath' is a chariot), who at a certain point in history massed together to form an army; these Hindu people are believed to have moved south to the state of Maharashtra where they integrated with some of the aboriginal tribes. During the mid-1600s they challenged the Muslim-ruled states, confronting the Mughal empire under the leadership of Sivraji.

The forests were leased in 1919 to the Calcutta-based Barua Timber Company, and in 1949 were acquired by the Orissa government. The Simlipal forest range was eventually declared a sanctuary in 1957, and in 1973 became a tiger reserve (having a core area of 846 square kilometres, or 326 square miles), with the government also declaring it a biosphere reserve to make it India's 15th. Simlipal was upgraded to a national park in 1980 and today receives 10,000 visitors every year.

Unfolding mountain vistas

Extending over a total area of 2750 square kilometres (1062 square miles), the park's sylvan forests are covered with tracts of Sal and interspersed by vast stretches of grassland, in turn crossed by gorges with their swift-flowing streams. Simlipal is known locally as 'mirable visu', a reference to its undulating hills and varied topography, soil and climate. Serene, lofty mountains form a backdrop – the Meghasani (1165 metres; 3822 feet) and Khariburu hills (1178 metres; 3865 feet) rise to the south, with Dhudhruchampa in the centre of the reserve, and the hills of Chahala and Nawana towering in the north. Innumerable rivers such as the Khairi, Budhablang, Polpola, and Panasia cross Simlipal and keep the forest floor moist all year round.

Wildlife and exotic flora

Simlipal's exotic flora embraces 1076 species of plants. Epiphytic and ground orchids are abundant (nearly 93 varieties have been identified), particularly around sites in the park like Meghasani, Jenabil, Bhanjabasa and Joranda. The most ornamental of the orchid species are Dendrobium, Pecteilis and Gigantea. Kash, an indigenous grass, flowers profusely.

Above right: Flowers of the Silk Cotton Tree (*Bombax ceiba*).

Opposite: Life-sustaining rivers such as the Khairi play a crucial role in this continent of extremes.

Map labels:
- Bisai
- = TIGER SANCTUARY
- **Simlipal National Park & Tiger Reserve**
- Manda
- Brundabah
- Entrance Gate
- Tulsibani
- Chahala Rest House
- Baripada
- Jashipur
- Barehipani
- *Joranda Waterfall*
- Joranda
- Lulung *Tourist Complex*
- Kaliani
- Nawana Rest House
- Kalikaprasad
- Gudgudia
- Dhudhruchampa
- Karanjia
- Jenabil Rest House
- Bhanjabasa
- N
- Khunta
- Delhi
- Upper Barakamra Rest House
- Udata
- Mumbai
- Thakur Munda
- Kaptipada

Location: In the district of Mayurbhanj on the Southeastern Railway route. Jamshedpur (140km; 87 miles) nearest airport and railhead. Bhubaneswar (320km; 200 miles) and Calcutta (240km; 149 miles) are main cities closest to Simlipal.

Climate: Torrential monsoons in May and June. Summer highs reach 45°C (113°F); winter minimum 4°C (39°F).

When to go: Simlipal best in the dry months; park is open 1 November to 15 June. It is worth spending several days in the park.

Getting there: Jashipur is gateway to Simlipal (via NH6); no bus service to the park, so jeeps must be hired. Park lies 50km (30 miles) from Baripada (NH5), which in turn is 30km (20 miles) from Lulung; buses run from Calcutta and Baripada to Jashipur. Simlipal also accessible from resort of Chandipur, near Balasore on Bay of Bengal.

Facilities: Basic forest rest houses in the park. Accommodation also available at Gudgudia, Lulung, Jamuari, Dhudhruchampa, and in maharaja's log cabin at Chahala. Aranya Niwas Tourist Complex run by Orissa Tourism Development Corporation (OTDC) is 10km (6 miles) inside Baripada entrance. Solar-power-operated stone lodges have fairly good catering facilities. Panthasala Tourist Bungalow at Bangriposi, 50km (30 miles) from Simlipal, can be booked by writing to the Tourist Officer, Baripada (visitors required to supply own provisions).

Wildlife: Indian Elephant, deer species, and Muggar Crocodile.

Landscapes: Varied topography of beautiful mountains, red loamy soils, rivers and streams flowing from mountains through forests.

Reservations: Contact the Field Director, Simlipal, Project Tiger, Baripada, Orissa–757002.

Above: Male Indian Elephants rarely exceed a height of 3 metres (10 feet). This beast is a *makhna* – the local name given to tuskless males.

Above right: The *Dendrobium aphyllum* orchid species; orchids grow in great profusion in Simlipal.

Opposite: The park's well-watered mountain landscapes give rise to exquisite waterfalls, one of which is Joranda, whose wispy plume falls for 150 metres (490 feet).

A 30-square-kilometre (12-square-mile) vegetation zone in the southern end of the park features a multitude of medicinal plants – Sarsaparilla, Pergularia, Vasaka are just some of them. The striking landscape of Nawana in the south, is adorned with miles of the indigenous mustard-yellow Alasi flowers.

The marshes and meadows of Simlipal are a haven for the park's wildlife. Around 430 Indian Elephant, 97 Tiger, 100 Leopard (Panther) and several Wild Boar find refuge here. Deer numbers are far greater, with 2500 to 3000 Spotted Deer (Chital) and 7000 to 9000 Sambhar. Rivers of the higher altitudes harbour Mahseer (Freshwater Shark) and Goonch (Trout).

Among the birds that can be spotted are Hill Mynah, Rose Finch, Indian Pied Hornbill, buntings, Red Junglefowl and Peafowl.

Near Jashipur, the gateway to the park, is the starkwhite Barehipani waterfall tumbling spectacularly from an altitude of 1308 feet (400 metres). It forms the source of the park's major river, the Budhablang. A rest house at Chahala is in the form of a log cabin named Eucalyptus Villa, and was built originally by the Maharaja of Mayurbhanj for his hunting expeditions. It is set against a backdrop of dense Eucalyptus jungle. An-

other waterfall, Joranda, is located 14 kilometres (9 miles) from Barehipani, and cascades from a height of 150 metres (490 feet).

Today, Simlipal's ecological resources are under constant threat from the local tribespeople encroaching on the land. The most primitive tribe are the Kharia Kondhs. Other groups include the Santhal, Sabhara, Bhumija, Saora, Hos, Mahali and Mankadia.

Members of the Orang tribe are characterized by their dark brown complexion, curly black hair and full lips. Their society is patriarchal and they co-exist as a family, surviving on a diet of rice and occasionally meat. The Orang hold strong beliefs in the spirit world, and worship natural elements such as the sun and wind.

The well-built Santhal people have similar features to the Orang, but are darker – almost black – in complexion. Still pursuing traditions that are culturally rich, they sing and dance on all joyous occasions to the sound of their drums, known as *madal*. Their main livelihood is the cultivation of rice and other cereals, but they sometimes eat meat, for which they hunt using bows and arrows. They are known to also eat snakes. The Santhal live in mud homes, whose walls are painted with hues derived from earth pigments.

PALAMAU SANCTUARY AND TIGER RESERVE

Jharkand's tiger sanctuary

The Palamau Sanctuary rests on the northwestern edge of Chota Nagpur plateau in the newly created state of Jharkand, whose eastern extent borders West Bengal. The region has a wealth of wildlife although some animals, such as the Indian Cheetah, which used to inhabit the jungles of the sanctuary, are today extinct. Palamau was set aside as a tiger reserve under Project Tiger in 1973 and established as a sanctuary in 1976, and extends across 1026 square kilometres (395 square miles). A proposal has been lodged to declare 225 square kilometres (88 square miles) of this area a national park.

The forest reserve of what was originally the Betla sanctuary in the northern section of the sanctuary is the most fascinating portion in terms of its wildlife. Here, the Betla forests are of the dry deciduous vegetation type with dominant stands of Sal (Shorea robusta) and bamboo. Set in undulating country, the forests resemble a nature park. The Koel River and its tributary flow at the sanctuary's northern fringe, so animals tend to congregate at the Auranga River for their source of water in the dry season. Besides the Koel, the Amanat and Kanhar rivers also flow through the northern, Betla section of the sanctuary.

Two types of tree in the forest are significant to both the wildlife and the local people: the Bael (Aegle marmelos) for its summer fruit, which also makes a refreshing drink for humans; and the Mahua (Mowra Butter tree) for its flowers – relished by herbivores. The Mahua fruits when fermented make an intoxicating brew.

During the summer months, most of the rivers in the sanctuary dry up. To ease the shortage of water for the wildlife, certain remedying measures have been made: the natural springs have been deepened, wells have been dug and artificial water sources created. The Hathbajwa watchtower and Madhuchuhan hide overlook waterholes and are excellent spots for visitors to watch the wildlife; they are assured of seeing many species of animals at dawn and dusk.

A successful conservation programme

Tribal groups in India have always lived in symbiosis with the indigenous forest, and any threat to the environment poses a threat to their daily rituals and habits. In the setting up of wildlife reserves, the human element requires cognizance.

Two different methods were applied in two reserves, Palamau Sanctuary and Tiger Reserve and Gir Lion Reserve in the state of Gujarat on the west coast of India. While the Madhari people and their cattle were relocated beyond the Gir forest boundaries in the latter, at Palamau a protected core area was identified and declared out of bounds for any exploitation. The tribespeople (there are three tribal villages in the sanctuary – Lato, Kujrum and Ranandag) were permitted to remain, with certain restrictions; they had to keep to the buffer

Above right: Indian Wolf (Canis lupus). India's only wolf sanctuary is near Baresand, on the outskirts of the reserve.

Opposite: The park's rivers, such as the Koel, cannot withstand summer's hot and dry conditions, and many dry up at this time of year.

Location: On the Chota Nagpur plateau of Jharkand State. The nearest airport is at Ranchi, 170km (105 miles) away. The nearest railhead is at Daltonganj, which is 25km (15 miles) from the sanctuary and 26km (16 miles) from Betla. Regular bus services to the sanctuary.

Climate: The sanctuary experiences an extreme climate: hot and dry in summer (maximum 48°C; 118°F), very cold in winter (minimum 3°C; 38°F).

When to go: Palamau can be visited all year round. Winter is pleasant, but in summer it is easier to spot wildlife at the waterholes.

Getting there: Daltonganj is the nearest town, 25km (15 miles) away. Car hire available here.

Facilities: Ample accommodation is offered in the form of a tourist lodge and forest rest houses in the Betla portion of the sanctuary. There are also rest houses at Kerh, Kechki, and Mundu in the park.

Wildlife: Of particular interest are migrating Indian Elephant, Tiger, Gaur, Chital and Sambhar. Jeeps can be hired to view wildlife. Trained-elephant rides can be booked from Betla.

Landscapes: The scenery at the edge of the Chota Nagpur plateau, with its undulating terrain and parkland-style forests, has a remoteness that is beautiful.

Reservations: Contact The Field Director, Project Tiger, Palamau Tiger Reserve, Daltonganj, Jharkand –822001.

Map labels: Delhi, North Koel, Betla, Barwadih, Wireless Station, Kerh, Mumbai, Wireless Station, Lat, Forest Rest House, Palamau Sanctuary & Tiger Reserve, Mundu, Kutku, Garu, = TIGER SANCTUARY, Koel, N, Maromar, Baresand, Adhey, Rud, Netarhat

zone around the reserve's protected core, where they could graze their cattle, and harvest bamboo, grass for thatching, wood for fuel, and wild fruits, roots and tubers for food. Members of the tribes were also employed for the construction of patrol roads, guard huts, watchtowers and other work in both reserves. Gradually, they developed an interest in the conservation programme and actively cooperated with management. In return, they benefited from the additional water sources developed within the reserves.

Indian Elephant and Tiger

An Indian Elephant population inhabiting the Betla section of the sanctuary increases every October and lasts until April as more of these giants migrate from the Baresand forests in search of water at the end of the monsoon season (Baresand is a village on the fringe of the sanctuary's vast core area). While these Elephant are the centre of attraction for park visitors, they create problems for local farmers as they destroy vegetation and raid the paddy fields. Gaur (Indian Bison) are plentiful and regularly spotted – particularly as they are not shy creatures. It is a similar case with Palamau's antelope

Above and opposite bottom right: India has an impressive count of over 2000 bird species, whose plumage ranges from drab to dazzling: here, a Jungle Crow (*Corvus macrorhynchos*) can't compete with the iridescence of the Whitebreasted Kingfisher (*Halcyon smyrnensis*).

Above right: Although the Tiger population in Palamau is substantial due to the ongoing efforts of Project Tiger, visitors are not likely to see them.

Right: Dry deciduous forest in the north of the park.

species: Sambhar, Chital, Muntjac (Barking Deer) as well as Wild Boar. Nilgai (Blue Bull) occur in a very small number. In the forests near Baresand, on the way to Mahuadar, is a wolf sanctuary. Named the Sarhadih Wildlife Sanctuary, it is the only one in the country.

Other animals in Palamau include Leopard (an accurate census is not available), Sloth Bear, Indian Wild Dog (Dhole), Striped Hyena and mongoose, as well as Rhesus Macaque and Common Langur (Hanuman Monkey).

Since protective efforts were established in the sanctuary under Project Tiger, a large percentage of Jharkand's Tiger population is sustained by Palamau.

In other parts of the state, they occur in isolated pockets but are never seen and do not have a long-term future. The preserving of this regal cat, which numbers around 50, is the focus of this sanctuary which is contiguous with the forests of Hazaribagh, a national park, and the nearest town, Ranchi.

Birdlife is abundant and varied, with about 140 avian species having been identified in the sanctuary. Commonly spotted species are Scavenger Vulture, Crested Serpent Eagle, Lapwing, Rose-ringed Parakeet, White-breasted Kingfisher, the Coppersmith and Large Green Barbet, Palm and House Swift, Mahratta Wood-pecker, Rufous and Yellow-bellied Flycatcher, orioles, Jungle Crow, swallows, Small Minivet, Tailor Bird and drongos. The Red Jungle Fowl and Peafowl are also plentiful. Many waterbirds are seen at the small Kamaldaha lake and other water sources during winter.

The ruins of two 16th-century forts built nearly 600 years ago by the local Chero tribal chieftains, whose descendents still live in the sanctuary, are an added attraction in this reserve.

There is also a modern hotel called Naihar lying on the outer fringes of the forest, which offers wonderful cuisine and good accommodation.

CENTRAL INDIA

Three significant mountain ranges roughly form the boundaries of Central India. Along the western edge of the subcontinent which parallels the Arabian Sea, a wall formed by the Western Ghats extends from north to south, while on the eastern edge facing the Bay of Bengal, the far more broken Eastern Ghats run along the coastline of Andhra Pradesh and Orissa. The Ghats stretch down into India's peninsula, converging in the Nilgiri hills of the southern state of Karnataka. The Vindhya range of the Deccan plateau separates Central India from southern Peninsular India. Madhya Pradesh – India's largest state – and the eastern portion of Maharashtra fall into this vast Central Indian region. The principal rivers, Narmada and Tapti, ultimately drain into the Arabian Sea; the Narmada forms a spectacular waterfall in the marble rock near Bhedaghat at Jabalpur, in central Madhya Pradesh.

Annual rainfall in Central India varies from 1270 to 1520 millimetres (50 to 60 inches). Extreme climatic conditions prevail here, with minimum winter temperatures dipping to almost freezing, while during peak summer the mercury often rises to 45°C (113°F).

Moist and dry Teak forests are mixed with deciduous forests of Sal, Mahua (Mowra Butter tree), Ber (Indian Jujube), and Dhak, whose common name Flame of the Forest aptly describes the bright orange and red sweetpea-shaped flowers that provide a burst of colour above this species' gnarled trunk. A number of fruit-bearing trees have strong medicinal value: the deep purple blackberries of the Jamun act as a blood purifier, the roundish green fruits of the enormous Bahera (*Terminalia bellerica*) relieve coughs and asthma, and the pale green fleshy fruit of the Amla contains calcium and is a great digestive; drinking water after eating this fruit freshens and sweetens the mouth.

The parks and tiger reserves of Madhya Pradesh include Kanha, Bandhavgarh and Pench, as well as Madhav National Park. Eastern Maharashtra's protected areas are the Melghat and the Tadoba National Park and Tiger Reserve.

Above right: The Spangled Drongo (*Dicrurus hottentottus*) is noted for its melodious birdsong.

Left: The Banjar River in Kanha is a major catchment area for the surrounding region.

TADOBA NATIONAL PARK AND TIGER RESERVE

Leopard heartland

There are still many wildlife refuges in India that remain tucked away from the constant parade of visitors. One of these is the Tadoba National Park and Tiger Reserve, which retains a unique charm. The park lies in the Teak belt of Central India which gradually extends into northern Andhra Pradesh.

Tadoba was once in the possession of the semi-nomadic aboriginal Gond rulers of Central India, who were in control of the region in the 10th and 11th centuries, and again in the 16th century. First set up as a reserve in 1935, the Tadoba National Park was legislated in 1955. The park became part of Project Tiger in 1995 when it added the adjacent Andheri Wildlife Sanctuary (625 square kilometres; 245 square miles) to its area. It protects around 45 Indian Tigers.

The national park itself is compact and has an area of 117 square kilometres (45 square miles). Its forests consist of mixed deciduous trees encircling the perennial Tadoba Lake, on whose shores stand a number of sprawling lodges. A road runs around the circular lake and is suitable for motor vehicles. Set amid serene rolling hills, the lake creates a lasting impression of the park's tranquil beauty.

Besides the abundance of Teak, other interesting tree species are the fragrant-bloomed Gardenia, Satinwood, *Diospyros montana*, Mahua (Mowra Butter tree), Mango and Jamun (Blackberry). Lofty Jamun also encircle the lake; beyond here the ground is marshy to the road. The forest floor is covered with shrubs, and clumps of bamboo are prevalent.

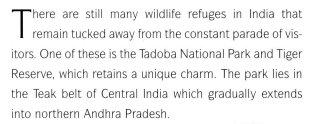
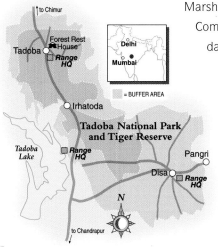

Waterfowl around the lake

Cattle Egret, common at the lake, perch in trees at the water's edge. At dusk, they follow the Wild Boar, roaming the lake perimeter in search of insects. Purple Moorhen and Jacana also make a regular appearance while Wood Owl and Lesser Owl retreat to the forests. Marsh Crocodile (also referred to as Common Indian) congregate in abundance in the lake waters.

Twilight at the lake

The park presently has few Tiger but Panther, or Leopard, are frequently sighted on drives in the late evening. There are six villages within the park and 53 at the fringes; the Leopards – of which there are presently about 30 in Tadoba – generally prefer to move around the periphery of human habitation to prey on domestic fowl, stray dogs and cattle. As dusk sets in, the Common Palm and Small Indian Civet are drawn to the lake. Jackal are fairly common, while Dhole (Indian Wild Dog) are seen every now and again. Gaur makes a seasonal appearance at twilight from March to May and the solitary Muntjac (Barking

Above right: Leopard, or Panther (*Panthera pardus*).

Opposite top: Tadoba's serene forest-lined lake.

Opposite far left: The waxy, sweet-scented Frangipani.

Opposite left: The large- and dense-leaved Teak (*Tectona grandis*) is fire-resistant, which has aided the tree's survival.

Location: In the district of Chandrapur in Maharashtra State. Nearest airport is Nagpur, 208km (129 miles) from the park. Nearest town and railhead is Chandrapur (45km; 28 miles).

Climate: Winters are cold (minimum 8°C; 46°F), while the summer months are searing (maximum 46°F; 115°F).

When to go: The summer months (March to June) and winter season (November to February) after the monsoon rains are the best times to visit the park.

Getting there: The park is accessible from Chandrapur, where jeeps can be hired. Tourists may enter in their own motor vehicles. There are also buses to the park.

Facilities: Chandrapur has its own lodges and catering facilities. There are rest houses, huts and youth hostels in the core of the forest, with canteen facilities. Platforms constructed in the trees serve as watchtowers. Night guided tours in jeeps and minibuses fitted with searchlights can be arranged with the Forest Department.

Wildlife: Leopard, Jackal, Sambhar, Chital, Common Langur, Nilgai, Wild Boar. Tiger are not very visible. Wildlife is best viewed at twilight and into the night, when animals emerge to feed.

Reservations: For permits and reservations, contact: The Divisional Forest Officer, West Chanda Division, Chandrapur (West Chanda), Maharashtra; or District Conservator of Forests, Tadoba National Park, Chandrapur, Maharashtra.

Precautions: It is advisable for visitors to carry mosquito repellent and mosquito coils while visiting the park; both are available locally.

Opposite: A female Common Langur (*Presbytis entellus*) assumes an instinctively protective pose with her young.

Right: During mating season, both male and female Median Egrets develop a long, silky plumage on their throat and wings to increase their attractiveness to the opposite sex.

Bottom right: The Marsh Crocodile (*Crocodilus Palustris*), known locally as Muggar, is the most common species in India.

Below: Nilgai, or Blue Bull (*Boselaphus tragocamelus*), is the largest member of the Indian antelope family; its name is derived from the blueish-grey hue of the male.

Deer) is occasionally spotted. Sambhar and Chital are quite common, the latter roaming in small herds but seen in their dozens at twilight. The Sambhar feed on aquatic plants and as darkness sets in, they arrive at the lake to graze. Nilgai (Blue Bull) number around 300. Indian Wild Boar, too, are seen, in regular groups of 30 or more. Unlike the states of Madhya Pradesh and Andhra Pradesh, the national parks of Maharashtra do not harbour Wild Elephant.

Because of the scorching midday heat, the animal residents of Tadoba tend to hide under cover of the park's foliage during the day to emerge after sunset. They eventually retreat into cover at daybreak.

Habits of the Hanuman Monkey

Several troops of Common Langur (or Hanuman Monkey) frequent the park. They appear round the tourist campgrounds and at an ancient open-air shrine standing at the edge of the lake, which is often visited by the local people. This was built by the Gando kings of Tadoba and honours the Indian gods Murlidhar and Krishna. Lord Krishna is one of the incarnations of Vishnu, and is among the most popular of the gods as he takes the most human form.

Although the Langur are tolerant of the presence of humans, they refuse to accept any offerings from visitors – and this habit is strongly discouraged. As dusk descends, they perch high up, close together on the branches of tall trees. Their bodies remain hidden by the foliage cover and only their tails hanging down are visible to observant nature-watchers. The Langur rise in the late morning. They scamper about in happy groups and wherever their wanderings take them in search of food, this eventually determines the tree they will roost in for the night. They frequently use the same tree for several nights. Common Langur eat a diet of young green shoots, berries and other fruits. Langur do not swim at all; they have a firm mistrust of water – even the shallows – and while drinking water from a river or stream, they keep carefully to the bank.

MELGHAT NATIONAL PARK AND TIGER RESERVE

Domain of the Indian Bison

Tucked away in the north of the state of Maharashtra, on the border with Madhya Pradesh, lies the tranquil Melghat park and reserve on the banks of the Tapti River, which acts as the state's northern boundary. The word Melghat translates as 'the meeting of ghats', ghat being a hilly tract – a reference to the Satpura hills. The area used to be a hunting ground for *shikaris* (royal hunters) of the past.

A sanctuary to begin with, Melghat today sprawls across 1676 square kilometres (654 square miles) on the southernmost ranges of the Satpura hills. This area consists of a buffer of 1314 square kilometres (510 square miles) and a core zone of 362 square kilometres (140 square miles); the latter makes up the national park and tiger reserve. In 1973 the Melghat Sanctuary fell under the wing of Project Tiger – one of nine tiger reserves already introduced to the scheme. Today, the national park section, along the hilly northern tracts, goes under the name of Gangamal and is kept relatively protected from human encroachment. The striking Chikaldhara plateau forms the highest area with Vairat Devi Point at the western extreme as the highest peak (1178 metres; 3865 feet).

Fauna of the park

The vegetation that's characteristic of Melghat National Park and an abundance of prey make it one of the best habitats in Maharashtra for the Indian Tiger. About 4 per cent of the dry Vidharba region in the eastern portion of the park comprises Tiger habitat, although in the areas frequented by these regal cats, visitors do not often get to spot them. However, there is generally ample evidence of their presence, such as the remains of a Chital kill or Tiger droppings and pug-marking.

The park's vegetation is dry deciduous forest composed mainly of Teak. The broad plateaus of the hill summits are clad in tall prairie grasses and Jaintic trees with, on the hillsides, dense tracts of bamboo occurring.

Of Melghat's fauna, the Gaur (Indian Bison) is the pride of the national park, and makes up the largest population of this herbivore in any of India's protected areas; numbers are around 1755. There are only small groups of deer in Melghat, but visitors have a fairly good chance of sighting Sambhar (1718 deer counted) and Indian Wild Dog (Dhole) which number just over 120 animals. Watchtowers and hides are located in appropriate places to enable naturalists to gain a clear view of the forest and its wildlife without disturbing the creatures.

Diverse Birdlife

The Melghat National Park and Tiger Reserve is marked by an absence of wetlands. Despite this, 270 avian species have been documented and the reserve is home

Above right: Although Melghat is a tiger reserve, these cats are extremely elusive here and not often seen.

Opposite: A Gaur, or Indian Bison (*Bos gaurus*), stands in deciduous forest, a habitat in which it thrives.

Location: In northern extreme of Amravati district of Maharashtra. Nearest railhead Badnera (124km; 77 miles) on main Mumbai-Nagpur railway route.

Climate: Winters cold (minimum 7°C; 45°F), summers scorching (42°C; 108°F). Monsoon season June to September.

When to go: October to February (winter) popular among local visitors. Make reservations well in advance on weekends and holidays.

Getting there: Buses from Badnera to Paratwada (Project Tiger headquarters), 60km (37 miles) to the north. Buses from Paratwada, Amravati and Akot to Chikhaldara, a tiny resort at south of park. Project Tiger Tourist Complex on banks of Sipna River, 1km (half a mile) from Semadoh (no buses); Information and Education Centre here.

Facilities: Forest rest houses throughout park. No lodges at Semadoh. Project Tiger offers dormitories and basic, low-budget double bed huts with Indian- (rather than Western-style) bathrooms. Green Valley resorts and Konarak, a basic lodge, in the town of Koklaz.

Wildlife: Indian Bison, Sambhar, Dhole, Sloth Bear. Avifauna includes Green Avadavat and endangered endemics. Project Tiger minibuses take visitors on early morning and late evening game-viewing drives; seats can be reserved.

Landscapes: Terrain rises from Tapti River to 1178m (3865ft) in the striking Gaurilagarh hills.

Reservations: For permission to visit and accommodation, contact: Field Director, Project Tiger, Melghat National Park, Paratwada, Amravati District, Maharashtra–444805.

Precautions: Human habitation between Semadoh and Chikhaldara is rare, so it is essential to carry plenty of water in summer – min. 2–3 litres (3.5–5pt) per person.

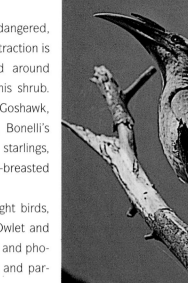

to some endemic species that are presently endangered, one of which is the Fairy Bluebird. The prime attraction is the Green Avadavat, which can be spotted around Lantana as it is attracted to the flowers of this shrub. Other species to look out for are Crested Goshawk, White-eyed Buzzard, Changeable Hawk Eagle, Bonelli's Eagle, storks, vultures, flycatchers, babblers, starlings, shrikes, nightjars, the Alexandrine and Red-breasted Parakeet, and Scarlet Minivet.

Semadoh in the park is a good spot to sight birds, particularly the Indian Grey Hornbill, Barred Owlet and Brown Fish Owl (it is not impossible to observe and photograph owls during daylight if one is vigilant and particularly patient).

Displacement of local tribes

Melghat is not merely a sanctuary for wildlife, but also reflects the heritage of India's ancient tribal cultures. The Tapti River and its tributaries flowing through Melghat's forests supply the aboriginal tribespeople – the Korku, Gawali and Gond communities – with over 30 per cent of their fresh water.

For centuries, the forests have provided shelter to longtime inhabitants, the Korku tribe, by yielding Mahua (Mowra Butter Tree) flowers, roots, bark, creepers, crabs and fish. The red Mahua flowers, which bloom during April and May, are very sweet and homemade wine made from these is relished by locals and tribespeople alike. These flowers also contribute to the diet of many animals, particularly the 180-odd Sloth Bear, which become intoxicated after eating them!

The recent demarcation of a third of Melghat's area for national park and tiger reserve protection, however, and the deaths – on a relatively large scale – of local tribespeople due to malnutrition is causing anxiety to the state government of Maharashtra. The Forest Department, on the other hand, has placed the blame firmly on the tribespeople for maintaining their age-old superstitions and cultural beliefs (they also claim that deaths have not occurred within the confines of Melghat's forests).

The Melghat National Park and Tiger Reserve has not yet received adequate public exposure and has consequently not received an influx of visitors comparable to other Indian reserves. This, in turn, has been to the advantage of Kanha, Bandhavgarh and Ranthambore.

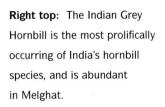

Right top: The Indian Grey Hornbill is the most prolifically occurring of India's hornbill species, and is abundant in Melghat.

Right centre: To catch a glimpse of the gorgeous shimmering plumage of the Fairy Bluebird is an exhilarating experience for visitors.

Right bottom: The deep hollow-sounding 'boom-o-boom' call of the Brown Fish Owl (*Bubo zeylonensis*) is positively eerie when it unexpectedly rents the forest stillness.

Below: The Crested Goshawk is a medium-sized raptor with short wings and it can be identified from a distance by its blackish-grey crest.

PENCH NATIONAL PARK AND TIGER RESERVE

Where legend meets landscape

Lying in Central India's Satpura range in the state of Madhya Pradesh, this national park and tiger reserve has derived its name from the swift-flowing Pench River that runs from north to south through the park. Pench has played its own role in Central India's historical past. In the late 1800s writer Rudyard Kipling was mesmerized by Pench's spectacular landscape, and he set his two *Jungle Books* in the natural grandeur of this forested tract nestled among the Satpura hills.

The park lies within a vast sylvan belt that includes the forest zones of the Seoni, Balaghat and Nagpur districts. The Pench River defines the outer boundary of the Seoni and Chhindwara districts in the park's upper reaches and forms the state boundary with Maharashtra in the south. The more prominent hills of the Seoni district have been given names such as Arjal Matta, Kalapahad, Chhindimatta and Kumbhadeo.

Pench was declared a national park in 1983, and the tiger reserve was legislated in 1992, at which time it became the 19th tiger reserve of India.

The national park and tiger reserve sprawls across an area of 757 square kilometres (292 square miles), of which the national park covers about 293 square kilometres (111 square miles) and the buffer zone comprises the remaining area of about 464 square kilometres (179 square miles).

It has been recognized that this forest tract has the potential to be restored back to its original diversity. A contiguous forest expanse extending south towards Maharashtra has been notified as the Pandit Jawaharlal Nehru National Park.

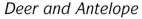

to Jabalpur

National Highway No.7

Delhi

Mumbai

Seoni

N

Sangoonkher Checkpoint

Pench National Park & Tiger Reserve

Forest Rest Camp

Pench

Totlah Dam

to Nagpur

Conservation of precious water

The construction of a reservoir on the Pench River, submerging a 54-square-kilometre (21-square-mile) area, has caused a significant change in the park. The reservoir lies on the southeastern boundary, surrounded by miniature hills and steep slopes. Because the national park lies on the winter migratory route of waterfowl, the reservoir is an ideal site for them and draws many migrating species. The forests of the park are crisscrossed by innumerable seasonal streams of the Pench River but during the summer, this river dries up. A myriad perennial natural pools, known locally as *dohs*, serve as waterholes for the park's fauna.

Deer and Antelope

The vegetation of this national park and tiger reserve consists of mixed deciduous forest, with Teak (*Tectona grandis*) and *Michelia champaca* being the prevailing species. A great variety of herbs and grasses within the forest sustain the large number of ungulates: Pench is home to high densities of Wild Pig, Nilgai (Blue Bull) and Chital, and in lesser numbers, Muntjac (Barking Deer), Chausingha (Four-horned Antelope), and Indian Bison. The Muntjac can often be spotted under the shaded

Above right: The Nilgai is common throughout Pench, although it tends to avoid the dense forests. Its herbivorous diet consists of leaves and fruits. A characteristic physical feature of this antelope is its pronounced sloping back.

Location: In the Seoni and Chhindwara districts of southern Madhya Pradesh. The nearest airport is Nagpur, 93km (58 miles) from the park. The town of Seoni, 19km (12 miles) away, is the nearest railhead.

Climate: Summer is scorching (maximum 43°C; 110°F) while winter is extremely cold (minimum 4°C; 39°F).

When to go: Although very hot, summer, from March to June, is the best time to see wildlife. November to February are pleasant.

Getting there: Pench reserve lies on National Highway No. 7 (NH7), between Nagpur and Jabalpur. A car is essential in the park; car hire in Jabalpur, Seoni and Nagpur. Visitors to Pench at present are true wildlife enthusiasts, although the park is gaining in popularity.

Facilities: Forest rest houses within the national park; no private lodges. Cooking facilities supplied for self-catering. Guides are necessary for touring the park.

Wildlife: Major attraction is great numbers of deer and antelope: Nilgai, Chital, Muntjac, Chausingha. Also Wild Boar and Indian Bison. Tiger present but sightings rare.

Reservations: For details and reservations, contact: The director, Pench National Park, Seoni District, Madhya Pradesh.

Above: Although captured here by the photographer's lens, these female Muntjacs (*Muntiacus muntjac*) are manifesting their intrinsic shy nature; they will generally avoid any human contact.

Right: Pench is characterized by its abundance of Teak (*Tectona Grandis*), a deciduous tree species. Generally, today, India's remaining Teak tracts are planted.

canopies of trees. Frequently seen are Chinkara (Indian Gazelle), slender, gracefully built antelope that are light chestnut in colour, deepening where this meets the animals' white underparts. The straight horns are ridged with rings. Their habitat is the thinner jungle zone, where they feed on cultivated crops, grains and leaves.

Sighting Tiger in the park is usually a chance encounter and is quite rare as they constantly avoid human contact and they remain very well camouflaged in their dappled environment.

Stringent conservation efforts have been adopted by the park authorities in Pench: the setting up of anti-poaching camps and patrols have greatly contributed to its now flourishing population of wild fauna.

Birdlife in Pench counts among its 125 species minivets, orioles, barbets, bulbuls, wagtails, munias and mynas. Small Blue Kingfisher dart along the Pench River, and Marsh Crocodile and freshwater turtles – such as Indian Softshell and Indian Roofed Shell – are abundant in the Totlah Dam.

In recent times, the declaration of the Pench forest as a national park and tiger reserve has created resentment amongst the local tribes as, in affording the forests complete protection, this prevents the people from collecting forest products such as Tendu fruits – which are tasty to eat – and leaves (the indigenous people roll them to make a *bidi*, which they smoke), lac (used in the preparation of lacquer), honey, and gum. A strict control is also imposed on the felling of trees and fishing. Proper eco-development of the park involving the combined efforts of local tribespeople and the park authorities has yet to be fully developed in the future.

KANHA NATIONAL PARK AND TIGER RESERVE

Rudyard Kipling's tiger country

Famed as India's 'Kipling country' after the Indian-born English writer Rudyard Kipling who achieved renown with his *Jungle Book* stories only after his death, the Kanha National Park and Tiger Reserve is spread over the Maikal range of hills, part of the Satpura mountains in Central India whose daunting hills rise above 3000 feet (900 metres).

The park comprises vast stretches of unbroken hilly forest on the Central Indian plateau in the state of Madhya Pradesh. It includes three forest ranges known as Kisli, Kanha and Mukki which are dominated by vast stands of tall Sal (*Shorea robusta*) and various *Terminalia* species; these are interspersed with well-watered valleys and flourishing grasslands.

Creating a sanctuary

A wildlife reserve was first established on the plateau in the Maikal hills in 1933, where the dry Teak zone of west Madhya Pradesh gives way to the evergreen moist Sal forests of the east. It also forms the catchment area of the Banjar River, which joins the Narmada at the town of Mandla to the north. The original park is bounded by a crescent-shaped hill range that rises to 900 metres (2950 feet) for three-quarters of its extent and cradles open undulating meadows dotted with Sal and tracts of bamboo. Many of these meadows originated as clearings that were created by the Gond and Baiga aboriginal tribes of the area, through their practice of shifting cultivation. These meadowlands are locally known as *maidans*. Madhya Pradesh has undergone many physical changes, the major contributing factor being the depletion of its mixed forests to the west and Sal forests to the east by felling for human settlement.

Kanha was declared a national park in 1955 and comprised a forest tract of 250 square kilometres (95 square miles). It became a reserve under Project Tiger in 1973. Two more sanctuaries in the nearby Balaghat district, Maikal and Supkhar, were merged with Kanha in 1976. The present overall area is 1945 square kilometres (745 square miles), of which 940 square kilometres makes up the core zone.

From Barasingha to Tiger

The wildlife in Kanha is a good representation of the general diversity of India's fauna. Indian Bison, or Gaur, roam in large herds in the park. This is the most robust of India's bovine family, with some bulls standing 1.8 metres (6 feet) at the shoulder. Cows are slightly smaller. The colouring of the bull is jet-black with an ashy forehead and white stockinged feet, while females are brownish. They can occur at high altitudes of up to 1830 metres (6000 feet) where they exist on a herbivorous diet. The highest point in Kanha, known as Bamhnidadar

Above right: Hardground Barasingha (*Cervus duvauceli branderi*) have learnt to adapt to less swampy conditions.

Opposite: *Mahout*-led elephant rides take visitors to view Tiger once they have been located in the park.

Location: In the Mandla district of Madhya Pradesh State in Central India. The park is accessible from Jabalpur (170km, or 105 miles, away) which also has the nearest airport and railhead. Nagpur is 270km (168 miles) from Kanha.

Climate: Summer temperatures are very high (maximum 43°C; 109°F) and winter is extremely cold (minimum 2°C; 36°F).

When to go: Best time to visit is March to June. Park closed during monsoon from beginning July to end October. Also closed midday to give respite to wildlife.

Getting there: Mandla is the district's main town (65km; 40 miles); buses travel between here and the park. The road from Nagpur to Kanha is bad; a car journey takes about five hours. Entrance gates at Kisli and Mukki, which have full canteen facilities. Just beyond Kisli gate, multiple food stores at Khatia.

Facilities: Forest Lodge managed by MPSTDC, forest rest houses, Baghira log huts of Madhya Pradesh (no self-catering required). Khatia has many private lodges, among them Kipling Camp, Krishna and Mowgli. Self-drive permissible with guide; jeep tours and elephant-back rides into Kanha. Khatia has an Interpretation Centre with displays and a sound and light show.

Wildlife: Regularly spotted are Tiger and Muntjac; Panther rarely. Chausingha and Nilgai, although present, are not often seen.

Landscape: Forested park nestles in horseshoe-shaped valley backed by spurs of Maikal hills and fronted by rolling meadows.

Reservations: Accommodation should be booked in advance. For general information, write to: The Field Director, Project Tiger, PO Mandla, Madhya Pradesh.

The map shows:
to Mandia, Delhi, Mumbai, Ronda, to Jabalpur, Bhimpur, Khatia, Entrance Gate, Kisli, Nila, Amlitola, Kanha, Indri, Bamhnidadar, Ghorila, Garhi, Supkhar, Banjar, Sondhar, Kanha National Park & Tiger Reserve, to Bilaspur, Entrance Gate, Mukki, ITDC Forest Lodge, to Nagpur, = BUFFER ZONE BOUNDARY

Above: A male Soft-ground Barasingha (*Cervus duvauceli*) can be distinguished from the Hard-ground species by the outward and upward curve of its antlers.

Below: While hunting, Indian Wild Dogs, or Dhole (*Cuon alpinus*), generally move together in packs.

Right: In the intense heat of summer, Tiger keep cool by immersing themselves in park waterholes and swamps.

('dadar' translates as 'extensive plateau'), creates a suitable habitat for these Gaur. They have no predators, although their calves are sometimes attacked by Wild Dog, Leopard and Tiger.

Kanha is particularly well known for protecting a rare species of Barasingha, or Swamp Deer (*Cervus duvauceli branderi*), which has adapted to a hard-ground habitat in contrast to its marsh-living cousin (*Cervus duvauceli*). Variation exists in the antlers of the two species: on the hard-ground deer species, the main branch first curves backwards then forwards, bringing the points of the antlers parallel with the top of the head. On the soft-ground species, the main branch is set at right angles to the head, curving outwards and resulting in a wider spread of the horns. Hard-ground Barasingha inhabit the grassy plains, being less dependent on water, while their cousins are seldom out of water, thus preferring the marshlands. Breeding habits are similar between the two subspecies, and both generally feed till late in the morning and again in the cool evening.

The adapted deer subspecies exists only in Kanha National Park, while Softground Barasingha occur in Uttar Pradesh and Kaziranga in Assam. The Barasingha population was at one point on the verge of extinction with a count of only 80 deer; conservation efforts adopted by the Forest Department in Kanha over past years have led to its stabilization. Wild Boar and the Black-naped Hare also exist throughout the park.

Although famous for its Barasingha, Kanha is known better as Tiger country. The elegant beasts are spotted regularly here, even during the day. As in most tiger reserves, in the very early hours of morning the elephant riders, or *mahouts*, penetrate the interior of the forest in search of the elusive Tiger. When an animal is successfully tracked down, the *mahouts* escort visitors to it on elephant-back. Walking is not permitted in the park, and visitors are allowed in with their own vehicles only if accompanied by an authorized guide.

Other members of the cat family in the reserve are Panther (Leopard) and the smaller Jungle, Leopard and Fishing Cat species. Also a major predator is the Indian Wild Dog, or Dhole. These animals move in packs of between five and 25 and collectively hunt even the larger animals, such as Sambhar. The Dhole has the long, lanky body of a wolf, but its legs as well as its muzzle are shorter, and its ears rounded at the tips. It is glossy brown in colour, with a long bushy black tail.

Interestingly, Kanha's Jackal – which generally are scavengers – are hunters. They move around in small families and kill Chital (Spotted Deer), small Sambhar and their fawns. Kanha's meadows are frequented by large deer populations where they graze in their hundreds. After the seasonal monsoon rains (July to October), the meadow  grasses flourish, becoming tall and green and leading to poor visibility for animal viewing. During the dry season (March), the grasslands are often completely burnt as a result of forest fires, and the entire meadowland is thus cleared. Deer are then clearly visible, grazing at dawn and dusk.

Legend of the lake

Kanha has its own historical legend attached to a small lake in one of the reserve's meadows. Dating back to epic times, it recounts the story of a king named Dashratha, whose kingdom extended across the whole of the Indian subcontinent. He hunted often with his bow and arrows, tracking his prey by listening intently for animal sounds. Once, while passing through a jungle, he heard the sound of an animal drinking water, so he shot his arrow. The next moment, he heard the moaning sound made by a man. He rushed to the spot to find a dying man named Shrawan; he had been hit by Dashratha's arrow and was groaning in pain. The man had come to fetch drinking water for his blind parents, and the sound that King Dashratha had mistaken for an animal drinking was of a pitcher being filled with water. The king carried Shrawan's dead body to his parents and begged them for mercy, but they died on the spot after hearing of the demise of their only son. The legendary lake is today called Shrawan Tal ('tal' being a reservoir).

Inset: The Sand Boa (*Eryse conicus*) is a non-venomous snake; it is nonetheless deadly as its method of killing prey is by constriction.

Below: The banks of Shrawan Tal are surrounded by Sal (*Shorea robusta*) forest.

Avian heaven

Kanha teems with avian life. Songbirds like the Racket-tailed Drongo and Magpie Robin enliven the forest with their sweet song, and before the monsoon arrives, Peacocks perform their spectacular displays throughout the forest. Two species of hornbill, the Common Grey and Malabar Pied, occur in large numbers. In winter, migrant birds such as Common Pochard, Lesser Whistling Teal and Black Stork congregate at the water-holes. Raptors spotted in the reserve are Shikra, Honey Buzzard, Sparrow Hawk, Lesser Kestrel, and the Crested Hawk and Crested Serpent Eagle, while several species of vulture, including the Long-billed and Scavenger Vultures, also make their home here.

Above: The high surrounding plateau, part of the Maikal (hill) range, creates a watershed for the Banjar River flowing through the valleys below.

Inset: Of Kanha's eagle species, the Crested Serpent Eagle (*Spilornis cheela*) is the most frequently spotted.

Clockwise from top left: Species such as Common Pochard, Lesser Whistling Teal, Red-crested Pochard, Whistling Teal, and Black Stork are all migratory water-birds that arrive in Kanha during the winter months to settle temporarily at the different wetlands.

BANDHAVGARH NATIONAL PARK AND TIGER RESERVE

Ancient stronghold of many kings

Bandhavgarh is the former land of valiant medieval kings – onetime bastion of the 12th-century Kalchuri dynasty – and is set in a vast expanse of verdant forest mantling the slopes around the ancient fortress that used to belong to the maharajas of Rewa. The park is equidistant from the four major towns of Madhya Pradesh State – Shahdol, Satna, Rewa and Katni – and rests in the cradle of the Vindhya range of hills.

First declared a national park in 1968 with an initial area of 105 square kilometres (40 square miles), an additional area of 343 square kilometres (132 square miles) was added in 1982. It was brought under the protection of Project Tiger in 1994 when 245 square kilometres (94 square miles) of Panpatha Wildlife Sanctuary were merged with the existing national park. Bandhavgarh is visited by thousands of national and international tourists annually.

The fort of Bandhavgarh dates back to Palaeolithic times (which extended up to roughly 4000 years ago) and has withstood the test of time. It is featured in the *Mahabharata* (an epic Sanskrit poem of India that is 2950 years old and focuses on two rivalling families), where it is referred to as Matsyadesh. During medieval times, the fort came into the possession of various Buddhist and Hindu dynasties. Until the late 12th century, the fort was a stronghold of the Kalchuri and Baghel Hindu dynasties, although the Muslim rulers, the Lodhis, possessed it temporarily. The temples, sculptures and pavilions evoke this bygone era; the fort is of

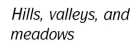

archaeological and mythological significance, featuring typical caves, rock paintings and carvings. There are also statues of the various incarnations of Vishnu, the Hindu god of stability. During the period in which Bandhavgarh was under the domain of a particular maharaja of Rewa, the forests became his preferred destination and virtually became his own personal game reserve.

Hills, valleys, and meadows

This country of 32 hillocks is crowned with flat plateaus and overhanging craggy cliffs. In turn, the hills are divided by green valleys and marshes, and the plains interspersed with meadows. The hills are composed mainly of permeable sandstones, allowing rainwater to percolate through. This has led to the formation of springs in the valleys and the marshes in the low-lying areas. Because of excessive water draining from the upper reaches of the park, some of the meadows have been turned into marshland. The plateaus and slopes are relatively drier.

Perennial streams and rivulets such as Charanganga, Janad, Damnar, Umrar and Bhadar, with their crystal-clear waters, crisscross the region, promoting fertile green vegetation on the riverbanks.

Above right: Iridescent dragonfly *Trithemis avrora*.

Opposite: A female Chinkara (*Gazella gazella*) pauses beside the ancient ruins of Bandhavgarh fort; the population has unfortunately decreased considerably in these forests.

Location: Set amidst Vindhya ranges, altitude varies from 44–811m (144–2660ft) above sea level. Khajuraho, 210km (130 miles) from park, is nearest airport; it is a five-hour drive from here to Tala (entry gate). Nearest railheads are Jabalpur (164km; 100 miles), Katni (102km; 63 miles) and Satna (112km; 70 miles) on the Central Railway and Umaria (32km; 20 miles) on the Southeastern Railway.

Climate: Winter nights are freezing (2°C; 36°F), summer unpleasantly hot (maximum 42°C; 108°F).

When to go: February to May is favourable; park remains closed from beginning July to end October.

Getting there: Private bus and car hire available from Umaria (32km; 20 miles), Amarpatan (80km; 50 miles), Shahdol (97km; 60 miles) and Rewa (105km; 65 miles), as well as from Khajuraho and Satna.

Facilities: Accommodation provided by the MPSTDC (White Tiger Forest Lodge) and many private lodges at Tala (Bandhavgarh Jungle Camp – former Maharaja of Rewa's palace – and Tiger Trails). Visitors may enter park in their own vehicles (petrol only as diesel is banned here); alternatively hire a taxi at Tala (park entry point). Park open from dawn to dusk. At entry gate, trained guides with interpretive skills can lead visitors through the park.

Wildlife: Chances of sighting Tiger high; also Chital, Sambhar, Nilgai and Chinkara. Elephant rides arranged by Forest Department.

Reservations: Prior booking essential; write to: The Manager, White Tiger Forest Lodge, Madhya Pradesh State Tourism Development Corporation, Umaria, Shahdol District, Madhya Pradesh; or Tourist Officer, Head Office, MPSTDC, 4th Floor Gangotri, T T Nagar, Bhopal.

Above: Blue-tailed Bee-eaters are generally spotted in the park's tall-grassed meadows.

Below: Visitors pass through dense forests on their way to the Chakradhara meadow.

The area's combination of hills, rivers and valleys, meadows and marshes has created a unique biodiversity evident in the varied, luxuriant vegetation. Bandhavgarh's forests are generally of the moist deciduous forest type. The sheltered valleys are clothed with moist evergreen Sal forests, while drier slopes and plains are covered in mixed forest. Dense tracts of bamboo are scattered throughout the valleys.

The Chakradhara and Rajbahera meadows are major features in the park, but uncontrolled growth of grass at Chakradhara is creating uncertainty for their future survival. Valleys that have deep, fertile soils covered in thick grasses are locally termed *vah*. Where these areas are marshy in nature, they support tall grass species. An interesting species of the marshy meadows is the insectivorous plant *Drocera*. A small herb with a leafy stem of long, linear leaves, its fruit contains seeds that attract microscopic organisms. The park's grasslands mainly consist of the Saccharuphragmites, Themeda and Heteropogon species. The ground vegetation of the riverine areas is dominated by various species of bryophytes (characterized by moss and liverwort-type plants) and pteridophytes (characterized by ferns, horsetails and club mosses).

Above: A special quality of Bandhavgarh is that Tigers are often seen in broad daylight.

Opposite: *Mahouts* washing their domesticated elephants.

Sighting the Bengal Tiger

Bandhavgarh's rich floral diversity, constancy of food, water and shelter, and the strict monitoring and prevention of encroachment by humans from outside the park has promoted a wealth of animal life. As far back as medieval times, the area was believed to have supported a healthy population of Tiger – sometimes referred to in India as the Royal Bengal Tiger.

The rare White Tiger used to occur here, but the last known creature was trapped in 1937, and there has been no report of a sighting since then.

The chances of visitors spotting a Tiger in Bandhavgarh are greater than in any of India's other forests. In peak summer, these majestic striped beasts can often be seen at the waterholes of Chakradhara, Gopalpur, Barwanala, Jurmani and Jamunia. At dawn, trained elephants and their riders go into the forest to track the Tiger. Once discovered, visitors are led back to the sighting on elephant-back. Other important cats in Bandhavgarh are Panther (Leopard), the Fishing, Leopard and Jungle Cat, and the rare Rusty-spotted Cat whose name accurately reflects its red dappled coat.

As many as 34 mammal species have been listed for this national park and reserve. A huge population – more than 8000 – of Chital (Spotted Deer) exists here, sharing the grasslands with Sambhar and (Muntjac) Barking Deer. Among the antelopes are Nilgai (Blue Bull) and Chinkara. Other major animals contributing to the wildlife diversity are Indian Wild Dog, Jackal, Wild Boar, Honey Badger, mongoose, porcupines and the Indian Hare. Central India's most common monkeys, the Rhesus Macaque and Hanuman Monkey (or Common Langur), chatter and swing lithely in the treetops.

The park sustains a particularly large number of butterflies – over 70 species – which are attracted to the marshes, wildflowers and dung piles of the park's herbivores. The many-hued species carry evocative names like Moon Moth, Common Rose, Blue Oakleaf and Blue Pansy. Shimmering dragonflies and damselflies are drawn to the limpid pools of water.

The Bandhavgarh National Park has a longer 'season' than the Kanha or Madhav parks because of a shorter monsoon, and the diversity of its habitat is reflected by the wide range of birdlife; nearly 250 avian species have been reported in the park. It provides a suitable habitat for different species of stork (White-necked and Lesser Adjutant) and hornbill (Malabar Pied and Common Grey), herons, cranes, as well as birds living in the tree canopies and birds of prey – most commonly, Crested Hawk and Crested Serpent Eagle, Honey Buzzard, Sikra, and Lesser Kestrel. In winter, the artificial waterholes of Bhadrashila, Gopalpur and Bathan attract migratory waterbirds such as Nakta, Lesser Whistling Teal, and Ruddy Shelduck. The smaller birds include Grey Tit, Baya Weaver Bird, Spotted Munia, the Green and Bearded Bee-eater, and of the flycatchers, the Varditar, White-browed, Fantail and Paradise species. and Bandhavgarh's three species of parakeet –

Above: From afar, the Black Ibis can clearly be identified by its scarlet crown.

Inset: Moon Moth.

Alexandrine, Blossom-headed and Rosering. The Peafowl, with its spectacular tail-feather displays, adds its own blaze of colour to the jungle.

The Bandhavgarh National Park and Tiger Reserve is worth visiting for its breathtaking beauty alone. A satisfying drive through the park – which needs to be undertaken over at least three days – can take in Chakradhara meadow, the sprawling *vah*, or grassed valleys, of Rajbahera, the serene tranquillity of the spot named Andheri Jhiriya, and the beautiful forested hills of Badhaini (the sights are not in any logical order). Thereafter, there is Ghoradaman's awesome wilderness, a view of the spectacular fort on the towering clifftops from the viewpoint at Seshsaya – counterbalanced by panoramic vistas of the park from the fort itself – and finally, the gentle coolness of the Jamunia stream.

Below: The local name for *Sterculia urens*, a soft-wood tree with a papery outer bark, is *keonji*.

Above: White Tiger Forest Lodge on the fringes of the park's forests offers visitors a comfortable stay.

MADHAV NATIONAL PARK

Shivpuri's royal heritage

The Madhav National Park, not far from the urban centre of Shivpuri, has managed to retain a virgin jungle state. Nonetheless, located as it is just over 100 kilometres (60 miles) from the city of Gwalior, the park is becoming a favoured destination for adventure-seekers drawn to its dense, original forests. It draws a steady stream of 20,000 visitors every year.

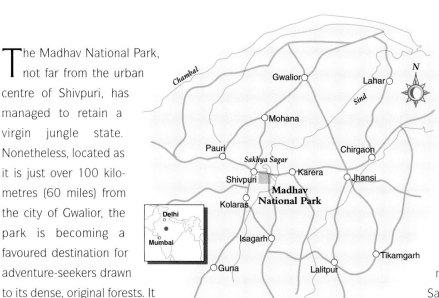

Once a royal hunting ground of the Islamic Mughal emperors ('mughal' means 'king') who ruled here till the mid-18th century, Madhav also witnessed the rise and fall of the Hindu Scindia rulers of Gwalior in the first half of the 19th century (Gwalior was a hill fort that was key to the control of the Central Provinces). The forests became the summer capital of the Scindia kings, during which time they used to shift their base from Gwalior to Shivpuri. The Maharaja of Gwalior took possession of the forest, in those days known as Shivpuri, and laid the foundations of a good network of roads to turn this into a private *shikargarh* (meaning 'hunting grounds') for himself and for the entertainment of his royal guests. During this time, Shivpuri was referred to as the 'jungles of Shipri' (the latter a contraction of 'Shivpuri').

In 1959, the Shivpuri National Park was established with an area of 156 square kilometres (60 square miles). It was renamed the Madhav National Park in 1977 in honour of Madhav Rao Scindia I, the former Scindia ruler of Gwalior. A later proposal was made to include an additional 182 square kilometres (70 square miles) and today the park extends over an area of 355 square kilometres (137 square miles).

Freshwater Snub-nosed Crocodiles

Madhav is bounded by two lakes, the crescent-shaped Chandapata and the Sakhya Sagar. Lying 8 kilometres (5 miles) from the town of Shivpuri, Sakhya Sagar is semi-circular in shape and filled with the little-appreciated Marsh, or Muggar, Crocodile. This reptile, also known as the Snub-nosed Crocodile, is primarily a freshwater species occurring in inland reservoirs and rivers with little current. Adults are light brown to uniform black and grow to 3.5 to 4 metres (11 to 13 feet), although larger specimens have been recorded. Muggars feed on snails, crabs, fish and turtles as well as mammals, small reptiles and waterbirds. Their wider throat and jaws enables them to swallow larger prey. These crocodiles breed by laying around 30 eggs, of which only 1 per cent survive.

A host of migratory birds

A large number of migrating birds choose the Sakhya Sagar lake as their temporary habitat during the winter months of December through February. They include pochards, pintails, jacanas, ibises, Greylag Goose, Lesser

Above right: Chausingha, or Four-horned Antelope (*Tetracerus quadricornis*), are quite visible to park visitors, although at times they do retreat into the tall grass.

Location: On the semi-arid plateau of Malwa. Small centre of Shivpuri is 7km (4 miles) from Madhav park and 115km (70 miles) from Gwalior. Gwalior and Jhansi (95km; 60 miles) are the nearest railheads.

Climate: Summer months are unpleasantly hot (maximum 43°C/109°F in May) while winter nights are very cold (minimum 3°C; 35°F).

When to go: The months between November and May best for visitors.

Getting there: Shivpuri lies on Agra-Bombay NH3. Regular bus services to the park operate from Jhansi, Gwalior, Indore and Bhopal.

Facilities: Park is open 06:00–19:00 (sunrise to sunset) each day; entry restricted from 11:00–15:00. Visitors can join a guided tour or hire a jeep accompanied by a guide. Accommodation available at the Tourist Village (3km, or 2 miles, from Shivpuri), MPSTDC-owned Chinkara Motel (8km, or 5 miles, from the park), as well as circuit houses (constructed for government officials) and dak bungalows (rest houses for park officials) in the park. There is an observatory tower.

Wildlife: Mainly herds of deer: Chinkara, Chital, Nilgai. Also Wild Boar and an abundance of migratory birds at the two lakes. Boat rides on the lake from the Sakhya Sagar Boat Club for wildlife viewing can be arranged through the Forest Department. Also of interest are the *chhatris* of the Scindia royal family and Narawar fort.

Reservations: For accommodation, contact: Tourist office, Government of India, Gwalior, Madhya Pradesh; or Director, Madhav National Park, Shivpuri, Madhya Pradesh–473551.

Whistling Teal, Pied Wagtail, Red Wattled Lapwing, and Painted Stork. In all there are 227 species of birds in Madhav, of which White-backed and Scavenger Vulture, Red Jungle Fowl, Peafowl, Tree-pie and Jungle Crow are only a few. During the searing summer, perennial streams and lakes provide the only source of water.

The park consists of tropical dry deciduous forest, which rests on a barren, rocky foundation and bears a close resemblance to the forest in Rajasthan's Ranthambore National Park. A vast grove of Khair (*Acacia catechu*) makes up a major portion of the forests, together with other major tree species such as Kardhai (*Anogeissus pendula*) and Sali (*Boswellia serrata*). Sali trees carry small white flowers each bearing five petals.

The park is popular for its relatively easy viewing of herds of deer, although Chital (Spotted Deer), for example, do not appear in herds as extensive as those of Kanha National Park despite being distributed through-

out Madhav (1900 deer have been recorded); they are also not as large nor do they have such beautiful coats. Of the other deer and antelope species, there is an abundance of Chausingha (Four-horned Antelope); there are 500 Sambhar, 700 Chinkara (Indian Gazelle), and 750 Nilgai (Blue Bull). Panther, or Leopard, and Indian Wild Dog are also inhabitants of the forests.

In Shivpuri's early hunting days, giant Tigers used to roam the forests, unlike today's threatened numbers. Visitors can undertake a guided safari by vehicle across an enclosed area of 9 square kilometres (3.5 square miles), which presently contains four Tigers and highlights recent efforts to breed these beasts in captivity.

Architectural relics

The historic George Castle in Madhav National Park is a magnificent architectural relic from the reign of the Scindia dynasty. It was built by the rulers for a proposed

Below: The best time for viewing migratory waterfowl in Madhav, particularly at Sakhya Sagar lake, is during the winter months of December through February.

Left: A tourist drawcard in Madhav is George Castle, a historic landmark dating back to the Scindia dynasty of the 19th century.

Centre: The Ruddy Shelduck belongs to a family of goose-like ducks whose plumage is usually brightly coloured.

Bottom: India's milder winter sun attracts Muggar Crocodiles (*Crocodilus palustrus*) to the riverbanks where they bask in large numbers.

Following pages: Tigers resort to the waterholes during the sultry Indian summers.

visit by King George V, although it was later used as a hunting lodge. It stands serenely at the highest point of the park, which makes for excellent views across the lake at sunset. The Martyr Memorial to the famous Indian revolutionary, Tantia Tope, who pioneered the 1857 Sepoy Mutiny ('sepoy' translates as 'ordinary soldiers'), also stands in the park. At the time, the Maharaja of Gwalior had demonstrated his loyalty to the British colonists, but his British East India Company troops chose to follow Tantia Tope; they were, however, defeated by the British rulers in fierce battles the following year. Historical sites in Shivpuri include the *chhatris* (meaning 'umbrella' and referring to the dome-shaped pavilions of the Indian mausoleums). Those of Maharani Sakhya Raje Scindia and Madho Rao Scindia, with their mosaic inlays and exquisitely crafted latticed-marblework (known as *jali* – literally, 'net'), have stood the test of time. These *chhatris* are an interesting mix of Hindu and Islamic design styles.

The Narawar Fort, built by King Nal, stands on a hillock 40 kilometres (25 miles) from Shivpuri. Its grounds extend for 8 square kilometres (3 square miles). It was built by King Nal, an Indian mythological figure appearing in the epic *Mahabharata*. The cascading Sultangarh falls fed by the gurgling waters of the Parvati River greet visitors on the way to the town of Shivpuri.

SEMI-DESERT INDIA

A vast desert country lies along India's western boundary. In terms of climate and physiography, this region is entirely different from the rest of the country; high temperatures, very low humidity and low precipitation are the primary characteristics. It can be divided into two zones: desert in its full sense and semi-desert. The desert zone, into which the Thar Desert of Rajasthan falls, features typical sand dunes and almost no vegetation. The semi-desert zone, which consists of part of Rajasthan and part of Punjab to the extreme north, is filled with thorny and less leafy trees. There are some mighty rivers in this region: the Indus, Jhelum, Sutlej and Beas all flow along the plains of Punjab, while the Sabarmati drains the upper Udaypur District of Rajasthan. All of these rivers empty into the Arabian Sea to the west of the Indian continent. One of the oldest mountain systems in the world, the Aravalli range, runs across Rajasthan, and its forests harbour many wild animals.

There is a slight variation in rainfall between the northerly state of Punjab and Rajasthan: the former receives an average annual rainfall of 200 to 500 millimetres (8 to 20 inches) while Rajasthan enjoys 600 to 750 millimetres (24 to 30 inches). Climatic conditions are extreme. In summer hot, powerful winds blow and the mercury rises to 50°C (122°F); in winter, it dips to freezing. Only trees that can survive on very little water survive here; they have long roots that penetrate deep into the ground to avail themselves of subsoil water. Predominant tree species are various acacias, Indian Jujube, Flame of the Forest, and various cacti. Although Punjab has very little wildlife, Rajasthan is rich in fauna. Desert Fox and reptilian life such as the Sidewinder Snake, scorpions, and various lizard species occur in the desert zone. The semi-desert thorn forests harbour Tiger, Leopard (Panther), Jungle Cat, Jackal, Sloth Bear, Common Langur (or Hanuman Monkey), Wild Boar, and various deer and antelope. The most important bird of this desert region is the Great Indian Bustard, which is also one of the most endangered birds in the country.

Both the Ranthambhore and Sariska tiger reserves and the country's finest bird sanctuary, Keoladeo National Park, are located in Rajasthan.

Inset: The Rhino-horned Beetle (*Lucanus cervus*) is well adapted to its desert environment.

Left: An expansive view from the old fort at Sariska, across a valley in the Aravalli hills.

RANTHAMBHORE NATIONAL PARK AND TIGER RESERVE

One-time domain of the maharajas

An awesome gift from Nature, the sprawling verdant forests of central India have, over the years, eventually been depleted and today, only a minuscule portion survives in the northwestern region. Before India gained Independence in 1950, the northwest was divided into several states that were under the domain of ruling Indian princes, or maharajas. They were merged into one state after Independence and came to be known as Rajasthan, the 'land of Rajputs'. The Rajputs, meaning 'sons of kings', were a military caste descended, according to legend, from the mythical warlike figure Kshatriya, and were renowned as great warriors from the seventh to the 12th centuries. They left behind them a rich legacy in terms of architecture and culture.

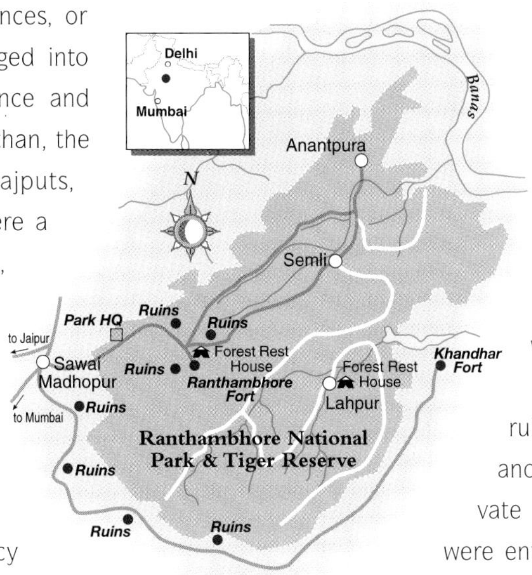

Princely states and dynasties

Ranthambhore National Park and Tiger Reserve lies in Rajasthan and memories of its regal past are evoked by the old turrets, mosques, wells, and other structures that are studded throughout the park. Overgrown with Peepal (*Ficus religiosa*) trees, they blend beautifully into their natural surroundings.

Originally a Hindu kingdom, with the fort established in 944, Ranthambhore came under Muslim rule intermittently over the next six centuries (increasing pressure from warring Arabs and Turks had eventually brought about Muslim power in much of northern India). The fort was taken over in 1301 by Ala-ud-din Khilji of the Bahmani dynasty, but the powerful Rajputs managed to regain control and Ranthambhore emerged as a powerful kingdom. During the 16th century, Muslim emperor Akbar was the most illustrious ruler of the Mughal dynasty which ruled India for more than 200 years. In 1569, in addition to Ranthambhore, Akbar took possession of the fort in Chittor, another princely state in Rajasthan, after 40 days of bloodshed between the Mughals and the Rajputs. The Mughals handed over the Ranthambhore fort to the Hindu rulers of the princely state of Jaipur, after which it remained with them until 1949, when Jaipur was merged with Rajasthan.

While under the protection of the ruling maharajas of Jaipur, the forest and its animals were maintained as a private hunting preserve, where royal guests were entertained. It was to be an extremely positive move when, later, in 1972, the preserve was taken over by Project Tiger.

Above right: Jungle Cat (*Felis chaus*).

Opposite top: Devotees come to pray for prosperity and everlasting union in marriage at the temple of Ganesh, situated on Raj Bagh lake.

Opposite bottom: Common Langur (*Presbytis entellus*).

Opposite right: This view of the Jogi Mahal, an old hunting lodge standing at the edge of Padam *talao*, can be seen from the ancient fort of Ranthambhore. It was built on the summit of a steep outcrop and offers sweeping vistas.

Location: The Ranthambhore park and reserve lies in the desert state of Rajasthan on the main Delhi-Mumbai railway line and is readily accessible from Jaipur (145km; 90 miles). Sawai Madhopur, the nearest railhead and gateway to the park, lies 11km (7 miles) away.

Climate: Summer (April–June) temperatures rise to 40°C (104°F). Winter nights are cold (8°C; 46°F).

When to go: The best time to go is in winter (December to February) and March/April. The park is closed during the monsoon period; it reopens on 1 October.

Getting there: The nearest town is Sawai Madhopur, which has a good bus service with many connections.

Facilities: Sawai Madhopur has excellent resorts and eco-lodges: Taj group-owned Sawai Madhopur Lodge (old hunting lodge of Maharaja of Jaipur); new Vanyavilas, super luxury tented resort owned by Oberoi Hotels. Rajasthan Tourism Development Corporation (RTDC) manages more basic and functional Hotel Kamadhenu and Castle Jhoomar Baori Forest Lodge.

Wildlife: Interesting array of fauna includes Tiger, Panther (Leopard), Hyena, deer, Sloth Bear, Wild Boar, and Jungle Cat. Prolific bird species. Ranger-led safaris in open-sided jeeps and Canters (20-seater, open-roofed trucks); drives around picturesque reservoirs (good for photography).

Reservations: For information and accommodation, contact: Field Director, Ranthambhore National Park and Tiger Reserve, Sawai Madhopur, Rajasthan–322001.

Map labels: Delhi, Mumbai, Anantpura, Banas, N, Semli, Park HQ, Ruins, Ruins, to Jaipur, Sawai Madhopur, Ruins, Forest Rest House, Ranthambhore Fort, Khandhar Fort, Forest Rest House, Lahpur, to Mumbai, Ruins, **Ranthambhore National Park & Tiger Reserve**, Ruins, Ruins, Ruins

Inset: Mango fruits.

Below: The aerial roots of *Ficus bengalensis*.

Below right: A Tiger's angry snarl is sometimes difficult to distinguish from 'flehmen' behaviour, a wide-mouthed grimace that opens up an organ above the palate, which is covered with sensory cells, allowing Tigers to process scents.

The Ranthambhore National Park and Tiger Reserve extends across the Aravalli and Vindhya mountain ranges. The park was first established as a sanctuary in 1955, and became one of the first eight sanctuaries to fall under Project Tiger. In 1955 it was established that the forest covered an area of 410 square kilometres (158 square miles). In 1984, an additional 104 square kilometres (40 square miles) of adjoining forest were combined with the sanctuary, and named the Sawai Man Singh Sanctuary. It was at this time that it became a national park and tiger reserve.

The park's forests consist of deciduous forest trees which include Dhak (Flame of the Forest) with occasional Renj, Ber (Indian Jujube), Sal, Mango groves, palms, and members of the fig family, the Banyan and Peepal. The entire forest is dominated by the massive battlements of Ranthambhore fort.

Ranthambhore has three artificial lakes, or reservoirs (termed *talao*) – Padam, Raj Bagh and Milak – which are essential for supplying water to the animal residents of the park.

An estimated population of 38 Tigers prowl the Ranthambhore reserve. Over the last decades, as a result of the reserve's preservation policies, the Tigers have become more active during the day, and Ranthambhore is now well-known for frequent sightings of these cats in broad daylight. It is generally believed that Tiger are

White-necked and Painted Storks, and spoonbills. A variety of ducks also migrate here from their Northern Hemisphere winter season.

Ranthambhore is also home to a large number of Leopard, which make up the second largest predator population in this forest. They are not as fearless as the Tiger, however, and sightings of them are infrequent. Other predators of Ranthambhore are the Striped Hyena, Jackal and Jungle Cat. Unfortunately Indian Wild Dogs were last sighted as far back as 1954.

Sloth Bears can be spotted in the Lakarda and Anantpura areas while driving through the park. In and around the lakes, Sambhar (India's largest deer species) are visible everywhere in large herds; Nilgai (Blue Bull) roam throughout the forests but their greatest concentrations are around the lakes; and Chital, which graze on lush green vegetation, are drawn to the water in hundreds during summer. Marsh Crocodiles, or Muggars, are often seen crossing from one lake to another. They prey on Sambhar, dragging the carcasses into the water in daylight. Chinkara (Indian Gazelle), hares and mongoose can be spotted at the edge of the water, and Common Indian Monitors are frequently sighted.

A former hunting lodge, the Jogi Mahal, stands in a serenely beautiful setting overlooking the Padam reservoir, with the two other lakes, Raj Bagh and Milak, visible at the opposite end; the latter dry up in summer. These bodies of water attract a large number of Chital, Sambhar and Nilgai, which in turn attract Tiger. There are views of the park from Jogi Mahal, and a drive around the reservoirs is every photographer's dream.

solitary, nocturnal creatures, but they appear to have undergone a change in this particular park and have become quite used to the sounds of human beings; they hunt during the day as well as at night. Common Peafowl, or Peacock, constitute a major prey species of this great cat. During the course of 1986, two tiger families were sighted and observed for a long time in jungle clearings, in daylight. One family with three cubs included a large male Tiger, which is very rare. Sighting one of these cats can never be an absolute certainty, but Ranthambhore has become a favourite haunt for wildlife photographers across the globe.

Profuse birdlife and wildlife

The park supports a wonderful bird population. This includes Bonelli's and Crested Serpent Eagle, Great Indian Horned Owl, Tree-pie, Paradise Flycatcher, and Pheasant-tailed Jaçana, while in the lower-lying forest undergrowth are Grey and Painted Partridge, sandgrouse, quail, Red Spurfowl, and Common Peafowl. Waterbirds spotted in and around the lake are the Black,

KEOLADEO GHANA NATIONAL PARK

Avian Paradise

The pristine marshy land of Bharatpur Bird Sanctuary, which has since been renamed the Keoladeo Ghana National Park (after the Hindu god, Keoladeo), encompasses an area of 29 square kilometres (22 square miles) and, since its inception in 1899, has been a haven for birds. It is a man-made avian paradise. During the 19th century, one of the maharajas of Bharatpur who occupied this marshy wetland set out to create a personal waterfowl hunting ground. Over time, it attracted thousands of wild fowl from around the world.

In 1956, the conservation-minded Maharaja Brajendra Singh declared the area a sanctuary. Much later, in 1981, it was upgraded to a national park to further protect the sanctuary. It has since been declared an important site under the Ramsar convention.

A constant supply of water in the park is sustained by a watershed in the region, which is drained by two nonperennial rivers, the Gambhir and Banganga, and their canals, Jatwalce, Bessmora and Chiksana. The Keoladeo wetland has been divided into eight segments with the construction of dykes which have sluice gates, so that seasonal water can be retained for longer periods and distributed evenly across a wide area. This provides a better feeding ground for migratory and resident wetland birds.

The powerful monsoon

The dominating factor of the park's ecosystem is the monsoon rain from July through September. The monsoon is preceded by dusty storms during April and May;

the first rain settles the dust and clears the air as the monotonous plains transform into verdant green prairies. September sees a stable reservoir of water develop (in the dry winter, evaporation of this water is at its maximum, the highest occurring in April and May; water remains in the form of puddles in burrows and pits, and a landscape of cracked earth is left behind). The combination of completely dry land, temporary swamps and flood plains creates an interesting habitat that is biologically rich with specific vegetation types and plant species. There are 227 floral subspecies in Keoladeo Ghana.

Winter haven for migrating birds

The park is also home to 369 avian species – it is the only winter haven for the highly endangered Siberian Crane. When the temperature drops, many species of wild duck can be seen floating in the wetland, where they reside till mid-March. These migratory waterfowl include pintails, Garganey, Shoveller, Marbled Teal, Red-crested Pochard, Mallard, and the Spotted-bill and Tufted Duck, to name only a few.

Above right: The birdlife is best viewed by boat.

Opposite top: Painted Storks nesting in *Acacia nilotica*.

Opposite bottom left: Sarus Cranes (*Grus antigone*).

Opposite bottom right: The future of the rare Siberian Crane (*Grus leucogeranus*) is presently under threat.

Location: Lies at an elevation of 360–370m (1180–1200ft) in the Bharatpur district of Rajasthan.

Climate: Summer temperatures fluctuate between 26 and 38°C (79 and 100°F); winter months (mid-November to February) pleasant.

When to go: Best period for sighting migratory birds is November to February, while monsoon and autumn (mid-September to mid-November) months ideal for viewing breeding birds. Drier months of March through May are best for viewing faunal life.

Getting there: Bharatpur lies 176km (110 miles) from Delhi and is 2km (1 mile) from park; it is the nearest railhead. Nearest airport is Agra, 54km (30 miles) due east of Bharatpur. Bus services link Bharatpur with major cities of Rajasthan and outside the state.

Facilities: Bharatpur has plenty of accommodation for different budget travellers: ITDC-run forest lodge; RTDC-run tourist bungalow; Laxmi Vilas Palace, 2km (1 mile) from park entrance; and Chandra Mahal Haveli 22km (14 miles) away (latter two classified as Heritage Hotels).

Avian life: Impressive list of colourful breeding, migratory and resident birds. Boats and bicycles for hire in wetlands. Rickshaws can be hired near the gate; drivers act as guides and are good in identifying birds (good for photography). Indian Rock Python can be seen at Python Point.

Reservations: Accommodation can be reserved with: The Wildlife Warden, Keoladeo Ghana National Park, Bharatpur, Rajasthan. The forest rest house operates a minibus; contact the Deputy Chief Wildlife Warden, Forest Rest House, tel: (05644) 22777.

Above: Keoladeo during monsoon season.

Inset: Spoonbill (*Platalea leucorodia*).

Right top: A pair of Rose-ringed Parakeets, these birds create holes in tree trunks in which to build their nests.

Right bottom: Indian Shags (*Phalacrocorax fuscicollis*) preparing to nest at sunset.

Below: The Indian Rock Python (*Python molurus*) generally attains a length of 3.5–4.5 metres (12–15 feet).

Between November and March, the migratory season for birds that come mainly from Siberia and China, 120 different species nest in the park. Among these are the Black-necked, White-necked, Open-bill and Painted Stork species, White and Glossy Ibis, spoonbills, Indian Moorhen, and the Pheasant-tailed and Bronze-winged Jacana.

The breeding period, during the rains in September and October, witnesses resident birds consuming an unbelievable 7 to 8 tonnes of food. Tree-residing birds include Rosering, Alexandrine and Blossom-headed Parakeet, Baya Weavers, pipits, swallows, and babblers. Keoladeo also sustains a good number of raptors: Osprey, the Marsh and Pale Harrier, Tawny and Fishing Eagle, Brahminy and Black-shouldered Kite, King and Bengal Vulture, and the Peregrine Falcon. The park is rich too in aquatic species, with local fish species such as Rohu, Catla, Bata, Calbasu, Mrigal, and eels.

The most frequently sighted mammals are Nilgai, Chital, Sambhar, the occasional secretive Leopard, jackals, and Wild Boar. Fishing Cat, Palm Civet, mongoose, porcupines and otters are also present. Beyond the Keoladeo Temple erected in honour of Lord Siva (an alternative name for Hindu god Keoladeo), Indian Rock Pythons can often be spotted at aptly named Python Point.

SARISKA NATIONAL PARK AND TIGER RESERVE

Desert Splendour

Perched on the prominent Aravalli hill range in Rajasthan, Sariska lies in the onetime state of the Rajputs. It was once a royal hunting ground for the maharajas of Alwar (the town of Alwar is 35km, or 22 miles, from the park). During the 6th to 13th centuries, Sariska's Lake Palace hotel just opposite the gate to the tiger reserve was a former hunting lodge where princes and their guests gathered for bird shoots. Sariska is the closest reserve to Delhi and today is a good weekend destination for both local and foreign visitors.

Set up as a sanctuary in 1955, it was declared a tiger reserve under Project Tiger in 1979. Its area was recently increased to make this the second largest tiger reserve in Rajasthan. It is considerably greater in extent than Ranthambhore, and though unlike it terrain-wise, Sariska bears a close similarity in terms of its dry deciduous forest and its animal life. Upgraded to a national park in 1982, the Sariska National Park and Tiger Reserve today sprawls over an area of 765 square kilometres (298 square miles) with the picturesque Siliserh lake lying along the northern edge. The reserve's core area is 480 square kilometres (187 square miles).

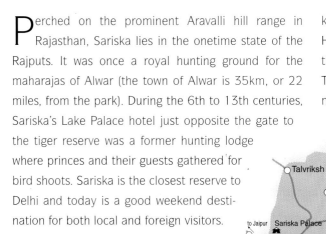

Macaque and Langur

A special feature of Sariska is its populations of monkeys. All monkeys in India belong either to the Macaque or Langur species, and north of the Godavari River in the state of Maharashtra, the Rhesus Macaque is the most widespread primate. The Common Langur (or Hanuman Monkey, from Indian mythology) is the only one of its

kind to range across India, from the foothills of the Himalaya in the north to Kanniyakumari at the southern tip of India, in Tamil Nadu. Sariska National Park and Tiger Reserve is the only region where both species of monkey are tolerant of human presence.

Major predators are Tiger and Leopard, which number 30 and 50 respectively. The Tigers of Sariska are largely diurnal in their habits (like those of Ranthambhore). The king of the jungle is often viewed in full sunlight, and chances of sighting this animal are fair once the influx of tourists has decreased during the peak of summer (March to May). *Machaans*, or watchtowers, have been installed in the park to enable tourists to view this magnificent beast. The numbers of their prey — antelope and deer species — are also on the rise, and are becoming increasingly visible.

Commonly seen carnivores are Jackal, Striped Hyena, Jungle Cat and Caracal. Of the deer and antelope species, herds of Sambhar, Chital, Nilgai, and Chausingha (Four-horned Antelope) will be seen, as well as Wild Boar. An anomaly is that Chausingha, endemic to India, exists in Sariska but is completely absent in Ranthambhore. Its distribution throughout India is quite unpredictable. Sariska harbours another antelope species, the little Chinkara (Indian Gazelle). Wildlife

Above right: The Sariska Palace, which once belonged to India's princes, was one of the country's largest hunting lodges. Its 27 rooms have been refurbished and the complex is run today as a Heritage Hotel.

Location: In the Alwar district in the eastern pocket of Rajasthan. Nearest airport is at Jaipur, 108km (67 miles) from Sariska; Alwar is nearest railhead, 21km (13 miles) away.

Climate: Summer months extremely hot and dry (maximum 47°C; 116°F). Winter more palatable at a maximum of 31°C (89°F), minimum 3°C (37°F). Monsoon brings heavy rain from July to September.

When to go: The best time to visit is between October and June. Summer, between April and June, although very hot makes observing wildlife much easier as animals are drawn to the waterholes.

Getting there: The principal town is Alwar (34km, or 21 miles, from the park), a four-hour drive from Delhi and a three-hour drive from Jaipur. Buses run to the reserve from Delhi, Jaipur and Alwar. Cars and jeeps available for hire.

Facilities: All types of accommodation available at Alwar and Sariska park. Upmarket Sariska Palace on highway just opposite entry gate to Sariska is run by former princely family (Heritage Hotel). At Siliserh, privately owned Lake Palace is a delight for visitors. The RTDC-run Tiger Den lodge is basic.

Wildlife: Semi-desert-type animals: Tiger, Striped Hyena, Jungle Cat, civet species, Sambhar, Nilgai, Chausingha. The best hours to view wildlife in the sanctuary are around 06:30 and 16:00.

Reservations: For information, contact: Field Director, Sariska National Park and Tiger Reserve, Alwar District, Rajasthan.

Above: The serene Siliserh Lake is situated at the northern edge of the Sariska Tiger Reserve.

Right: Common Kingfisher (*Alceo atthis*).

viewing is best carried out from the hides which are situated near the waterholes and from where visitors can take photographs.

Due to annual water shortages when only the waterholes of the upper plateau contain water from the monsoon rains, the Forest Department creates artificial waterholes along the roadside in the lower tourist zone to attract the animals. Visitors should settle themselves in these hides in the early afternoon as the animals come to drink water before sunset. Walking within the sanctuaries of northeast India is comparatively safer than south India as visitors do not face the risk of being confronted with wild Elephant, which are absent from Sariska.

The Siliserh lake lying between Sariska park and Alwar teems with migratory birds on cold winter days. Marsh Crocodiles conceal themselves in the lake's waters and frequently bask in the sun.

Sariska's vegetation of dry deciduous forests consists of trees such as Dhak (Flame of the Forest), Khair (*Acacia catechu*), Goira (*Acacia leucophlaea*), Tendu, Ber (Indian Jujube), and Surwal.

The many species of birds that fill the park include the Common Peafowl, Grey Partridge, quail, sandgrouse, Tree-pie, White-breasted Kingfisher, Golden-backed Woodpecker, Crested Serpent Eagle and Great Indian Horned Owl.

There are places of historical interest on Sariska's fringes. The ruins of the carved Neelkanth temples, which date back to medieval times from the sixth to the 13th centuries, are located 32 kilometres (20 miles) into the park. The deity presiding over the temple is Lord Siva, who in Hindu mythology is a creator, and a destroyer of evil. The Kankwari fort 20 kilometres (12 miles) away, within the park boundaries, is reputed to have been used by the Mughal emperor of India, Aurangazeb, to imprison his brother Dara Shikoh after defeating him in order to usurp the throne of India.

Above: Large herds of Chital, or Spotted Deer (*Axis axis*), are drawn to the waterholes of Kalighati on summer evenings.

Above right: Peacocks, or Common Peafowl as it is known in India, is the most beautiful of the pheasant species. It is also the national bird of India, and occurs in abundance in Sariska.

Right: A Striped Hyena (*Hyaena hyaena*) pup tests out the safety of the surrounding territory from the security of its den.

Below left and right: The Rhesus Macaque (*Macaca mulatta*) is the most commonly occurring of India's monkey species.

COASTAL INDIA

T he Indian coastal region as defined in this chapter comprises two biotic (relating to living organisms) zones, namely the eastern and the western coastal zones. The eastern coast encompasses the regions south of West Bengal and east of Orissa, as well as the Andaman and Nicobar islands in the Bay of Bengal, while the western coastal zone is formed by the Gujarat seaboard, the south portion of Maharashtra and the little state of Goa, all edging onto the Arabian Sea. Major portions of the south Indian states can also be counted as part of the coastal region but due to their own unique biotic characteristics, these states are not included here and appear later under Peninsular India. The eastern coast receives more rain than its western counterpart – 2500 millimetres (100 inches) annually – while in the west this varies between 1520 and 2030 millimetres (60 and 80 inches).

A moderate climate prevails in both zones, although temperatures of the west coast are milder than the east. Lush tropical vegetation lines the Arabian Sea coastline with, among other palm species, Coconut and Talipot Palms and thick shrubs and climbers making up the principal vegetation. The eastern coast features a rich variety of mangrove trees in the deltaic region of the Bay of Bengal as well as fruit-bearing Mango, Jackfruit and Coconut Palm.

The Gir forest in Gujarat is the last stronghold of the Asiatic Lion, while the coastal mangrove swamp forests of the Sunderbans in the far south of West Bengal hold the largest number of Indian, or Bengal, Tiger in the country. The Asiatic Wild Ass is strictly endemic to the Rann of Kutch (also Kachchh), an enormous expanse of salt marsh in Gujarat. Dolphins, porpoises, turtles and the Dugong inhabit the seas around the Andaman and the Nicobar islands – believed to be a former hill range that has been submerged leaving tropical isles – and the Chilika lagoon on Orissa's east coast supports many migratory waterbirds, as well as dolphins along the sea edge.

Left: India's shores are lined with Coconut Palms (*Cocos nucifera*) – visible in the foreground – and Palmyra Palms (*Borasus flabellifer*) – a pair rises on the horizon to the right. The former bears large green fruit and has feathery leaves, while Palmyra leaves are fan-shaped.

SUNDERBANS NATIONAL PARK AND TIGER RESERVE

Tigers in the mangroves

The Sunderbans delta has been formed by the meeting of India's two great river systems, the Ganges and the Brahmaputra, which cross eastern West Bengal State and Bangladesh to drain into the Bay of Bengal. Created by sediments washed down from the Himalayas, it is the world's largest intertidal area – covering approximately 2600 square kilometres (1000 square miles) and is undoubtedly the most dynamic river basin that exists today. The Sunderbans is the largest prograding delta (constantly changing in a series of stages) in the world and holds the largest expanses of mangrove vegetation. In India, the Sunderbans covers an area of 4264 square kilometres (1660 square miles), defined by an imaginary demarcation line devised by (and named after) two surveyors, Dampier and Hodges, which extends in the north between the estuaries of the Hooghly River to the west and the Ichamati-Raimongol rivers to the east. The delta here is spread over two districts of 24 *parganas* to the north and 24 *parganas* to the south (a *pargana* is a subdivision of a district, generally containing many villages). The main trunks of both the Ganges and Brahmaputra cross Bangladesh to empty into the sea.

In 1973, the Sunderbans Tiger Reserve was established under the protection of Project Tiger with an overall area of 2585 square kilometres (1010 square miles) and a core zone of 1330 square kilometres (520 square miles). In 1984, the area was proclaimed a national park and in 1985, the entire Sunderbans delta was designated a World Heritage Site. A buffer zone to the north of the park and tiger reserve contains a sanctuary of around 360 square kilometres (140 miles) called the Sajnekhali Wildlife Sanctuary.

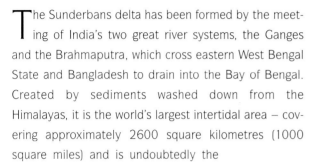

An awe-inspiring delta

The Hooghly River divides itself into innumerable streams to form narrow creeks which flow through the islands of this huge delta. Mudflats separate the creeks, some of which are very wide, while others are as narrow as canals.

There are 54 islands within the national park. Major branching streams traversing the Sunderbans have names like Matla, Bidyadhari, and Raimongal. This waterlogged habitat is regularly flooded and is characterized by its salinity and its intense humidity.

Above right: Estuarine Crocodile (*Crocodilus porosus*), also known as Saltwater Crocodile.

Opposite top: Local fishermen paddle their sailing vessels, known in India as *dingi*, through the Sunderbans delta.

Opposite bottom left: Kankra (*Bruguiera gymnorhiza*), with its stilt-like roots, is a typical mangrove species.

Opposite bottom centre: A close-up view of the pneumatic root system of the region's mangroves.

Opposite bottom right: Muddy islands are covered with mangrove species, among them the Phoenix Palm.

Location: In the Ganges deltaic region of eastern West Bengal. The nearest airport is in Calcutta, 112km (70 miles) from the Sunderbans. The nearest town is Gosaba, 50km (30 miles) away. There is a railhead at Canning.

Climate: Summer is very humid (35°C; 95°F) in December to February, while winter months are cool (15°C; 59°F).

When to go: October to February is the best time to visit.

Getting there: There are several gateways to the Sunderbans: Canning is 48km (30 miles) from Calcutta and is well-connected by trains and buses; Basanti is 110km (68 miles) from Calcutta and is connected by buses. Boats to Sajnekhali from Canning or Sonakhali.

Facilities: Permission to enter the park by boat should be obtained from the Project Tiger office, Canning. Guides are provided at Sajnekhali Tourist Centre. Accommodation available in the tourist lodge (raised on concrete pillars) at Sajnekhali.

Wildlife: Different deer species, Estuarine (Saltwater) Crocodile and Gangetic Dolphin. Abundant sea- and waterbirds.

Reservations: For accommodation, contact: The Field Director, Sunderbans Tiger Reserve, PO Canning, South 24 Parganas District, West Bengal.

Precautions: The use of mosquito repellent creams and mosquito coils is advised.

Heavy southwest monsoons

The region's main feature is a typical heavy monsoon season that experiences excessive humidity and lasts for almost half of the year. Summer in the Sunderbans stretches from mid-March to mid-June. The monsoon then arrives, brought by the southwest winds and lasting till September, though sometimes it extends to mid-October. The region receives intermittent rain all year round. Occasionally, cyclonic storms lash the delta during October and November, accompanied by high tides and waves capable of causing great destruction.

December to February are the winter months, during which time the rivers become serene and quiet; it is perhaps the best period to navigate the delta's mangrove swamps. In April–May, violent thunderstorms known as 'Nor'westers' approach from the northwest. They are often accompanied by hailstorms.

Right: The Smooth-coated Otter (*Lutra perspicillata*) frequents freshwater habitats – rivers, lakes and streams – where it feeds on fish.

Below, from left to right: The mangrove swamps provide a suitable habitat for the Mudskipper (*Periothalmus barbarus*); a Freshwater Turtle (*Pelochelys cantorii*); the female turtle will lay between 100 and 150 eggs in a protected hollow; at low tide, an army of crabs invades the exposed mudflats, among them the Fiddler Crab.

Saltwater mangrove shores

Vegetation in the Sunderbans falls into the littoral forest type – mostly mangrove species growing in the shallow waters of the seashore. The lower tidal zones of the delta feature what are known as primary colonizers, the *Sonneratia* and *Avicennia* species, belonging to the saltwater mixed forest type and possessing submerged roots which bind the soil together; these roots tolerate high salinity. Above this tidal zone stretches an area characterized by the Rhizophora species, *Bruguieria* and *Excoecaria careops* forest, of which the Phoenix Palm is typical. The Rhizophora species, with their tangled aerial roots, are the most familiar of the mangrove trees. A mangrove of note is the Sundari from which the name Sunderbans is derived, in addition to the Hental, Baen, Goran, Golpata, and Passur species – in all, 64 species of mangroves occur in the delta.

Because the river system of this deltaic region is so interconnected with the Bay of Bengal's waters, high and low tide occur twice daily. During high tide, the entire mangrove forest – the highlands excluded – is submerged in water. When the tidal water recedes, it leaves soft alluvial soil behind.

Indian's largest tiger population

The Sunderbans are famous for their Tiger numbers – the park boasts the highest population of this regal cat in India. Research shows that cubs are born after the rains, between February and May each year, and according to the last census, there are 273 Tiger in the park today. This predator has proved itself well able to adapt to any environment and the saline, waterlogged mangroves are no exception. Wild Boar and Chital form its staple diet but, unlike in other parks of India, the Tigers also catch fish and crabs from the rivers in the delta to supplement their diet. The swampy environment indeed makes it difficult for Tiger to pursue their prey, and the proximity of human habitation to the animals' habitat does cause conflict, so they do periodically become man-eaters.

Other wildlife species occurring here are the Rhesus Macaque and the Fishing Cat. This stout, nocturnal cat is around 130 centimetres (4 feet 3 inches) in length and has grey fur infused with brown. It lives near rivers, tidal creeks and reedbeds, preying on calves, fawns and – true to its name – sometimes fish.

Naturally, birdlife of the Sunderbans is characterized by water- and seabirds. Some of the more unusual species are Whimbrel, Goliath Heron, Large Egret (*Ardea alba*) and Median Egret (*Egretta intermedia*), Black-headed Gull, River and Whiskered Tern, Stone Curlew, Golden Pochard, and pintail ducks. The reserve has its share of raptors, among them White-bellied Fishing Eagle, Pallas's Fishing Eagle, and Brahminy Kite.

Turtles and Estuarine Crocodiles

The Sunderbans National Park harbours a few endangered reptiles, among them the Olive Ridley Turtle, which emerges from the Bay of Bengal to lay its eggs on shore. Another endangered reptile, the tortoise *Batagur baska*, is very rarely spotted.

In winter, huge Estuarine, or Saltwater, Crocodile (*Crocodilus porosus*) emerge from the cold waters to bask in the sun on the riverbanks. These carnivorous ocean-going reptiles, which grow to 6 metres (over 19 feet), swim as far as 64 kilometres (40 miles) out to sea. They lay between 25 and 90 eggs of which only 1 per cent survive. They have a life span of 25 to 50 years.

Aquatic mammals of the rivers and estuaries are the commonly occurring black, finless Little Indian Porpoise which has a rounded snout, as well as the Irrawaddy, Plumbeous and Gangetic Dolphin species. The latter is often sighted from boats in the upper streams, away from the estuary. A freshwater mammal, the Gangetic Dolphin is differentiated by its head which lengthens into an elongated beak. The young have pointed, conical teeth which become bony projections with age. They live in the rivers of the Ganges, Brahmaputra, Indus and larger tributaries, never entering the sea. The Common Otter is the sole aquatic carnivore of the delta.

Watchtowers are located within the tiger reserve, at Sajnekhali, Sudhanyakhali, Netidhopani, and Burirdabad. Visitors can hire launches, both for guided tours or private excursions, and motorboats from different entry points to the park – Canning, Basanti, Basirhat and Namkhana. West Bengal Tourism has established the Sajnekhali Tourist Lodge on Sajnekhali island, which also has a visitor centre with a nature interpretation facility.

CHILIKA LAKE

Where migratory birds come to feed

A narrow sandy stretch, parallel to the coastline of the state of Orissa on India's east coast, separates Chilika from the Bay of Bengal. It is the largest lagoon in India, and features unending stretches of wetlands partly surrounded on its inland, western side by the verdant hills of the Eastern Ghats, with lonely long beaches where the wind whispers through dark, rocky islands that are surrounded by waterbirds and dolphins.

The lake extends over an area of just over 1100 square kilometres (425 square miles). Fresh water drains the higher regions and flows into the lagoon, which, combined with water flowing through a narrow mouth from the sea, results in a brackish water ecosystem – the largest in Asia – supporting a diversity of flora and fauna.

Birdwatching naturalists are drawn to Chilika after the monsoon since the lagoon is a haven for a large number of migratory waterbirds. At the same time, the islands and their vegetation are also an ideal habitat for resident birds. In recognition of its significance as an ornithological habitat, Chilika was declared a Ramsar site in 1981.

There are four small settlements situated along the banks of the lake from where one can explore the area: Satapada, a small, sleepy fishing hamlet near the mouth of the lagoon; Balugaon; Barkul; and Rambha.

Nalbana Island

The most spectacular area for birdwatching is Nalbana ('nal' means 'reed', 'bana' forest) Island, which lies closest to Balugaon. The biggest of the 34 islands sprinkled across the lagoon, it has an area of 10 square kilometres (4 square miles) and is easily approached by motorboat hired from Balugaon. During the monsoon months of July through September it remains submerged but emerges during the dry winter from November to February, becoming a veritable paradise for ornithologists and naturalists as a host of migratory species from Siberia and central Asia descends on and around the vegetation-covered mudflats. In winter, Nalbana is visible from a distance by the thousands of birds wheeling on the horizon.

Some important species are Brow-headed Gull, Large Egret, Grey Heron, Great Crested Grebe, Pratincole, Rosy Flamingo, Pheasant-tailed Jacana, Pallas's Fishing Eagle, and of the pelicans, the Spot-Billed, Grey, Great White, and Rosy species.

Due to the fluctuating water levels, boats are not always able to reach the dry land areas directly, so visitors may have to wade through the shallows before reaching solid ground. Apart from Nalbana, several other islands which also teem with birdlife are accessible from Satapada.

Above right: Spotted-bill, or Gray Pelican (*Pelecanus philippensis*), are gregarious birds; they visit Chilika in their thousands in winter.

Opposite: Local fishermen on Chilika Lake use gill nets to catch fish; species include Flatfish, Hilsha and prawns.

Location: Arching across the districts of Puri and Ganjam, along the coast of the state of Orissa. The nearest airport is at Bhubaneswar, 100km (60 miles) from Chilika.

Climate: Summer is moderately hot (maximum 32°C; 86°F), winter is mild (minimum 10°C; 50°F).

When to go: The winter months (December to March) are best for observing migratory birdlife.

Getting there: By road via NH5; Balugaon, Barkul, Chilika and Rambha via Khallikote are all strategically located on Chilika Lake along the Howrah–Madras route of the Southeastern Railway. The nearest railhead for the Barkul settlement is at Balugaon. Bus services from all the above centres.

Facilities: Orissa Tourism Development Corporation (OTDC) offers reasonably priced accommodation on Satapada island, 50km (30 miles) from the well-known beach resort of Puri, and at the settlements of Barkul and Rambha. Both have railway stations on the Calcutta–Chennai railway line. OTDC also offers comfortable tourist bungalows at Panthanivas and the Ashoka hotel at Balugaon offers accommodation. Motorboats can be hired; guides are necessary.

Avian life: The lagoon, one of the biggest inland lakes in India, is a sanctuary and winter haven for thousands of migratory birds.

Permits and reservations: Tourists can obtain assistance and further information from the following centres: Tourist Office at Panthanivas, Rambha, Chilika, Orissa; or Tourist Office, Station Road, Berhampur, Orissa.

Above left: Ruddy Shelduck (*Tadorna ferruginea*) tend to live in pairs.

Above centre: Colonies of Grey Heron (*Ardea cinerea*) establish themselves in Chilika during the monsoon season.

Above right: The Bronze-winged Jacana (*Metopidius indicus*) is a common wader on the lagoon.

Right: Teal are a migratory species which arrive from lands as distant as Lake Baikal in Siberia. The many varieties include the Gray, Common, Large Whistling, Falcated, Marble and Baikal Teal species.

Dolphin spotting

In terms of the aquatic fauna, encounters with dolphins are the most exhilarating. Irrawaddy Dolphin are often seen from boats while cruising on the lagoon. Although they are deep-water mammals, they rise to the surface to breathe in oxygen, their arched backs visible to visitors. Their nose is much shorter than that of the Gangetic species, also spotted here.

The more remote parts of Chilika, its surrounding fishing hamlets and the forested islands still support a number of smaller wild animals such as the Golden Jackal, Striped Hyena, Jungle Cat, the grey-brown Small Indian Civet, Palm Civet, Bengal Fox, Black-naped Hare, and Common Mongoose.

Waterfowl residents of the lagoon

When boats carrying visitors enter the great expanse of the lagoon during winter, thousands of wild duck greet them. Among the migratory duck species, Northern Pintail, Gadwall, Wigeon, Red-crested and Common Pochard, Ruddy Shelduck, Tufted Duck and shovellers, flock to the boats in their chain formations. Among the common birds seen around the Barkul settlement are the Common Drongo, Pied Bush Chat, Blue-tailed Bee-eater, and White-browed Ground Thrush. Nocturnal species include the Spotted Owlet and Indian Jungle Nightjar. The reedbeds of the lagoon sustain a variety of migratory waterfowl; among them the more common residents are Black-winged Stilt, Black-tailed Godwit, Redshank, and Red Wattled Lapwing.

Later in the day, the lagoon becomes turbulent due to incoming tides, so it is advisable to visit by boat in the very early morning and return by early afternoon.

Nesting turtles

The sandy beaches along the Bay of Bengal side of the narrow sandbar are an important location for Olive Ridley Turtles. They arrive from the Indian Ocean in their hundreds and thousands in the winter to nest in the sand along certain stretches of the beach. The mass arrival of these nesting turtles is known as *arribada*. During December through March this strange phenomenon,

which can be witnessed by visitors, occurs near the mouth of the Rusikulya River near the settlement of Rambha, where between 10,000 and 30,000 turtles crawl out to the high-water mark to nest. They dig holes up to 60 centimetres (2 feet) deep in which to lay 100 to 150 eggs, which they then cover with sand. Hatchlings arrive about seven weeks later and start moving immediately toward the sea, guided instinctively by the light radiating across the eastern horizon. Another species that occurs here is the Indian Flapshell Turtle.

Ten species of lizard, including the Bengal Monitor, have been recorded in and around the lagoon. The most interesting is the Barkul Island Limbless Skink, which was first recorded in the early 20th century on Chilika's island of the same name. This lizard is characterized by the absence of legs and leads a burrowing life.

Above left: Gadwall (*Asas strepera*) is a species belonging to the wild drake family.

Above centre: The reddish-brown head and grey-and-white colouring distinguishes the male Wigeon (*Anas penelope*) from the female.

Above right: Great Crested Grebe (*Podiceps cristatus*) migrate to Chilika in the winter months (December to March) from the upper Himalaya.

Left: Along the shores of the Bay of Bengal, winter heralds the nesting season for tens of thousands of Olive Ridley Turtles.

Invertebrate life in the lagoon is enormously diverse, with prawns and crabs playing a significant role as sustenance for the local population. Today the ecosystem is being increasingly threatened by intensive fishing, industrial pollution and siltation as a result of deforestation occurring on the catchment area of the rivers which drain into the lake. More recent is the mushrooming of the shrimp and prawn culture ponds all around Chilika which, in addition to disturbance to the environment, could pollute the lagoon with aquacultural chemical discharges. Local NGOs have successfully halted some large projects, but no initiatives are being taken by the state government.

MIDDLE BUTTON ISLAND NATIONAL PARK

Dolphin wilderness

The Andaman and Nicobar islands comprise a chain of 293 emerald-green isles scattered across the Pacific Ocean from New Guinea to India's Bay of Bengal coastline. The total length of this island chain is 725 kilometres (450 miles). Apart from Car Nicobar, most of the largely remote islands are hilly – with an average altitude of 1220 metres (4000 feet) – and covered with dense, verdant tropical forests that have generally remained virgin and unspoilt. An interesting feature of the Andaman and Nicobar islands is the region's aboriginal people and their mysterious customs and behaviour. The western part of South Andaman is a vast forested area of 700 square kilometres (275 square miles) which is inhabited by the Joroans, a ferocious Negroid people who live naked in the forests and presently number 250. On Strait Island, to the north of South Andaman, only 20 tribes remain, having gradually been reduced due to epidemics caused by disease. The most vulnerable are the Jarwa and Ongi (a Mongoloid people), whose dwindling numbers are on the verge of extinction. Numbering 102 individuals, the Ongi, although primitive, have adapted to wearing clothing.

Several sanctuaries and national parks have been established on the innumerable Andaman and Nicobar islands. Significant national parks are the South, Middle and North Button islands (which lie north of Port Blair), Saddle Peak and Mount Harriet. Middle Button was declared a national park in 1979 (South Button in 1977; North Button in 1979). The North Button National Park lies 200 kilometres (125 miles) from Port Blair, the administrative capital of the Andamans on the east coast of South Andaman, and is 4400 hectares (10,870 acres) in size. Middle Button is 100 hectares (247 acres), while South Button covers an area of 300 hectares (740 acres).

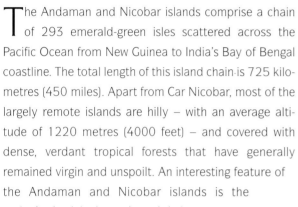

Blue Whale, dolphins and turtles

Unlike other islands in the chain, Middle Button National Park does not have any original land mammals. A few Chital deer, introduced in the mid-1960s, may be spotted. In contrast, marine life is diverse and rich, with the prime attraction being dolphins and sea turtles such as the Green, Leatherback and Olive Ridley. Common Dolphin occur in large groups and are the fastest of the oceanic mammals, capable of attaining over 30 knots. They communicate extensively with each other in the ocean depths.

Although the Blue Whale does occur here, it is very rare. It is generally around 23 metres (75 feet) in size from snout to tail fluke, and its blue colour is interrupted by white only on the tips and underpart of its flippers. It feeds on krill, a small, shrimplike crustacean. Blue Whales become sexually mature at four to five years, and pregnancy occurs every two or three years; there is no fixed breeding season. Also rare in these waters is the Dugong, or Sea Cow. With a flattish belly and rounded

Above right: Common Dolphin (*Delphinus delphis*).

Opposite: Pristine coastline of the Andaman islands.

Above and far right: Partly due to their relative remoteness, these islands have retained their unspoilt nature and have managed to avoid exploitation through tourist activity. As a result, they are becoming increasingly attractive today for nature lovers and underwater enthusiasts.

Above right Dugong are seldom spotted by visitors as they are very shy creatures; they feed in shallow waters on sea grasses.

back, Dugongs have a massive head and no neck, resembling Eared Seals. A distinctive feature is their small mouth with an upper lip – an extensive horseshoe-shaped fleshy pad – that projects over the lower lip. Clumsy and sluggish in movement, little is known of their breeding habits.

The ocean is full of live corals, shoals of magically coloured marine fish, sea anemones, urchins, and snails. Snorkelling is a popular activity here and there are many snorkelling facilities around the Buttons.

Birdlife of Middle Button includes the White-bellied Sea Eagle, Andaman Wood Pigeon, Andaman Teal and Andaman Hill Myna. Recently naturalists are finding increasing interest in the little explored wilderness of the bays and beaches of these Andaman islands.

DHANGADHRA WILDLIFE SANCTUARY

Where the wild ass roams

Gujarat – on the west coast of India, facing onto the Arabian Sea – is known as the Jewel in the West for its Gir National Park, sprawling beaches along a picturesque coastline, its historical Jain temple city (consisting of 863 temples) at Palitana, and its burgeoning industrialized cities of Ahmedabad, Vadodara and Surat with their blend of traditional and oriental influences. The Dhangadhra Wildlife Sanctuary in Gujarat was set up in 1973 to protect the Asiatic Wild Ass, and is therefore better known as the Wild Ass Sanctuary. It rests in the Little Rann of Kutch which lies south of the Great Rann of Kutch (or Kachchh), and has an area of 4953 square kilometres (1910 square miles).

The vast, flat saline wasteland of the Rann of Kutch in northwest Gujarat is a unique treeless wilderness with scanty vegetation. A part of the Rann is frequently inundated by seawater, and during the southwest monsoon rains from July to September, the entire area is flooded. During this time the Rann is constantly lashed by rain from the Arabian Sea, driven by high winds sweeping across the land. The wilderness tract becomes a region of swamps and marshes which are punctuated by small highland pockets that have evaded being submerged; these are called *bets*.

Typical saline vegetation

The variegated vegetation of the Little Rann of Kutch consists of mangrove scrub, Rann saline thorn scrub and *Salvadora* scrub forests. Along the coast low mangrove scrub, occurring in dense forest patches, is prominent

and frequently remains submerged by tidal currents. Other species dominating here are coarse grasses and stunted vegetation such as *Acanthus ilicifolicus* and the mangrove species *Avicennia alba*, a food source for the wild asses. Tracts constantly inundated by seawater are covered by Rann saline thorn scrub comprising mainly *Acacia* species, *Calotropis procera* and *Prosopis juliflora* (Mesquite). The *Salvadora* scrub, well-suited to the arid saline soils existing in the Rann of Kutch, is also made up of *Calotropis procera* and *Salvadora persica*.

Endangered wild ass

The endangered Asiatic Wild Ass, a member of the wild horse family and popularly known as *onager*, has its only home in India in the Rann. These beasts roam in herds of 40 to 50. They stand high at the shoulder and are chestnut-brown and white in colour. They are fast runners although they do not fear humans and are not threatened by the sound of vehicles. Photographers can slowly approach *onagers* while viewing them through the lense of a camera without intimidating them.

When their saline territory becomes flooded, the Asiatic Wild Ass migrate to the higher-lying land. At this

Above right: The Asiatic Wild Ass (*Equus hemionus*) carries a short erect mane, from the base of which a dark stripe runs along the spine from neck to tail. In keeping with its arid environment, this ass survives on a diet of coarse grass.

Location: In the Little Rann of Kutch in Gujarat, west coast of India. Accessible from the railhead at the settlement of Dhangadhra, which has connections to Ahmedabad and Rajkot via Surendranagar. Rajkot is the major town (140km; 87 miles).

Climate: Southwest monsoon rains from the Arabian Sea strike the Rann from May to September, flooding the entire wilderness zone. Summer maximum is 40°C (104°F); winter minimum is 8°C (46°F).

When to go: The best period to visit is from December to June; sanctuary closed from July to November.

Getting there: The wildlife sanctuary is 209km (129 miles) from the city of Ahmedabad. Dhangadhra is the closest town (22km; 14 miles). Visitors need to drive to the park.

Facilities: Limited accommodation is available outside the park, with canteen facilities. Private facilities at Desert Courser (Camp Zainabad). Jeeps are necessary in the park; vehicle hire or transport arrangements can be made with the Forest Department at Dhangadhra.

Wildlife: Asiatic Wild Ass, Blue Bull, Blackbuck, Chinkara. Visitors may catch rare glimpses of fox and Indian Wolf. Driving in an open jeep across the desert landscape is a mesmerizing experience.

Reservations: For accommodation, contact: The Sanctuary Superintendent, Dhangadhra District, Surendranagar, Gujarat State; or Desert Courser, Camp Zainabad (near Dashada), Ahmedabad–382751.

Map labels

NATIONAL HIGHWAY NO. 15
Delhi
Mumbai
Radhanpur
Santalpur
Sami
Nanda
Sankesh
Adesa
Pung Bet
Little Rann
Mardakh Bet
Jalandar
Bhachau
Chitrod
Dhangadhra Wildlife Sanctuary
Dasada
Surajbari
Kesmari Bet
Jalandar
Zainabad
Tikar
Kharaghoda
to Ahmedabad
Kandla
Halvad
Kuda
Bajana
Viramgam
Gulf of Kutch
Dhangadhra
N
Morvi
= MARSH
= RANN OF KUTCH SANCTUARY AREA
= WILD ASS SANCTUARY AREA
Wadhwan
Wankaner
to Rajkot

time, the *bets* protruding from the water are populated with extensive numbers of these asses. In total, their count has increased to over 1000.

The Rann is also home to the Nilgai (Blue Bull), two antelope species – Blackbuck (Indian Antelope) and Chinkara (Indian Gazelle) – Desert Cat, wolves, and foxes. The Desert Cat (*Felis libyca*) is the size of a domestic cat, and is recognizable by its pale yellowish fur with spots. It survives in this arid environment on rodents and birds.

Several species of aquatic and terrestrial birds find shelter in the saline marshes. Pelicans and desert birds such as the Houbara Bustard, sandgrouse and lark species add colour to the generally monochromatic desert landscape.

Above: The Asiatic Wild Ass, which roams in large herds through the Rann of Kutch, freely migrates across the international border between India and Pakistan.

Left: During the rainless summer and winter seasons, the muddy plains of the Little Rann of Kutch become parched and cracked from the scorching sun.

GIR NATIONAL PARK

Last stronghold of the Asiatic Lion

More than 2000 years ago, the Indian (Asiatic) Lion played a role in Indian history even before the Tiger thrived on the subcontinent. The lion's vast habitat spread from southern Greece in the northwest to Pala-mau in the state of Bihar (now Jharkand) in eastern India.

Ashoka, one of the greatest of the Mauryan emperors, who was in power from 272 to 232BC, left a series of inscriptions of his edicts on pillars and rocks across India. Some of Ashoka's edicts describe the lion capital of Sarnath and these stand in north Bihar.

Ashoka became famous for his strongly expressed views on Buddhist pacifism, and his edicts encouraged his people to follow the code of dharma – that is, a moral, pious and virtuous life.

Before the focus on protection shifted to the Tiger, the Asiatic Lion was the national animal of India. Today it remains an emblem of the Republic of India.

Lion – a threatened species

The Asiatic Lion (also known as West Asian or Persian Lion, depending on its precise habitat), was fast disappearing from many areas in India. The Gir forest in Saurashtra, in India's Gujarat State, formed part of the onetime princely state of Junagadh in India's pre-Partition days. At the turn of the 19th century, the Lion of Gir were on the verge of extinction as a result of poaching and shooting; it was believed that not more than 20 Lion existed in Gir at the time. The rulers of Junagadh enforced a strict ban on the shooting of this

cat and later, a limited quota of three animals per year was permitted to be shot at the discretion of the Nawab (Muslim prince) of Junagadh. These measures worked remarkably well and the Lion population subsequently increased. A census held in 1936 established a count of 287 animals; a subsequent census indicates that the Gir forest holds a minimum of 175 but not more than 275 Asiatic Lion.

Presently, Saurashtra's original Gir forest has shrunk from 3070 square kilometres (1195 square miles) to 1150 square kilometres (444 square miles). In the mid-1900s, Gir was connected to the forest sectors of Girnar, Barda, Mitiyala, Alech hills, Dhank and Chorwad by corridors of forest, grassland and scattered hamlets. This enabled the Lion to roam freely throughout the region. It was during this period, in 1965, that Gir was registered a wildlife sanctuary, confining its existing cat population to the core sector of the forest. After acquiring this status, the subsequent implementation of the Gir Lion Sanctuary Project in 1972 aimed to protect the Asiatic Lion and its habitat as well as improve the living conditions of the Maldhari people. The sanctuary was upgraded to a national park in 1975.

Asiatic Lion did also occasionally exist in the Girnar and Mitiyala forests and some coastal forest before the 1990 census. Here, too the situation has improved

Above right: Asiatic Lion (*Panthera leo parsica*).

Location: In southwest region of the Saurashtra peninsula, Gujarat. Nearest airport is Keshod, 50km (30 miles) from the park. It is also accessible by rail from Sasan Gir (1km, or half a mile, from the park) on the Western Railway.

Climate: Summer temperatures are hot and humid (43°C; 109°F); winter nights are freezing (4°C, or 39°F, at night; 24°C, or 75°F, during the day).

When to go: The park is closed from monsoon (June to September) till mid-October. A pleasant time to visit is December to May (although May is hot, wildlife viewing is good).

Getting there: Nearest town, Veraval, is 42km (26 miles) away. At a distance of 65km (40 miles), Junagadh is well-connected with Delhi and Bombay by train and bus. Buses and jeeps for hire at the Gujarat Tourism Office at Diwan Chowk in Junagadh.

Facilities: GSTDC-run Lion Safari Lodge at Sasan Gir village has canteen facilities and dining hall. The deluxe Gir Lodge run by Taj Group of Hotels is very comfortable. Guides necessary in the park; hired at entry gate. Visitors can take petrol vehicles (diesel not permitted) on prescribed routes only.

Wildlife: The only retreat in India of the Asiatic Lion. Also present, Panther, Striped Hyena, many deer species, Indian Wild Boar and Marsh Crocodile.

Reservations: For information and accommodation contact: The Deputy Conservator of Forests, Wildlife Division, Sasan Gir, Gujarat–362135.

Map labels: to Junagadh; Dhari; N; to Keshod & Junagadh; Kamleshwar Dam; Kamleshwar; Delhi; Mumbai; Crocodile Breeding Farm; Sasan Gir; Kankai; Entrance Gate; Shirwan; Gir National Park; Tulsishyam; Banej; to Una; to Veraval; Jamvala; = LION SANCTUARY BOUNDARY

considerably, and prides of Lion are now permanently settled in these areas – at present, there are four independent Lion populations. In the past they were relocated to Gir but they repeatedly migrated back to the coastal forests in search of food and a permanent territory. They were finally settled here permanently after the 1990s.

Habitat of the Asiatic Lion

The Asiatic Lion is no less majestic than its African counterpart, although there are some differences in appearance. The Indian species is much shaggier, its coat and the fringe of its belly are denser, and the hair of the elbow and tail tuft longer. The largest recorded Asiatic Lion measured about 2.9 metres (9 feet 7 inches) in comparison with 3.2 metres (10 feet 7 inches) for the African Lion. The Indian cat, however, inhabits only a tiny fraction of the vast territory that is covered by African Lion.

Unlike most wild cats, which are solitary animals, the Lion exists in groups, or prides. It spends up to nearly 20 hours sleeping during the day and may feed only once or twice in a week. In comparison with the Tiger, Lion were never present in as large numbers as the former cat, and were quick to fall prey to hunters. Disadvantages the Lion has versus Tiger are its need for open grassland habitat (Tiger are more adaptable and can also exist in dense forest and the shrubby semi-desert forests of the Aravalli hills) and it lacks the Tiger's crafty nature, essential for survival. The disappearance of open grassland and scrub forests, the rise in agriculture, improved firearms for hunters and encroaching human settlement throughout its territory are some of the factors which contributed to its extinction in other areas of India.

The Asiatic Lion can be observed at dawn and dusk. As these cats are not shy or fearful, visitors can watch them from their motor vehicles. But like all predators, sighting a Lion is not always guaranteed. There is a proposal by the Forest Department to set up a safari park in a fenced-off area of around 405 hectares (1000 acres) to allow for easier observation.

Threat of human encroachment

One of the national park's major problems is its human population and their cattle herds. The herders of this region, a tribe called the Maldhari, reside on the fringe of the sanctuary with the result that their domestic buffalo are prey to, and substantially reduced in number by, the park's Lion. The cattle population is estimated at 20,000; at the same time these domestic animals compete for food and territory with the wild ungulates.

The Gujarat government has launched a scheme to try to relocate the Maldhari settlers, which involves building a wall around the sanctuary and providing them with new water sources outside the protected area.

Gir's other wildlife

Today, Gir's self-sustaining stable ecosystem nurtures over 450 plant species, 350 varieties of bird, 32 species of mammal, 24 kinds of reptile and more than 2000 species of insect. Herbivores in the park – Chital, Chausingha (Four-horned Antelope), Nilgai (Blue Bull), Sambhar, Chinkara (Indian Gazelle) and Wild Boar – have risen in number from a total of 9600 in 1974 to more than 38,200 in 1995. The smaller carnivores are Jungle Cat, Jackal, and Striped Hyena. Gir also shelters a large population of Panther (Leopard); they are seen here more than in any other national park. Their prey includes stray domestic dogs and the Maldhari's cattle.

The wildlife of the Gir forests is best viewed by touring in a jeep, as the roads are very rough for sedan vehicles. The best drives from Sasan, a park entry point, lead to sites named Baval Chowk and Kankai, Chodavdi, Tulsishyam and Kamleshwar dam.

A great number of Marsh (Muggar) Crocodiles bask in the rivers of Gir and particularly in the Kamleshwar dam. There is a crocodile breeding farm, popular with visitors, at Sasan from where these reptiles are relocated to the lakes and rivers of Gujarat.

Above: When it flies, the Indian Roller (*Coracias bengalensis*) reveals the dazzling blue on the underside of its wings.

Below: Domestic Buffalo grazing and bathing in the park's waterholes has been known to spread disease among the wild animals.

Below right: The Striped Hyena (*Hyaena hyaena*) generally prefers open country, where low hills and ravines offer shelter in protective hollows.

The park's vegetation consists of Dry Teak (*Tectona grandis*) and deciduous forest of Banyan, Jamun (Blackberry) and Flame of the Forest (also known as Palash or Dhak) as well as scrub of *Acacia* and *Euphorbia* species.

A varied wealth of birdlife lives in the forests: Paradise Flycatcher, Black-headed Cuckoo, Grey Drongo, Pied Woodpecker, Coppersmith, Indian Roller, Crested Swift, Fish Owl, Black Vulture, Shaheen Falcon, and Bonelli's and Crested Serpent Eagle are just some of the birds of the tree canopies. On the forest floor are Painted Sandgrouse, Rock Bush Quail, Grey Partridge, and White-necked Stork.

The park has a sound infrastructure with good facilities. A forest bungalow and ITDC forest bungalow in the sanctuary require early prior reservation.

Above: Domestic cattle in Gir's forest have become a serious problem, as they denude the grasses that act as grazing for the park's wild herbivores.

Left: The five-petalled flowers of Amaltas (*Cassia fistula*).

Overleaf: A female Asiatic Lion (*Panthera leo parsica*) and her brood relieve their thirst in the cool of the day.

BHAGWAN MAHAVIR WILDLIFE SANCTUARY AND MOLEM NATIONAL PARK

Refuge for a wealth of wildlife

The tiny state of Goa on India's west seaboard is a coastal paradise offering holidaymakers invigorating sea air, sprawling beaches, and history combined with fiesta, food and *feni* (a liquor typical of Goa distilled from coconut milk or cashew nuts). Despite its size, the state of Goa embraces three sanctuaries: Bondla, Catigao near Konkan, and the Bhagwan Mahavir Wildlife Sanctuary and Molem National Park.

Located near the state boundary with Karnataka to the south, Bhagwan Mahavir is Goa's largest sanctuary. The original preserve (named Molem after the settlement nearby) was formed in 1967 with an area of 240 square kilometres (94 square miles), and covered the forested hilly slopes of the Western Ghats. The national park was established in 1978 and today comprises the core of the existing sanctuary, an expanse of 107 square kilometres (42 square miles). The park's forest is contiguous with the adjoining wildlife sanctuaries of Karnataka – the Anamod Ghat, Kadra and Dandeli sanctuaries. Large herds of wild Elephant find refuge here, so many of them migrate from Karnataka to Bhagwan Mahavir National Park in search of fresh grazing. Only around one 'tusker' and two Tigers are permanent residents in the park.

Moist forests and epiphytic orchids

Bhagwan Mahavir, minuscule in relation to India's other parks, sustains diverse, exotic-looking flora. Moist deciduous forests occur together with wet evergreen forests along the riverbanks.

Deciduous tree species are characterized by thickets of *Strobilanthus* **species**: *Carvia callosa* and *Nigirianthus warriensis*. These two canopy-forming trees flower only every seven years. Trees of the moist deciduous forests are predominantly Arjun (*Pentaptera arjuna*), Jamba (*Xylia xylocarpa*), *Adina cordifolia* and various *Dillenia* species. Tall grasses flourish together with plants from the Zingiberaceae family. Members of the climber family include the gigantic *Bauhinia anguina* species, *Vahlii* and *Entada pursaetha*, while epiphytic forest species include orchids such as Vanda, Cymbidium and Dendrobium. Drosera, an insectivorous plant, also survives in the forest. The higher reaches of the Western Ghats consist of patches of Wild Banana. Trees like Mango, Pun (*Callophyllum tornetorum*), Jambal (a *Eugenia* species), Olea, *Diospyros* and thorny bamboo grow in dense pockets throughout the park.

An enormously diverse fauna

Wild fauna species typical of north India, such as Hog Deer and Marbled Cat, have been recorded in the sanctuary. Other rare species populating Bhagwan Mahavir include the Indian Pangolin, Slender Loris and Leopard Cat. Herbivorous animals are Gaur and Indian Elephant, and two primates, Bonnet Macaque and Common

Above right: The *Cymbidium mastersii* orchid species.

Opposite: Tropical coastal vegetation in Bhagwan.

Location: Located along the Panaji–Belgaum Highway on the border between the states of Goa and Karnataka. The park is easily accessible from Dabolim airport at Panaji, 80km (50 miles) away.

Climate: The cimate is moderate all year round (summer maximum 32°C, or 90°F; winter minimum 15°C, or 59°F).

When to go: The best birdwatching season is winter, between December and February, when migratory birds nest in the park. It is also the mating season of Indian Bison. Wildlife viewing is at its best in summer (March to May) when the animals are drawn to the few remaining waterholes.

Getting there: The east–west NH4A passes through Molem, where the park is located. Nearest significant town is Ponda, a major road intersection, 30km (19 miles) away. Regular buses from Panaji and Ponda; jeeps can also be hired here.

Facilities: Rest house and tourist cottages available within the park. There are canteen facilities.

Wildlife: Indian Elephant, Leopard, Indian Bison, Bonnet Macaque, and many deer species.

Reservations: Contact the Range Forest Officer, Wildlife Subdivision, Molem, Goa–403410.

Langur. The Bonnet Macaque is so-called for its crown of long dark hair that radiates out from a whorl on the top of its head, while the forehead has short hair neatly parted in the centre. Similarly with other species, it eats leaves, fruits, spiders and insects. Although it is the same size as the Rhesus Macaque, the Bonnet monkey's tail is longer. A gregarious creature, it is not afraid to come into relatively close contact with humans.

Deer varieties are numerous, with Sambhar, Chital (Spotted Deer), Hog Deer, Barking Deer (Muntjac), and Mouse Deer (Chevrotain) all occurring here. The smaller creatures include hares, bats and the Malabar, Three-striped Palm and Five-striped Palm Squirrel species.

Among Baghwan's carnivores are Tiger, Leopard – including the rare Black Leopard – Jungle Cat, the Palm, Large Indian and Small Indian Civet, Jackal, Striped Hyena, Wild Dog (Dhole), foxes, and Small Indian and Common Indian Mongoose.

The Black Leopard is merely a colour mutant of the common Leopard (*Panthera pardus*) and its diet and habits reflect those of the latter. No precise numbers of this cat have been recorded. Sloth Bear, Ratel (Honey Badger) and Smooth Indian Otter also fall within Baghwan's extensive range of animal species. A unique characteristic of the park's fauna is that they vary in number all year round because of migration from the adjacent forests.

Forest bird and reptile life

The forest habitat harbours 300 species of bird. Gorgeous in colour are the large colonies of rare Malabar Hornbill, lorikeets, and the enchantingly named Fairy Bluebird. Crow Pheasant and Bush Quail forage on the forest floor, and among raptors are Sikra, Crested Serpent Eagle and White-eyed Buzzard Eagle.

Of the park's reptiles, Estuarine Crocodile (*Crocodilus porosus*) live in saltwater creeks in the forest. Rarely seen reptiles are the Flying Snake and Flying Lizard; the former 'fly' very short distances, jumping from branch to branch in the trees. They are nonpoisonous.

Deadly reptiles

King Cobra, Rock Python, Russell's Viper, Wolf Snake, Ornamental Snake, Vine Snake, Sand Boa and Blind Snake are just some of the species living in the forests.

The King Cobra, an endangered species, is India's most poisonous reptile. From 4.5 to 5 metres (15 to 16½ feet) in length, it does not have a hood but rears upright when agitated, and can kill an elephant with a single strike from its fangs. The brightly patterned Russell's Viper, too, is deadly. Its venom attacks red blood cells, causing renal failure; many local people in India's remote villages die from the bite of a Russell's Viper or a Krait. Other venomous snakes to watch out for here are the Saw-scaled and Green Viper.

Rock Python, on the other hand, which can grow up to 4.5 metres (15 feet) kill larger prey such as deer by constriction. Their favoured diet is field rats and birds.

The park's marked Route No. 3 takes visitors to the Dudhsagar Falls in the southeast corner of the park. They are the highest in India, and their name 'sea of milk' is derived from the white foam produced by the falls' stepped drops. There is a railstop at Dudhsagar to view the falls. It is also an ideal trek for birdwatchers, who can walk to the head of the falls with a guide (three hours). Trekkers need to be watchful for King Cobra.

Left: The Common Giant Flying Squirrel (*Petaurista petaurista*) is a nocturnal animal, seldom seen in daylight.

Right: The Five-striped Palm Squirrel (*Funambulus pennanti*) is India's most common squirrel species.

Below: The Slender Loris (*Loris tardigradus*) has no tail; it weighs only 280 to 340 grams (4 ounces).

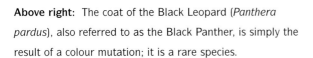

Above right: The coat of the Black Leopard (*Panthera pardus*), also referred to as the Black Panther, is simply the result of a colour mutation; it is a rare species.

Right: Only the tail end of this King Cobra's (*Ophiophagus hannah*) prey, a small snake, is visible in its lethal fangs – which contain the largest amount of venom among all snake species. King Cobras can kill an adult Elephant with a single penetration of their fangs.

PENINSULAR INDIA

eninsular India, popularly known as the Deccan (after the great plateau that stretches across the south of India) covers the vast region separated by, and including, the Western and Eastern Ghats, which eventually meet in the Nilgiri Hills ('blue mountains') to the south. The four southern states fall within Peninsular India: Andhra Pradesh, Tamil Nadu on the east, and Karnataka and Kerala on the west. Significant physical features encompassed in this zone are the Upper Mahanadi River (which rises in the south of Madhya Pradesh and flows east into the Bay of Bengal); the eastern hills of Orissa; the Cardamom hills in the Western Ghats; and the Deccan lava (black volcanic lavas solidified from eruptions through the earth's crust almost 70 million years ago, and formed along a fault line running the length of the west coast).

The climate here differs from the Coastal Indian region because of its two monsoons. The northern part of the peninsula enjoys more rainfall than its hilly southern counterpart – 1500 millimetres (60 inches) as opposed to 1000 millimetres (40 inches) in the south. Nonetheless, the heavy rainfall nurtures tall and leafy tree species: Teak, Mahogany and Indian Rosewood are all famous for their excellent timber, and Sandalwood for its fragrance.

Peninsular India is unique for its endemic fauna – species such as the primates Slender Loris, Nilgiri Langur, and the Lion-tailed and Bonnet Macaque, in addition to the shaggy, goatlike Nilgiri Tahr and Malabar Giant Squirrel.

Nagarjunasagar Srisailam, in Andhra Pradesh, is the largest reserve in the country. Major park destinations in Karnataka are Bandipur National Park and Tiger Reserve, Nagarhole National Park, and Ranganathittoo Bird Sanctuary, while Tamil Nadu embraces the well known Mudumalai Wildlife Sanctuary, Kalakad-Mudenthurai Tiger Reserve, and Vedanthangal Bird Sanctuary. Periyar National Park and Tiger Reserve in Kerala is perhaps the most sought-after nature destination of the region.

Above right: Displaying its supreme expertise in the art of camouflage, this Common Chameleon emerges from the disguise of the branch's dappled green leaves.

Left: The wild, untamed landscape typical of the Western Ghats in Tamil Nadu.

RANGANATHITTOO WATERBIRD SANCTUARY

The Ganges of south India

In the south of the state of Karnataka, a number of verdant tropical islands lie in the Cauvery River, bristling with a great variety of birds. This is the Ranganathittoo Waterbird Sanctuary, a remarkably picturesque spot near the medieval town of Srirangapatna, which has been built on another island downstream and is indelibly associated with Tipu Sultan, a wealthy and powerful Islamic ruler of Mysore (the old name for Karnataka) during the late 1700s. The city of Mysore, not far from the sanctuary, also still retains its historical royal charm.

The mighty Cauvery – popularly known as the Ganges of south India – branches to encircle Srirangapatna and the island holding the minuscule sanctuary.

An early breeding season

One of the most distinctive features of Ranganathittoo, established in 1940, are the groves of leafy Screw Pine, with their long, sharp-edged leaves, favoured by birds which perch and nest in the branches. An unusual occurrence at Ranganathittoo is how early in the season the birds begin their nesting rituals – they nest with the first shower of the southwest monsoon rains in June. In the other south Indian states, Andhra Pradesh and Tamil Nadu, waterbirds begin nesting when the northeast monsoon sets in at the end of October.

The assurance of an abundant supply of food is essential during this breeding season. A number of irrigation channels and low-lying patches of wetland ensure that there is rarely a shortage of prey in the shallow waters after the first rains arrive. Birds prepare to sit on their eggs while others set about feeding their already hatched young chicks. Breeding birds of Ranganathittoo embrace the following species: cormorants of all three species (Common and Little Cormorant, and Indian Shag), Open-billed and Painted Stork, White Ibis, the Pond, Grey and Night Heron species, cattle egrets, true egrets of all three species, and spoonbills.

Nesting habitats

River Terns and Great Stone Plover tend to perch on rocks and along the river edges. In the middle of the river, a flat-crowned tree species, *Terminalia arjuna*, provides the major nesting habitat for Open-billed Stork; they also like to nest on Screw Pines (which often grow in dams and reservoirs).

Six *Terminalia* species grow in India. A large tree with deep-brown hard bark, it carries clusters of leaves and produces single seeds. It also bears fleshy, stringy fruits with hard skins. All *Terminalia* species are of medicinal value to the local population.

Terminalia arjuna trees are favoured too by cormorants, darters and egrets for nesting purposes. Egrets also nest in bushes, trees (among them Screw Pine), and even in sedges, while Spoonbills nest in the broad-leaved shrubs that line some of the islands. The cormorants of

Above right: Darter, or Snakebird (*Anhinga rufa*).

Opposite top and bottom: Boat trips enable visitors to closely approach heronries and other waterbird colonies.

Location: Near Mysore (16km; 10 miles) in Karnataka. Mysore is the nearest airport, with the closest railhead being Srirangapatna.

Climate: The southwest monsoon brings rainfall from June to September; the northeast monsoon from November to February. Summer is hot and humid (maximum 37°C; 99°F) while winter is mild (minimum 18°C; 64°F).

When to go: Best months are between July and September, after summer (April to mid-June). It is cooler, attracting nesting birds.

Getting there: Srirangapatna is close to the sanctuary (3km; 2 miles). Buses from Bangalore (110km; 68 miles) and Mysore (19km; 12 miles) to Srirangapatna, and from here to sanctuary. Visitors can drive to Ranganathittoo from Mysore; car hire facilities here.

Facilities: Comfortable hotels in Mysore: Metropole and KSTDC-run Mayura Hoisala; also, luxurious Lalitha Mahal Hotel and eco-friendly Green Hotel (former palace). Boats for hire for excellent birdwatching.

Birdlife: Large colonies of cormorants, darters, egrets, storks and ibis can be watched at very close range, either on foot (south bank of river) or by boat.

Additional activities: At Srirangapatna, Tipu's summer palace Daria Daulat Bagh (1784) has frescoes and small museum; ornate mausoleum, Gumbaz; two Hindu temples.

Reservations: For accommodation contact: The Assistant Conservator of Forests, Wildlife Subdivision, Mysore, Karnataka.

Clockwise from top: Indian River Tern (*Sterna ausantia*), Great Stone Plover (*Esacus magnirostris*), Asian Open-billed Stork (*Anostomus oscitanus*), Black-crowned Night Heron (*Nyciticorax nyciti-corax*), and Asian Darter (*Anhinga melanogaster*).

south India are characterized by the absence of two large whitish-yellow circular patches above the thigh region, which in the cormorants of north India are quite distinct. And specific to Ranganathittoo's darters is the fact that their nests may hold up to five or six chicks, in contrast to darters of other national parks which sustain two or three nest-chicks.

A large-sized colony of Flying Fox – India's biggest fruit bat – exists on the largest island in the Cauvery River within the sanctuary. These bats feed on juicy fruits like mango, guava and banana.

There are plenty of Marsh (Muggar) Crocodile inhabiting the Cauvery River, where they live off birds, fish and molluscs. They tend to disappear immediately into the water when approached.

Above: Flying Fox, or Fruit Bats (*Pteropus gigantus*), form noisy colonies which roost in the treetops in the daytime.

Below: The White Stork's (*Ciconia ciconia*) red legs and beak contrast strongly with its pure white plumage.

NAGARHOLE NATIONAL PARK AND WILDLIFE SANCTUARY

Tiger and deer, monkeys and snakes

That the forests of south India are surviving today is quite unique – despite the fact that they occur parallel to the coast, they are flourishing along the high hills of the Western Ghats. The vast forests belonging to the Mysore plateau in the state of Karnataka stretch between the Western Ghats and the Nilgiri hills to the south. Karnataka's two national parks – Nagarhole (pronounced Nagara-holay) and Bandipur – are divided by the Kabini River, a tributary of the great Cauvery. Nagarhole is to the north of the river, while Bandipur lies to the south. The mountains mantled by their spectacular forests extend across into Mudumalai National Park in Tamil Nadu and down to Wynad Wildlife Sanctuary in Kerala State (Wynad actually extends along the western extent of all three parks, Nagarhole, Bandipur and Mudumalai).

About one-third of Nagarhole's area is designated as a Wilderness Zone, strictly prohibiting interference with the ecosystem in the form of forestry and tourism. The remaining portion of the forest has been developed into three Tourism Zones, with facilities for wildlife tourism; these are named Nagarhole, Karapura and the third, still in the planning stages, will be called Moorkal.

Due to their close proximity, Nagarhole and Bandipur have many similar features, but at the same time there are sharp contrasts in the weather, flora, mammals, reptiles, and birdlife. Nagarhole has an astonishing wealth of wildlife throughout its 250 square miles (640 square kilometres) of forest.

Tall-canopied forests

Rainfall in Nagarhole is higher than in Bandipur, so its moist, deciduous forest is more dense and abundant. The forest canopy is created by the tallest trees, which tower up to about 30 metres (98 feet). The uppermost canopy is dominated by the spectacular timber trees Mathi (*Terminalia tomentosa*), Nandi (*Lagerstroemia lanceolata*) and Tadasalu (*Grewia tilacfolia*). Two of the most expensive sources of timber in this jungle are the dark Rosewood (*Dalbergia latifolia*) and Teak (*Tectona grandis*). The lower forest canopy is composed of fruit trees, which attract a great number of wild animals. Beneath this canopy, shrubs are dense and varied. Flowering shrubs like Lantana and Lupatorium grow profusely in the clearings created by logging.

Forest fauna

Open grassy swamps in the forest, where the soil is perpetually moist, ensure that there are glades of succulent grass all year round. These attract ungulates such as Gaur (Indian Bison) – a common sight to visitors in the Nagarhole and Karapura tourist zones as they pass in their jeeps or vans.

Above right: The luxurious Kabini Tourist Lodge is perched on the bank of the picturesque river of the same name.

Location: Mysore, at a distance of 90km (55 miles) away, is the entry point to the Nagarhole and Bandipur parks. The nearest airport is Bangalore (220km; 135 miles), while Mysore is the nearest railhead.

Climate: Nagarhole receives heavier rainfall than Bandipur (1600mm; 65in); there are two monsoons.

When to go: A favourable time to visit the park is between October and March (part-monsoon season, part-winter).

Getting there: The nearest towns are Kutta, 7km (4 miles) away, and Mysore. Buses run from both towns to the park. Car hire in Mysore and park itself.

Facilities: Visitors should plan properly and book well in advance. Kabini Tourist Lodge offers accommodation in their lodge and in large tents with beds; located at the Karapura settlement (southern park entrance 5km, or 3 miles, from here). Tourists are taken into the forest in jeeps or vans on guided drives at least twice a day. A park guard accompanies visitors and identifies wildlife for them. *Machaans* (watchtowers constructed from logs) near waterholes.

Wildlife: Indian Elephant, Tiger, Leopard (Panther), Sloth Bear, and four deer species. Excellent birdlife (250 species); viewing also by motorboat or coracles.

Reservations: For further information, contact: Jungle Lodges and Resorts Limited, 2nd Floor, Srinagar Shopping Centre, MG Road, Bangalore–560001.

Similarly with Bandipur, the forest is the ideal place to spot hundreds of Elephant, in both small and large herds, throughout the year. When summer (March to June) approaches, they range further in search of food and water. During this period, they can be best viewed on the banks of the Kabini River. Here, a large herd of these pachyderms, either crossing the river with their playful young or congregating at the riverbanks around sunset, is a familiar sight.

A deer haven

Four species of deer inhabit the park. Sambhar roam throughout the region in small groups, and are seen in such large numbers that one tends to take them for granted; the same goes for Chital, India's spotted deer. These beautiful animals gather in hundreds around the forest headquarters in the evening, and occur in clusters around the tourist rest houses, even in the late hours of morning. Muntjac (Barking Deer) can also be viewed from close quarters. This species has earned its name from its remarkably loud bark, not unlike that of a dog,

Above: Indian Elephants in a mock fight at a waterhole; this is not aggressive behaviour, although it may appear so.

Right: Nagarhole's grass-lands are the favoured habitat of herds of Chital, or Spotted Deer (*Axis axis*).

which alerts others to any marauding predators. The Mouse Deer (Indian Chevrotain) is tiny and entirely nocturnal. As a result, these animals are rarely seen.

The Chausingha, or Four-horned Antelope, is the most remarkable ungulate of Nagarhole National Park. It is almost the size of a Muntjac but has longer legs. It is the only 'four-horned' antelope in the world – the male carries two regular horns, each of which has an extra projection extending slightly forward, creating the appearance of four horns. It is unfortunate that many of the park officials accompanying visitors on night drives fail to differentiate between this deer and the Muntjac.

Deer, Wild Dog and Tiger

Dhole (Indian Wild Dog) are prevalent in Nagarhole. Here, they prey on Sambhar and Chital. Smaller animal species are Wild Boar, Black-naped Hare (frequently sighted here), Giant and Flying Squirrel, and fruit bats. And if it's Sloth Bear visitors are after, these can be spotted in the Karapura Tourist Zone.

The treetops close to local settlements and tourist-designated zones (there is a greater abundance of fruits here) are the domain of the secretive and nocturnal Slender Loris, the Common Langur and Bonnet Macaque. The tiny Slender Loris (20 to 25 centimetres, or 8 to 10 inches, in height) sleeps in deep tree foliage during the day so is rarely seen by visitors. In appearance it has very large eyes ringed in black, proportionately large ears and a pointed snout; it has almost no tail. This primate is fond of Lantana berries, small birds, lizards, tree frogs, and small insects.

Although Bandipur Tiger Reserve counts as one of the original nine established under Project Tiger, it is in Nagarhole that one has the chance of coming across a Tiger, although the likelihood of sighting this cat in broad daylight is a lot less here than in some of the northern Indian parks. The latest census records around 50 Tigers. The elusive Leopard is also present, and in areas such as Karapura is sighted quite often. Among the smaller carnivores are Jackal, the Jungle, Leopard and Rusty Spotted Cat, Small Indian and Palm Civet, and mongoose. Sometimes, one will be lucky to encounter a group of Smooth Indian Otters (*Lutra perspicillata*) in the Kabini reservoir, which was created by damming the river in the 1970s; this reservoir separates Nagarhole and Bandipur. There are also Marsh Crocodile and Monitor Lizard here. Forest snake species include Rock Python, Krait, cobras, Rat Snake, Wolf Snake, and Russell's and

Bamboo Pit Viper. Turtles and frogs are quite common. The Nagarhole National Park, and particularly the Karapura Tourist Zone, is excellent for wildlife watching during the dry season of March to May. Guided tours in jeeps and open-sided trucks are popular. During the monsoon months of June to September and November to February, the forest is a rich, luxuriant green but the roads become slushy and muddy and sometimes visitors may be forced to remain in their rest houses.

Right: Members of the Jenu Kuruba tribe; its people live in harmony with the surrounding forests of Nagarhole and have gained renown as honey-gatherers.

Below: A jeep travels along majestic bamboo-lined roads; open-sided jeeps afford visitors excellent wildlife viewing.

BANDIPUR NATIONAL PARK AND TIGER RESERVE

Legacy of the Mysore maharajas

The vast tracts of the magnificent forests of Karnataka are the legacy of the maharajas of Mysore, under whose privileged management the sanctuary used to teem with wildlife. Today, the forests protect a large population of Indian Elephant, Gaur and other large mammals.

As stated earlier, Bandipur and Nagarhole form one continuous ecological zone that also includes Mudumalai in Tamil Nadu and Wynad in Kerala. In the drier seasons, the animals of the forests move from one area to another in search of food and water, blissfully ignorant of man-made inter-reserve and interstate boundaries.

Visitors enter the Bandipur and Nagarhole national parks via the old royal capital of Mysore. Bandipur, established in the early 1930s in the shadow of the Western Ghats, first covered an area of 60 square kilometres (23 square miles). It was a part of the former Venugopal Wildlife Park (803 square kilometres; 310 square miles) which used to be the shooting preserve of the early Mysore rulers. Today, Bandipur's Tiger Reserve, established as part of Project Tiger in 1974 and expanded to 690 square kilometres (266 square miles), stands in what used to be the Venugopal Park. It is one of the finest tiger reserves in India.

About one-third of the combined tiger reserve and national park (comprising the core area of 335 square kilometres, or 130 square miles) has been designated a Wilderness Zone, thus prohibiting tourism and forestry within its confines.

Dry deciduous forests

The topography of the park consists of an undulating land of rocky hills and valleys. Kabini River, a tributary of the Cauvery, is the largest river in this tract and flows southwards through the park. A dam for irrigation was built across the Kabini in 1974, creating a spectacular reservoir which separates Bandipur and Nagarhole.

In the pre-monsoon summer months of March/April and October/November, food and water shortages pose a serious problem for the herbivores. Bandipur's eastern extent receives the lowest rainfall, resulting in dry, deciduous forest with patches of open grassland while the tiger reserve portion is characterized by tropical dry deciduous forest. The more severe easternmost stretches of Bandipur, near Moyar gorge, are composed of rocky soils and vegetation dominated by thorny shrubs. The more densely forested southern half of the region with its higher rainfall supports, besides Teak, mainly Sandalwood, Jamun (Blackberry), Rosewood, Silk Cotton and groves of bamboo. The forest is fairly open, with clearings of tall and short grasses.

Above right: The Peacock's call resembles a metallic trumpetlike sound, repeated several times in a varying pitch.

Opposite: A lone Elephant shares its fast-dwindling grazing grounds with a handful of Bonnet Macaques; Elephant are often seen crossing the national highway on their migrations.

Location: On the Mysore–Ooty Highway, from where the Deccan plateau rises to meet the mountains of the Western Ghats, in the district of Chamrajnagar, Karnataka. Bandipur has nearest airport (190km; 118 miles); nearest railhead is Mysore, 65km (40 miles) away.

Climate: Moderate climate (32°C, or 90°F, in summer; 18°C, or 64°F, in winter). Summer rains arrive late and are called 'mango showers'. Monsoon strikes twice a year – southwest monsoon from June to September, northeast monsoon from November to February.

When to go: March to June and September to November is best.

Getting there: Gundulpet is the nearest town (20 km, or 12 miles, from the park). Buses operate regularly on the Mysore–Ooty Highway via Bandipur; taxis can be hired from Mysore and Ooty.

Facilities: Accommodation is available in forest lodges, cottages and forest rest houses in the park; canteen facilities. Bush Beta Wildlife Resort very comfortable. Elephant rides for hire. Guided jeep tours; no private vehicles permitted in park.

Wildlife: Indian Elephant, Gaur, Sloth Bear, four deer species.

Landscapes: Composed of igneous metamorphic rocks; clayey-black and red-loamy soils. Mountain-flowing rivers such as the Kabini, Nugu and Moyar have carved valleys, and cloud-covered peaks of Nilgiri hills form a splendid backdrop to the park.

Reservations: For further information and accommodation contact: The Field Director, Bandipur Tiger Reserve, Mysore–570004.

Map labels

to Hunsur
Kabini Reservoir
Kabini
Nugu Reservoir
Nugu
to Mysore
Bandipur National Park & Tiger Reserve
Delhi
Mumbai
Gundre
Kokankote Betta
Bargi
N
Kalkeri
Gundulpet
to Chamrajnagar
Hangola
Mulehole
Bachalli
Beermbadi
Bandipur
to Sultan's Battery
Moyar
to Ooty

Right: The Indian Giant Squirrel (*Ratufa indica*) is not a shy creature and is seen around human settlement.

Below right: A pair of Common Indian Monitors (*Varanus bengalensis*) perform a mating dance.

Bandipur National Park and Tiger Reserve sustains an enormous bird population. A checklist records over 200 avian species in the region. Bird-watchers could spot Rock Pigeon, Collared and Spotted Dove, Alexandrine Parakeet, lapwings, cuckoos, Brain Fever Bird, White-breasted and Common Kingfisher, Little Grey Bee-eater, hornbills, bulbuls, woodpeckers, flycatchers, orioles and drongos. Of the terrestrial birds, they might catch sight of Cattle and Little Egret, Brahminy Duck, fantails, Spot-billed Duck, Grey Partridge, Common Peafowl, Grey Junglefowl, and Bush Quail.

Elephant and bison

The Bandipur National Park and Tiger Reserve has one of the best planned road networks of India's parks, which offers excellent wildlife viewing. Bandipur is one of the best remaining habitats for Indian Elephant since they migrate through the corridor between Nagarhole, Mudumalai and Wynad, and it is estimated that over 1000 Elephant, in both small and large herds, inhabit the Bandipur and Nagarhole forests. During the two monsoons, when food and water are abundant, the Elephant are evenly distributed, but with the arrival of summer (April and May), they migrate to the banks of Mulehole River, the Nagarhole Tourism Zone and Mastigudi on the banks of the Kabini. It is not unusual to come across a herd of Elephant calmly crossing the highway to get to the other side of the forest.

Gaur (Indian Bison) is another major attraction in the park. The bison population was almost destroyed by an outbreak of rinderpest in 1868, but this animal has made a spectacular comeback.

An abundance of deer

Five species of deer inhabit Bandipur's forests. The largest of them is the Sambhar, a shy creature that prefers thick cover and comes out late in the evening. During the monsoon, large groups of 10 to 20 Sambhar can be seen by visitors. Large stags with fine antlers occasionally roam through the park. A large population of Chital, India's most common deer species, exists here. This handsome spotted deer is the least shy of the species, congregating in large numbers in and around the tourist guest houses from dusk to dawn. It is also frequently spotted in roadside clearings. The small reddish-fawn-coloured deer, Muntjac, has a surprisingly loud bark which breaks the stillness of the night, sounding the alarm to other deer for predators on the

prowl. Mouse Deer, or Indian Chevrotain, are tiny, rabbit-like creatures which are rarely spotted owing to their nocturnal habits, and Chausingha is the fourth deer species occurring here. Wild Dog, or Dhole, reside on the fringes of the forest reserve where they hunt ferociously for deer.

Bandipur also protects Leopard, Sloth Bear, Indian Wild Boar, Striped Hyena, Jackal, Palm Civet, Common Mongoose, and Black naped Hare. Bonnet Macaque and Common Langur are the two most frequently seen ape species. Among the reptiles, the Common Indian Monitor is the largest species existing in the park.

Below: The diet of the Common Palm Civet (*Paradoxurus hermaphroditus*) comprises small mammals, birds, and even fruits; it eats at night.

MUDUMALAI NATIONAL PARK AND WILDLIFE SANCTUARY

Sanctuary in an ancient range of hills

The Mudumalai National Park and Wildlife Sanctuary lies in the hilly terrain of the Western Ghats in India's southeasternmost state, Tamil Nadu. The word 'mudumalai' translates as 'the ancient hill range' and the essence of the word is relevant in all three south Indian languages of the states of Tamil Nadu, Kerala and Karnataka.

Mudumalai is spread over part of the Nilgiri hills. These 'blue mountains' are an extension of the Western Ghats, and their majestic height and range create extensive tablelands or plateaus, and grassy downs with deep forested ravines. A vast tract of wilderness on the northeastern slopes of the Nilgiri hills, originally known as Wynad, is divided between the three parks in their three different Indian states – Wynad Sanctuary in Kerala, Bandipur in Karnataka and Mudumalai in Tamil Nadu.

Mudumalai is split by the Mysore–Ooty Highway which runs north to south, following the path of the Moyar River, the most prominent one, together with its tributaries, in the sanctuary. Unlike the other streams, the Moyar does not dry up in summer. It also forms the northern boundary of Mudumalai, separating the sanctuary from Bandipur National Park and Tiger Reserve.

Mudumalai was established as far back as 1940. More forest land was incorporated into the sanctuary in 1956, and it presently comprises an area of 324 square kilometres (125 square miles). Mudumalai encompasses the forest zones of Kargudi, Theppakkadu and Masinagudi, all of which are renowned for their pristine, natural state. The vegetation is extremely diverse because of variations in temperature and rainfall in different parts of the sanctuary. Mudumalai receives more rainfall than Bandipur which in turn contributes to its dense vegetation. Forests range from tropical, semi-evergreen and deciduous to tracts of bamboo and thorny bushes. The park features a large number of moist deciduous Teak and Eucalyptus plantations. There are also bamboo plantations which provide raw material for the rayon silk mills.

Migrating Elephant and abundant deer

Although the Moyar River forms an administrative and political division, the animals frequently move freely between Bandipur, Mudumalai and other neighbouring forests. It is a common sight to catch large herds of Elephant crossing the Mysore–Ooty Highway on their migration to other forests. These migratory corridors become particularly active when water sources dry up and the pachyderms move to greener pastures.

The park's Gaur population was drastically reduced in the aftermath of the 1968 rinderpest epidemic, but it is slowly growing, and these herbivores can be seen in small groups headed up by two or more dominant bulls.

The fauna in Mudumalai National Park and Wildlife Sanctuary is quite similar to that of Bandipur, although the setting is different. The Giant Squirrel is a common inhabitant in Mudumalai, while Chital (Spotted Deer)

Above right: Bonnet Macaque (*Macaca radiata*) mother and baby – this species is very social, moving in highly organized troops in a well-defined territory of around 5 square kilometres (2 square miles).

Location: In Nilgiri hills at around 350–1220m (1150ft–4100ft). Route between Mysore and hill resort of Ooty runs through Mudumalai. Nearest airport is at Coimbatore, (160km; 99 miles). Ooty (better known as Udhagamandalam) is nearest railhead (64km; 40 miles).

Climate: Both summer and winter are moderate (summer 32°C, or 90°F; winter 18°C, or 64°F).

When to go: Wildlife viewing best between February and June.

Getting there: Nearest town is Gudalur (16km; 10 miles). Buses between Mysore and Ooty, and Ooty–Gudalur and the park.

Facilities: Park closed in middle of day (open 06:30–09:00 and 16:00–18:00). Private cars not permitted; jeeps and vans available through Forestry Department; must be accompanied by guides. Forest rest houses and guest houses at Masinagudi (restaurants and shops), Kargudi, Theppakkadu, and Abhayaranyam in the park. Private accommodation offered by Bamboo Banks Farm guest house 18km (11 miles) from sanctuary; Jungle Hut also offers cottages. Park has extensive network of fair-weather roads.

Wildlife: Indian Elephant, Gaur, Wild Boar, Wild Dog, Chital and Sambhar. Tours in vans available, but best way to visit the park is to take an elephant ride (arrange through rest houses). Night safaris and trekking opportunities.

Landscapes: Mudumalai has a diverse terrain of hills, ravines, valleys, waterfalls and swamps.

Reservations: For information and accommodation (reservations need to be made early), contact: Wildlife Warden, Mahalingam Building, Conoor Road, Udhagamandalam, Tamil Nadu.

Above: Generally the Indian Wild Dog, or Dhole (*Cuon alpinus*), resembles the domestic dog, the major difference being that its body is longer and lankier, similar to that of a wolf.

Left: The gorge of the Moyar River in the Nilgiri Hills is deep and narrow, with the riverbed lying at 300 to 600 metres (1000 to 2000 feet) above sea level.

Below: The delicate blooms of the *Rhodomyrtus parviflora*, which grows in the Moyar Gorge.

and Sambhar are the two most visible deer species. Chital wander in small groups in the southwest of the park, with much larger groups in the southeast, near the well-watered grasslands of the Masinagudi area. Herds of more than 100 Chital can often be observed at Viewpoint, near Masinagudi. Barking Deer (Muntjac) share the same forests as the Chital, while Sambhar roam throughout the park. Mouse Deer (Chevrotain) are seen more in this park than anywhere else in India. There are *machaans* (watchtowers) and saltlicks at the waterholes.

Although Tiger exist in the park, glimpses of this cat are rare. Leopard may be spotted in the Kargudi area. Seen often in packs at the fringes of the park near human habitation are Indian Wild Dog, a major predator. Striped Hyena, Jackal and Small and Common Palm Civet are also inhabitants of Mudumalai, while Wild Boar are regularly spotted along the streams, on the banks of ponds or crossing the roads. India's forested tracts provide Sloth Bear with termites, honey and mahua flowers, while rocky outcrops and boulder clusters offer overhangs and crevices in which to shelter.

Of the monkeys, Bonnet Macaque and Common Langur (Hanuman Monkey) are likely to be seen in the clearings of the open woodland around Theppakkadu in the north and Kargudi in the centre of the park.

The park's smaller creatures are the Indian Giant and Red Giant Flying Squirrel, Black-naped Hare and porcupines. The only reptile that is regularly spotted along the road on the way to the Moyar powerhouse is the Common Indian Monitor.

Colourful woodland birds

The Mudumalai National Park bristles with woodland birds. Birdwatchers will spot Racket-tailed Drongo much easier here than in Bandipur. Other species include the Malabar Trogon, Malabar Grey Hornbill and Malabar Great Black Woodpecker whose glorious crimson crest contrasts vividly with its jet-black body. During summer, many songbirds like barbets, cuckoos, mynas, and parakeets fill the forest with their sweet notes. The Crested Hawk Eagle is the main predator of the forests, and the Crested Serpent Eagle may also be spotted. There are many different owl species in the park, although owls are completely nocturnal and visitors are most unlikely to catch sight of them. As a result, the Common Scops, Little Scops and Tiny-eared Owl are more often heard than seen by visitors.

Primitive settlements exist within the park boundaries and the Moyar hydroelectric power station is situated on the outer park premises. Mudumalai has some picturesque scenic attractions, among them the Moyar waterfall which can be viewed from an observation point. Another waterfall, on the Segur River, is located outside the sanctuary, to the east. Theppakkadu has a famous Elephant camp where, it is said, more Elephant were born in captivity than in any other region in India. This is worth a visit.

Above: The Moyar waterfall is not particularly long, but its situation within beautiful verdant forests makes it a tourist attraction.

Inset: The Indian Porcupine (*Hystrix indica*) is highly adaptable to both moist and arid environments and it inhabits both open vegetation and forest areas.

VEDANTHANGAL WATERBIRD SANCTUARY

A significant breeding ground

Just 80 kilometres (50 miles) away from Chennai in the northeast of the state of Tamil Nadu is the Vedanthangal Bird Sanctuary, a refuge for migratory and resident birds. The sanctuary is believed to be the oldest protected area in India; its legislation took place in 1798. During those early years, the sanctuary was preserved by the local population and subsequently by the government for over 250 years. Vedanthangal derives its name from a hamlet lying in Tamil Nadu's Chengalpattu district.

The waterbird sanctuary covers an area of 2 square kilometres (1 square mile) and has a small lake – or what is termed a 'tank' in India – the Karikili Tank, at its centre. The sanctuary is created out of a grove of trees comprising Kadappamaram (*Barringtonia acutangula*) which grow in the lake, their roots and trunks remaining submerged during most of the rains. This tree produces elongated flowers composed of four petals, and later, fibrous berry fruits.

To the west of the reservoir, there is a raised *bund*, or embankment, with a broad path that is lined with rows of shady trees on either side. Nesting colonies of waterbirds can be seen in the treetops.

A time for nesting

The nesting season of the birds starts in late October, during which time breeding occurs, and lasts till about March; the height of the season is December and January. Chicks remain in their nests until they have attained a certain maturity. The breeding period is sustained by an abundance of aquatic food provided by a number of shallow expanses of water and reservoirs lying in the vicinity. In February the birds, mainly local migrants, disperse to their summer feeding grounds.

The main nesting birds include the Common and Little Cormorant and Indian Shag, the three species of true egret, Open-billed Stork, White Ibis, spoonbills and darters. Some of the migratory birds to be seen are Black-winged Stilt, several duck species and occasionally Grey Pelican. During July–September's monsoon, an enormous, congested colony of herons, which includes the Grey, Pond and Night Heron, is established here because of the increased aquatic food sources.

The White Ibis is a relative of the spoonbill and maintains the same habits. This bird is distinguished by its flight pattern in which its long neck is extended in front and the legs stretched out behind. Like the stork and spoonbill families it is a silent bird and is only noisy during mating. Two or three families of young are raised in succession during the breeding season.

Best observed in the very early mornings and at dusk between 16:00 and 18:00, the birds setting out and later returning in their flocks after gathering nesting material to replenish their nests are a splendid sight.

Above right: Spoonbill (*Platalea leucorodia*).

Opposite: A flock of Cormorants (*Phalacrocorax carbo*).

Location: In the state of Tamil Nadu. Readily accessible from Chennai, the state capital (80km, or 50 miles, away), which has the nearest airport, Meenambakkam. It is also the closest railhead.

Climate: Both summer (maximum 34°C; 93°F) and winter (minimum 15°C; 59°F) are quite moderate.

When to go: The best months are from late November to December (height of the breeding season). Between late October and February is when migrating birds arrive and subsequently return to their home territories.

Getting there: Visitors can stay overnight in Chennai and drive to Vedanthangal for the day. Car hire facilities and buses to the park.

Facilities: Accommodation for varying budgets in Chennai. A forest rest house is located beside the reservoir in the park; meals provided.

Birdlife: The sanctuary is famous for its wealth of year-round resident waterbirds and migratory species which nest here during their breeding season. Best viewing times are dawn and late afternoon/twilight hours.

Reservations: For accommodation contact: The Wildlife Warden, Adyar, Chennai, Tamil Nadu.

(Map labels: Delhi; Mumbai; to Chennai (Madras); Vedanthangal Waterbird Sanctuary; Karikili Tank; N; to Tindivanam)

MUNDANTHURAI-KALAKKAD WILDLIFE SANCTUARY

A botanist's heaven

In the extreme south of Tamil Nadu lies the Mundanthurai Wildlife Sanctuary. Although it does not often feature on popular tourist maps of India, it is an adventure simply getting to this sanctuary, and it offers naturalists and botanists the opportunity to study south India's rainforest habitat.

The sanctuary was created in 1962, and comprised a tract along Tamil Nadu's western border with Kerala to the east, covering 67 square kilometres (26 square miles).

Mundanthurai Sanctuary is also on the banks of the Tambraparni River, which is the site of the Manimuttar ('river of pearls') hydroelectric project. The preserve has recently been extended to include the Kalakkad Wildlife Sanctuary. Established in 1976, Kalakkad's area is about 224 square kilometres (87 square miles) with a core area of 82 square kilometres (32 square miles) and it adjoins Mundanthurai to the south.

Rainforests and elusive fauna

The virgin forests of Mundanthurai Wildlife Sanctuary form a tract of authentic rainforest, whose lofty dominating trees with their buttressed boles are a major attraction for botanists. The vegetation consists of semi-evergreen and secondary moist mixed deciduous forest, as well as thickets of cane and bamboo.

Many rare species inhabit the sanctuary – including unusual primates such as Nilgiri Langur, Lion-tailed Macaque and Bonnet Macaque, and the shaggy-coated wild goat, Nilgiri Tahr. Common Langur (Hanuman Monkey) and Bonnet Macaque are seen by visitors in many parts of the sanctuary, while the Nilgiri Langur is confined to the Taruvattamparai zone. The Lion-tailed Macaque exists in larger numbers from higher up the Ghat road to the top of the Valaiyur hill, where the rainforests begin. A distinguishing characteristic of the latter macaque is its mane of long dark-grey or brownish hair growing from the top of its cheeks and its 25- to 28-centimetre-long (10- to 15-inch) tail. It has a glossy black coat. The Nilgiri Langur's tail is much longer at 75 centimetres (2½ feet); it is also brown-black in colour but the head is a yellowish-brown. These monkeys breed in April and June, and the gestation period lasts for approximately six months.

Indian Elephant and Gaur are absent in Mundanthurai but Nilgiri Tahr, Leopard, Tiger and Sambhar occur, while eagles and vultures soar in the skies above. Mundanthurai was originally intended as a Tiger sanctuary, but here, particularly, the regal cats are wholly nocturnal as a result of the considerable human traffic that persists in the sanctuary from tribes and local villagers, so they are never spotted.

Above right: The Nilgiri Tahr's ideal habitat is the grassy upland occurring above the forest level.

Opposite: The name Nilgiri, meaning 'blue mountains', derives from the blue hue of the range as seen from afar.

Location: In the district of Tirunelveli in the state of Tamil Nadu. The temple town of Madurai has the nearest airport, 203km (126 miles) from the sanctuary. The town of Tirunelveli (45km; 28 miles) has the nearest railway station.

Climate: The valley and hill slopes of Mundanthurai receive an annual rainfall well over 2000mm (79in) as a result of a particularly heavy monsoon. Summer maximum is 37°C (99°F) and the winter minimum 15°C (59°F).

When to go: Best time to visit is from September to November.

Getting there: By road, sanctuary is within easy reach of Tirunelveli town. Buses travel frequently from Tirunelveli to Mundanthurai; car hire is available.

Facilities: An old-fashioned rest house stands right above the Tambaravarani River, which is scenically charming. Meals are arranged only after prior notification. Vans not provided for visitors in the park.

Wildlife: Rare species present – Nilgiri Tahr, Nilgiri Langur, Lion-tailed Macaque.

Landscape: Unique virgin rainforest habitat.

Reservations: For further details and accommodation, contact: The Wildlife Warden, Sengottai, Tirunelveli District, Tamil Nadu.

PERIYAR NATIONAL PARK AND TIGER RESERVE

A sylvan tract in the Western Ghats

In the quiet wilderness of the southernmost Western Ghats, in the state of Kerala, lies the sprawling Periyar National Park and Tiger Reserve. Historically, Periyar goes back a long way. In 1895, Periyar lake had its beginnings under the guiding hand of the Maharaja of Travancore, who was an avid nature lover. The first game warden of the forests that today make up Periyar was an S C H Robertson, appointed by the maharaja himself. Delighted by the biodiversity of these forests, he developed the Nellikampathy Sanctuary which in 1950 was eventually renamed the Periyar Tiger Sanctuary. It was later legislated to include a tiger reserve under the Project Tiger scheme in 1978, and today covers a vast expanse of 777 square kilometres (480 square miles). The Tiger habitat is concentrated in the core area of the national park (declared in 1982).

The last census confirms the population of these elegant cats at around 35 to 40, and visitors do spot them. Annually, 450,000 people visit the park.

The serene Periyar lake stretches for 26 square kilometres (10 square miles) and is surrounded by waterways that have formed inbetween the hills and islands. The dam constructed in 1895 was enlarged into a lake during British rule and provides a perennial source of water for the wildlife in the reserve. The national park is today surrounded by spice gardens and plantation estates. It has a recorded 1936 floral species and possesses the only south Indian conifer, *Podocarpus wallichianus*. In addition, 145 species of fragrant orchids bloom here.

From Lion-tailed Macaque to Flying Lizards

Periyar's sylvan environs offer a refuge to many mammals, reptiles and amphibians, and 316 avian species. The threatened Lion-tailed Macaque and Nilgiri Langur occur here, as does the Flying and Malabar Giant Squirrel. The elusive Nilgiri Tahr, which is present in the park, unfortunately is rarely spotted. Visitors can watch Indian Elephant swimming and submerging themselves in Periyar lake. Large numbers – believed to be more than 1000 – inhabit the forests.

Periyar's herbivores – Gaur (Indian Bison), Sambhar, and Wild Boar – spend much of their time wandering along the lakeside, particularly during the dry seasons of March and April. They can be viewed from boat launches which carry visitors on lake cruises. The lake carries a large population of turtles, among them the Travancore Tortoise and the Black Turtle. Leopard, Indian Wild Dog, Barking Deer and Mouse Deer may also be spotted in Periyar. Visitors will see Common Indian Monitors sunning themselves on rocks, and should be watchful for Indian Rock Python and King Cobra which are

Above right: Ornamental Snake (*Chrysopelea ornata*).

Opposite: Periyar lake lies in the heart of the park.

Location: Set amid the high ranges of the Western Ghats in the state of Kerala. The national park is accessible by air from Cochin (200km; 125 miles). Madurai is 140km (87 miles) from the park. The nearest railhead is at Kottayam (114km; 70 miles), while the nearest town is Kumily, 3km (2 miles) away.

Climate: Both summer (maximum 29°C; 84°F) and winter (maximum 21°C; 70°F) are moderate.

When to go: A favourable time to visit is between October and April.

Getting there: By road, head for Thekkady from Madurai, Tamil Nadu's temple town, then the district town of Theni. An hour's drive takes motorists to the Thekkady forest rest house in the hills. Beyond this is Periyar. Buses from Thekkady to the park; jeep hire available.

Facilities: Accommodation in Thekkady forest house at the outer fringes of the sanctuary; Aranya Nivas Hotel in the park at the lake; Edapalayam Lake Palace and Periyar House, both near the lake. Lake Palace was once the summer residence of the Travancore royal clan. Resorts include The Spice Village and Taj Garden Retreat; Shalimar Spice Garden also worthwhile. The Forest Department operates seven boats for cruising on Periyar lake.

Wildlife: Great herds of Indian Elephant, Gaur, Wild Boar, Sambhar and other deer species. Also elusive Lion-tailed Macaque and Nilgiri Langur.

Reservations: For further information and accommodation, contact: Field Director, Project Tiger, Kankikuzhi, Kottayam, Kerala.

Map labels:
Aumill · to Madurai · Wildlife Preservation Office · to Kottayam · Thekkady Park Headquarters · Periyar House · Aranya Nivas Hotel · Edapalayam · Lake Palace · Manakavala Rest House · Watchtower · Watchtower · Watchtower · Azhutha · 1159m · 1302m · Periyar Lake · 1030m · Mullakady Rest House · Mullavar · Thanikudi Rest House · Watchtower · Periyar National Park & Tiger Reserve · to Moozhiyar · Sabarimala Temple · Delhi · Mumbai · Periyar · N

prevalent here. Unusual species in Periyar are the Flying Snake and Flying Lizard which glide from the branches of trees. The former – slender and very fast but nonpoisonous – is 1 metre (3 feet) long with its black back beautifully marked by yellow or white cross-bands as well as speckles and red rosettes, while the latter is orange- or yellow-coloured.

The watchtowers are an excellent way to view the wildlife in the early mornings and twilight hours; these are situated at Edapalayam and Manakavala.

Kingdom fit for ornithologists

With its aquatic environment, protected nesting sites, and abundant fruits, berries, fish, and insects, Periyar provides the ideal conditions for breeding birds. This avian kingdom has attracted ornithologists from all corners of India and has been visited by legendary Indian ornithologist, Dr Salim Ali, to document its bird species.

Darters, cormorants, ibises, and Grey Heron perch on dead branches projecting from the lake. In addition to these, kingfishers, the Racket-tailed Drongo, and the Great Malabar and Grey Hornbill frequent the waters.

Above: The Flying Lizard (*Draco dussumeeri*), also known as Flying Dragon, lives in plantations of coconut and betel (a tropical flowering climbing plant).

Colourful butterflies and moths, carrying evocative names like Common Crow, Indian Fritillary and Tamil Lacewing, hover over wildflowers such as the Lantana and Lupatorium species. Of these, the Atlas Moth (not endemic to India), is recorded in the Guinness Book of World Records as the largest in the world; it can be spotted in the tiger reserve.

Rehabilitating poachers

Of interest in the park is a recent eco-development project, the Thekkady Tiger Trail, undertaken jointly by the Forest Department and private sector. It offers visitors trekking with overnight camps led by armed forest guards, and poachers who have been reformed as naturalists and tour guides. Funds raised contribute to the livelihood of these former poachers.

Inset: Atlas Moth (*Attacus atlas*).

Below and opposite: Periyar lake was created by the damming of the forested valley, hence the dead tree stumps projecting from its waters. Tourist boats pass through spectacular forest tracts of the Western Ghats.

NAGARJUNASAGAR–SRISAILAM TIGER RESERVE

Primeval forest of the Deccan

One of the largest tiger reserves in India is the Nagarjunasagar–Srisailam Sanctuary, which extends over an area of 3568 square kilometres (1390 square miles). Topographically, it consists of rugged terrain with meandering gorges cut by the Krishna River through the Nallamalai hills of central Andhra Pradesh.

Declared as a sanctuary in 1978, the forest tract became part of Project Tiger in 1983. This tiger reserve is truly representative of the arid interior characterized by the ancient Deccan plateau, with its cliffed ridges and valleys, plateaus and deep gorges, covered with mostly dry mixed deciduous forest, patches of dry scrub forest and bamboo thickets. Tree species include *Terminalia tomentosa*, *Adina cordifolia*, Teak, Redwood, Kendu, bamboo and grasses. The forest is inhabited by a number of aboriginal tribes, among them, the Lambada and Chenchu tribes. They are dependent on goat-keeping and agriculture, but their simple hunter-gatherer lifestyle is being severely disrupted as a result of the government's so-called tribal welfare policies.

Eco-development in progress

Generally, the Nagarjunasagar–Srisailam Tiger Reserve cannot be compared with other national parks of India. The park does not enjoy the privilege of having been a royal preserve in the past; rather it has been the domain of aboriginal tribes. The reserve's true wilderness areas and abundant sources of food contribute to its problems as it provides a safe haven for political terrorists.

Environmental degradation has also led to several areas becoming drought-prone. A recent threat to the sanctuary is posed by the local cattle herders who are occupying the verdant reserve. These two factors – the perilous threat of terrorists and encroaching grazers – continue to undermine the tiger project. Rampant illegal felling of timber is also causing heavy destruction to the forests. The Forest Department of Andhra Pradesh has launched a number of self-motivated eco-development schemes with a view to generating employment for the local population in order to lessen their dependency on the forest.

The reserve provides a habitat for a varied number of wildlife – Indian Wild Dog, Jackal, Wild Boar, wolves, foxes, Ratel (Honey Badger), and Indian Giant Squirrel. Many of India's deer and antelope species are also present here. Visitors are likely to see Spotted Deer, Sambhar, Barking Deer, Chausingha (Four-horned Antelope), Chinkara (Indian Gazelle), Nilgai (Blue Bull), and Blackbuck (Indian Antelope).

The 1979 census count recorded the presence of about 40 Tiger in the sanctuary. These, however, are nocturnal and sightings are therefore rare.

Nearby Srisailam has the ruins of a second-century fort and a series of temples that can be visited.

Above right: The antlers of Chital stags carry three tines.

Opposite: Bamboo varies in size from shrubs to woody trees.

Location: Reserve is spread over five districts of Andhra Pradesh State: Guntur, Rakasam, Kurnool, Mahboobnagar and Nalgonda. Srisailam is the main gateway to the reserve. Nearest airport is Hyderabad, 216km (134 miles) from the reserve.

Climate: At times, winters are bitterly cold (minimum 7°C; 45°F); summer maximum is 40°C (104°F). Monsoon rains occur from June to September.

When to go: Winter is ideal (from November to March).

Getting there: Town of Srisailam lies 190km (118 miles) from Kurnool, 216km (134 miles) from Hyderabad and 220km (137 miles) from Guntur. Cars can be hired from Kurnool; buses from Hyderbad (6 hours); train to Marchelna.

Facilities: Forest rest house and cottages (Devasthanam) in town of Srisailam, which is a strictly vegetarian town; travellers will savour the Andhra cuisine. The Forest Department does not provide vehicles for park tours. Jeeps can be hired from commercial centres at negotiable rates. The park only allows entry to visitors authorized by the Field Director. The reserve prohibits vehicular traffic at night.

Permits and reservations: For permission to enter park and prior reservation of the rest house, contact: The Field Director, Project Tiger, Nagarjunasagar–Srisailam Tiger Reserve, Sunnipenta–Srisailam–518102.

Precautions: The road between Hyderabad and Srisailam remains closed to traffic overnight from 21:00 to 06:00, so visitors should avoid this particular route at night. Visitors are advised to check first with the authorities that it is politically safe to travel.

NEPAL HIMALAYA

Nepal, since 1990 a multiparty democracy, is strategically located between India and China and covers an area of 147,181 (57,400 square miles). The Nepalese Himalayas cover one-third of the entire Himalayan mountain chain which itself stretches over 800 kilometres (500 miles), representing 16 per cent of the total land area of Nepal. This mountain range makes up the northern border of the country and its most remarkable feature is that out of 14 of the world's major peaks, nine occur in this region. They include the world's highest, Mount Everest, at 8848 metres (29,030 feet), Kangchenjunga, Makalu, Cho Oyu, Lhotse, Gaurishankar, Annapurna, Manaslu and Dhaulagiri.

Major rivers cut through the valleys of the main Himalayan chain, with deep gorges ranging from 1500 to 2500 metres (4900 to 8200 feet). In central Nepal, the gorge of the Kali Gandaki River is perhaps the deepest in the world.

Nepal features all the principal climatic and vegetation types. In the south, vegetation is typically tropical and subtropical, with Sal being the predominant tree species. Between 2000 and 3500 metres (6500 and 11,500 feet) are temperate forests, then the higher alpine meadows which during spring are covered with medicinal plants such as Primula, Meconopsis, Saxifraga, Anaphalis, anemones, and irises. Tree ferns like Pandanus and *Cycas pectinata* are a feature on the foothills and along the banks of the rivers in east Nepal.

The alpine region supports the striking Snow Leopard, while the subalpine region, from 2500 to 4000 metres (8200 to 13,000 feet), is inhabited by Clouded Leopard, Red Panda (Cat Bear) and the goat-antelope species Serow and Goral. Large herbivores – Great Indian One-horned Rhinoceros, Indian Elephant and Gaur (Indian Bison) – live in the foothills of the terai region.

For this book, Nepal's two most significant national parks have been selected, both of which have been designated World Heritage Sites. The Royal Chitwan National Park, situated in the lower terai region, has a great biodiversity and is considered one of the best managed parks of Asia. Sagarmatha National Park lies at the highest altitude in the world.

Inset: *Rhododendron lepidotum*, a dwarf rhododendron species of the upper regions.

Left: In this Nepalese valley the Narayani and Gandak merge to form a single river.

ROYAL CHITWAN NATIONAL PARK

Trekking among undulating hills

Situated in the subtropical inner terai lowlands of south-central Nepal, Chitwan used to be the hunting ground of the then-rulers of Nepal, the Ranas (1846 to 1950), who would invite the kings and ruling princes of India, Britain and other European countries to hunt in these forests. This ruthless slaughter of wild animals continued for many years right up until 1950, when a virulent form of malaria eliminated Chitwan's human population. This resulted in the fall of the Ranas, after which a drive to eradicate malaria in the region was initiated, and by 1960. a decade later, Chitwan was declared a malaria-free zone.

In 1962 a small portion of the Chitwan forest was declared a rhinoceros sanctuary. This was upgraded to a national park, with an area of 544 square kilometres (212 square miles), in 1973, and in 1979 the park was extended to a total of 932 square kilometres (360 square miles). Royal Chitwan National Park was designated a World Heritage Site in 1984.

Hills and watered plains

The park spreads across the foothills of the Himalayas' Siwalik range and is mostly hilly terrain, with the highest elevation rising to 600 metres (1970 feet). A large portion is made up of the plains from three large rivers: the Rapti, Reu and Narayani. The Rapti and Reu meet on the park's western boundary where they merge with the mighty Narayani River, which has gouged a deep gorge through the Siwalik foothills to enter India. Here, the river is known as the Gandak, and ultimately merges

with the Ganges. Several oxbow lakes, marshes and swamps have been created by numerous seasonal narrow water canals. Major lakes, or *tal* (reservoir), are Tamor, Lame, Dhakre and Devi, with the latter being the largest and most beautiful.

Seventy per cent of Chitwan's vegetation consists of dense Sal forest with the remaining portion made up of 20 per cent grassland, seven per cent riverine forest and three per cent Sal with Chir Pine (the latter covers the top of the Churiya range). The grasslands form a diverse and complex community of over 50 species. One of them, the Elephant Grass, can reach 8 metres (26 metres) in height, while shorter species such as *Imperata* are used for thatching roofs. The riverine forests feature Khair (*Acacia catechu*), *Dalbergia sissoo* and Simal (Silk Cotton trees).

From Sloth Bear to King Cobra

There are 43 species of wild mammal in Royal Chitwan National Park. Although the prime attraction of these forests is the Great Indian One-horned Rhinoceros and Tiger, this region is among the very few where Sloth Bear (*Melursus ursinus*) is so easily seen. The Sloth Bear, an

Above right: Kash, a grass species, flowers in autumn.

Opposite: Visitors at Tiger Tops Jungle Camp, preparing to embark on a guided trek on elephant-back.

Location: In the Chitwan district of south-central Nepal. Kathmandu is 165km (100 miles) from Chitwan park. The nearest entry point is Saurah, at the fringe of the park.

Climate: Minimum winter temperatures may drop to 2°C (36°F); maximum summer temperatures rise to 35°C (95°F).

When to go: September to May.

Getting there: Kathmandu is well connected with Bharatpur, the nearest airport. Regular bus services are available from Kathmandu to Saurah, where jeeps are available for hire. Elephants can be hired at Saurah to enter the forest.

Facilities: There are plenty of lodges at Saurah. In the Saurah region, Gaida Wildlife Camp and Rhino Residency & Hotel Park offer good accommodation. Six lodges and camps in the park; best deluxe park lodges are Tiger Tops and Temple Tiger.

Wildlife: Great Indian One-horned Rhino, Tiger, Sloth Bear, Indian Elephant, Gaur, various deer species. Aquatic wildlife includes Gangetic Dolphin, and Gharial and Marsh Crocodile.

Additional activities: The Tharu Cultural Show, which is worth seeing, takes place daily at Saurah.

Reservations: Write to: Tiger Tops Jungle Lodge, Box 242, Basondhara, Kathmandu; or Temple Tiger Jungle Lodge, Box 3968, Kamaladi, Kathmandu; or Gaida Wildlife Camp, Box 2056, Naxal, Kathmandu.

Above: Despite its name, the White-throated Kingfisher (*Halcyon smyrnensis*) has a glorious iridescent plumage.

Above right: The Narayani, one of the park's three major rivers, has created a broad meandering plain that's in contrast with the surrounding hilly landscape.

omnivorous creature, inhabits almost all of India's forested tracts, favouring rocky outcrops and overhanging boulders which offer shelter during the heat and seasonal rains. These bears stand up to roughly a metre (3 feet) at the shoulder and have an elongated snout that enables them to seek out termites. They also favour honey and the flowers of the Mahua (Mowra Butter tree). A marvellous experience is to come across a mother carrying babies on her back.

Of the larger mammals, the forest also harbours Indian Elephant, Leopard and Gaur (Indian Bison). Deer and antelope species present are Chital, Sambhar, Barking and Hog Deer, and the Chausingha (Four-horned Antelope), while the smaller animals which may be spotted by visitors are Himalayan Palm Civet, porcupines, the Pangolin and Malayan Giant Squirrel. Gangetic Dolphin frolic in the main rivers and two crocodile species lurk in the waters – the Gharial, which is endangered in Chitwan, and the Marsh (Muggar) Crocodile, which can be spotted in abundance on the banks of Lame *tal*. A Gharial breeding project has been established at Kasera Durbar where, since 1980, Gharials have been artificially hatched and then released in batches into the wild.

Spectacled, Monocled and King Cobra, Vine Snake, Rat Snake, and the Common Indian Monitor are prevalent among the reptiles.

An enormous variety of birds – around 450 species – flits among the forest foliage. Vigilant birdwatchers could see Bengal and Lesser Florican, Changeable Hawk-eagle, Shikra, Indian Moorhen, and the Common Peafowl and Red Junglefowl. Waterbirds count the Large, Median and Little Egret, Grey-headed Fishing Eagle, and the White-breasted, Stork-billed, Pied and Common Kingfisher among its species, while the prettier birds are the Rosering, Alexandrine, Red-breasted and Blossom-headed Parakeets.

Left: A trained elephant and its *mahout* succeed in tracking down a Great Indian One-horned Rhinoceros (*Rhinoceros unicornis*). The stealth of the elephant's movements and the height advantage that the *mahout* has combine to make the search more effective.

SAGARMATHA (EVEREST) NATIONAL PARK

At the top of the world

In Nepali language, Sagarmatha – referring to the Everest peak – means 'head of the sky'. Similarly, the Tibetan name for Everest, Chomolungma, means 'goddess mother of the earth'. To the world at large, the Sagarmatha park is more popularly known as Everest National Park. It is situated to the northeast of Kathmandu, in the district of Solu Khumbu.

In terms of the world's physical formation, the mountains of Sagarmatha National Park are young, moulded as they were during the Cenozoic period, which is the world's most recent geological era begun around 65 million years ago. They are broken up by deep gorges and glacial valleys. This section of the spectacular Himalayan mountain chain, an area of 1148 square kilometres (445 square miles), was declared a national park in 1976 and was declared a World Heritage Site by UNESCO in 1979. The park's northern boundary is defined by the main divide of the great Himalaya which form the international boundary with Tibet, an autonomous region of China. In the south, the park extends to the Mongo and Dudh Kosi rivers, while its eastern flank is contiguous with the Makalu–Barun National Park.

World-famous mountain peaks

Sagarmatha National Park encompasses the catchment basin of the Dudh Kosi, Bhote Kosi and Imjakhola rivers which drain the slopes of the Sagarmatha and other peaks of the area. Apart from Mount Everest (8848 metres; 29,030 feet), the highest peak in the world, other great peaks of the area carry names such as Lhotse, Cho Oyu and Nuptse. The park's lowest elevation occurs at Jorsalle at 2848 metres (9345 feet).

There are a number of human settlements within the park, the main ones being Namche Bazar, Khumjung, Khunde, Thame, Shyangboche, Pangboche and Phortse. A population of 3500 Sherpas, a people of Mongolian origin, lives in these villages. A number of them have become famous for their Buddhist teachings. The Khumbu Sherpa community traditionally based its economy on the trade of livestock but since 1950, mountaineering expeditions and trekking have increased considerably, and Khumbu Sherpas have as a result become heavily dependent on tourism.

For trekkers only

Travel to, and exploration of, the national park is generally undertaken on foot, but visitors can gain quick access if preferred by helicopter from Lukla airport to the Shyangboche airstrip within the park. From here, on foot, the park headquarters at Namche Bazar are a two-day trek away. Two alternative approaches to Namche Bazar can be made from Jiri in the southwest or through the Arun valley in the southeast, but this constitutes a 10- to 12-day trek. Those visitors who forego the helicopter trip and choose to enter

Above right: The Red Panda, or Cat Bear (*Ailurus fulgens*), sleeps in trees during the day, and descends to the ground in the evenings in search of sustenance.

Location: In northeast Kathmandu, Solu Khumbu district. The nearest town and airport is Lukla (a 50-minute flight away), situated at a height of 2850m (9350ft); regular air service from Kathmandu.

Climate: In summer, above 3000m (9800ft): 6 to -10°C (43 to 14°F); below 3000m: 10 to -5°C (50 to 23°F). In winter, above 3000m: 0 to -25°C (32 to -13°F); below 3000m: 5 to -21°C (41° to -6°F).

When to go: The best time to visit is from September to May because the skies are clear.

Getting there: Park is explored on foot; trekkers to Namche Bazar (park headquarters) start off from Kathmandu. Alternative 10- to 12-day treks from the south. Helicopter to Shyangboche airstrip available from Lukla airport.

Facilities: All grades of accommodation as well as food supplies are available at the fringes of the park in the villages of Namche Bazar, Shyangboche, Pheriche and Lobuche. Hotel Everest, located at the Shyangboche airstrip, has magnificent views.

Wildlife: Yak, Himalayan Black Bear, Red Panda, Barking and Musk Deer. Many colourful pheasant species.

Permits and reservations: Permits required for trekking. Essential to make prior reservations for accommodation. Contact the Tourist Service Centre, Bhrikuti Mandap, Kathmandu.

Below: The Khumbu Himal seen from the Gokyo River valley. The word Himalaya can roughly be translated as 'abode' (laya) 'of snow' (hima).

the park by trekking should allow a span of two weeks within Sagarmatha. Ideal sites to visit are the Gokyo valley, Lobuche-Kala Pattar base camp, and the Chukung and Thame valleys. Travellers need to be well equipped for camping, and should carry food supplies and sufficient fuel. It is advisable to arrange guides and porters from Kathmandu (trekking unaccompanied is not recommended; tourists do often find the steep, rugged mountain terrain of the Himalayas very strenuous to tackle).

Fauna and flora

There are mainly two types of forests in Sagarmatha park. In the 3000- to 4000-metre (9800- to 13,000-feet) zone of the subalpine forest region, the main tree species are Blue Pine, Hemlock Spruce, Silver Fir, and three rhododendron species, *Rhododendron arboreum*, *R. triflorum* and *R. lepidotum*. Above 4000 metres (13,000 feet) are a number of significant grasslands.

Because of the altitude, Sagarmartha's animal species are specially adapted to the climate and occur nowhere else in India. The park supports 34 mammal, 199 bird and five reptile species – the latter are the Himalayan Pit and Green Pit Viper, the Bearded and Agamide Lizard, and Skink.

On the lower ridges visitors will see Yak whose populations have been domesticated, Himalayan Black Bear and Muntjac (Barking Deer). In the higher areas Snow Leopard is shy and rarely spotted, but Red Panda, Musk Deer and Yellow-throated Marten, a member of the weasel family, are common.

The Musk Deer as a species falls between the deer and antelope. Males have canine teeth but sport no horns, and are generally solitary creatures except in the mating season, which occurs in summer. This deer has a musk gland (occurring only in the males), located beneath the skin of the abdomen. The gland produces a pungent odour when fresh, but when dried it gives off a musk scent. In order to meet relatively high energy requirements, Musk Deer prefer a quality diet comprising young leaves, buds, flowers and fruits.

More than 115 species of bird have been recorded in this region of the Himalayas. The colourful plumage of Chukor Partridge, Satyr Tragopan and Monal Pheasant can be spotted in the undergrowth while birds of the air include Nepal Kalij, Robin Accentor, Orange-billed Chough, and the Black and Orange Flycatcher.

Above: Mount Everest, or Sagarmartha – the Nepalese name for this peak – is the highest, and most famous, mountain peak in the world; it is clearly visible from the park.

Opposite bottom left: Trekkers in the park pass a *stupa* (a domed structure that contains Buddhist relics); this serves as a place of worship for Buddhists.

Opposite top right: These wild Yaks (*Bos grunniens*) have adapted to the coldest and most desolate of mountains. In the most bitter winters, many of them die of starvation.

Opposite bottom right: A Sherpa woman adjusts trekkers' equipment on the back of a pack animal; the women have a reputation for being very hard-working, and they are more visibly active than the men.

USEFUL ADDRESSES

General

Ministry Environment & Forests
Government of India, Pariyavaran Bhawan
Cgo Complex, Lodhi Road
New Delhi–110003
tel: 91-11-4361669
website: envfor.nic.in
e-mail: secy@menf.delhi.nic.in

Nepal Tourism Board
Tourist Service Centre
Bhrikuti Mandap, Kathmandu
tel: 977-1-256909
website: www.welcomenepal.com
e-mail: info@ntb.wlink.com.np

The Director, Project Tiger
Govt. of India, Min. of Environment
& Forests
Bikaner House, Annexe V
Shahjhan Road, New Delhi–110011
tel: 91-11-3384428
website: envfor.nic.in/pt/proj.html
e-mail: dirpt-r@hub.nic.in

Northern India

World Wide Fund for Nature-India
172-b, Lodhi Estate
New Delhi-110003
tel: 91-11-4633473
fax: 11-4626837
e-mail: wwfindel@unv.ernet.in

Ranthambhore Foundation
19, Kautilya Marg
Chanakyapuri
New Delhi–110021
tel: 91-11-3016261
fax: 11-3019457
website: www.ranthambor.com
e-mail: tiger@vsnl.com

Corbett Foundation
Wildlife Protection Society of India
Thapar House, 124 Janpath
New Delhi–110001
tel: 91-11-3320572
fax: 11-3327729
website: www.wpsi-india.org
e-mail: wpsi@nde.vsnl.net.in

Ibex Expeditions
(Adventure, eco, travel & cultural tours)
G66 East of Kailash
New Delhi–110065
tel: 91-11-6912641/7829 or 6828479
fax: 11-6846403
website: www.ibexexpeditions.com
e-mail: ibex@nde.vsnl.net.in

Eastern India

Assam Valley Wildlife Society
Pertabghur Tea Estate
PO Chariali, Sonitpur District
Assam–784176

Western India

**Bombay Natural History
Society**
Shahid Bhagat Singh Marg
Mumbai
Maharashtra–400023
tel: 91-22-2821811
fax: 22-2837615
website: www.bnhs.org
e-mail: bnhs@bom4.vsnl.net.in

Sanctuary Asia
602 Maker Chambers V
Nariman Point
Mumbai
Maharashtra–400021
tel: 91-22-2830061
fax: 22-2874380

Southern India

Chennai Snake Park Trust
Guindy, Chennai
Tamil Nadu–600022
tel: 91-44-2350821
e-mail: cspt1972@md5.vsnl.net.in

M S Swaminathan Research Foundation
3rd Gross Street
Taramani Institutional Area
Madras
Tamil Nadu–600113
tel: 91-44-2351698

INDEX

**Bold type denotes
photographs**

Adjutant Stork 39, 48
Agamide Lizard 170
Alexandrine Parakeet
84, 98, 112, 150,
168
Andaman Hill Myna
128
Andaman Teal 128
Andaman Wood
Pigeon 128
Asian Darter (*Anhinga
melanogaster*) 144
Asian Open-billed
Stork (*Anostomus
oscitanus*) 144
Asiatic Lion (*Panthera
leo parsica*) 117, 131,
132, 133, **134–135**

Asiatic Wild Ass
(*Equus hemionus*)
117, **129**, **129**, 130,
130
Asiatic Wild Buffalo
alt. Water Buffalo
(*Bubalus bubalis*)
39, 48
Assamese Macaque
(*Macaca assamensis*)
42, 56, **56**, 57
Assamese Myna 44
Atlas Moth *Attacus
atlas*) **160**
Baer's Pochard 59
Baikal Teal 124
Bamboo Pit Viper
147
Barasingha
Softground *alt.*
Swamp Deer

(*Cervus duvauceli*)
35, **34**, 36, 48, **90**
Hardground (*Cervus
duvauceli branderi*)
89, 90
Bar-headed Goose 48
Barred Monitor
Lizard 33
Barred Owlet 37, 84
Batagur baska 121
Baya Weaver 97, 112
Bearded Bee-eater 97
Bearded Lizard 170
Bearded Vulture *alt.*
Lammergeier 25
Bengal Florican 36,
39, 48, 64, 168
Bengal Fox 124
Bengal Monitor
Lizard 125
Bengal Vulture 112

Bharal *alt.* Blue
Sheep (*Pseudois
naygaur*) 27, 28
Binturong *alt.* Bear
Cat 42
Black Baza 56
Black Bulbul 42
Black Flycatcher 171
Black Gorgetted
Laughing Thrush
33, 42
Black Ibis 97
Black Leopard
(*Panthera pardus*)
138, **139**
Black Partridge 37
Black Stork 61, 92,
93, 109
Black Turtle 159
Black Vulture 133
Blackbird 55

Black-breasted
Sunbird 54
Blackbuck (Indian
Antelope) **12**, 13,
130, 163
Black-capped Sibia
54
Black-crested Cuckoo
33
Black-crowned Night
Heron (*Nyciticorax
nyciticorax*) **144**
Black-headed Cuckoo
133
Black-headed Gull 121
Black-naped Hare 90,
124, 147, 150, 153
Black-necked Crane
59
Black-necked Stork
112

Black-shouldered Kite 112
Black-tailed Godwit 124
Black-winged Stilt 124, 155
Blind Snake 138
Blood Pheasant 25
Blossom-headed Parakeet 61, 98, 112, 168
Blue Rock Thrush 48, 55, 60
Blue Whale 127
Blue-headed Flycatcher 44
Blue-tailed Bee-eater 96, 124
Blyth's Baza 33, 44, 60
Bonelli's Eagle 84, 109, 133
Bonnet Macaque (Macaca radiata) 137, 138, 138,141, 147, 150, 151, 153, 157
Brahminy Duck 150
Brahminy Kite 112, 121
Brain Fever Bird 150
Bronze-winged Jacana (Metopidius indicus) 112, 124
Brow-headed Gull 123
Brown Fish Owl (Bubo zeylonesis) 37, 84
Bush Quail 64, 138, 150
butterflies
    Blue Oakleaf 97
    Blue Pansy 97
    Common Crow 160
    Common Rose 97
    Indian Fritillary 160
    Moon Moth 97
    Tamil Lacewing 160
Capped Langur (Leaf Monkey) 44, 53, 56
Caracal 113
Cattle Egret 79, 150
Changeable Hawk Eagle 84, 168
Chausinga alt. Four-horned Antelope (Tetracerus quadri-cornis) 12, 13, 85, 99, 100, 113, 132, 147, 150, 163, 168

Chestnut-bellied Nuthatch 54
Chestnut-fronted Shrike Babbler 55
Chinese Pangolin 60
Chinkara alt. Indian Gazelle (Gazella gazella) 12, 86, 94, 95, 97, 100, 109, 113, 130, 132, 163
Chir Pheasant 28
Chital alt. Spotted Deer (Axis axis) 33, 36, 48, 60, 64, 70, 74, 80, 85, 91, 97, 100, 109, 112, 113, 115, 120, 127, 132, 138, 146, 146, 147, 150, 151, 153, 163, 168
Chukor Partridge 171
Civet 60
Clawless Otter 64
Clouded Leopard (Neofelis nebulosa) 42, 44, 53, 53, 56, 59, 165
Collared Bush Chat 48, 54, 61
Collared Dove 150
Comb Duck 44, 48
Common (Golden) Jackal (Canis aurens) 62
Common Chameleon 141
Common Cormorant 143, 155
Common Dolphin (Delphinus delphis) 127, 127
Common Drongo 124
Common Giant Flying Squirrel (Petaurista petaurista) 139
Common Grey Hornbill 92, 97
Common Indian Hare 49
Common Indian Mongoose 49, 150, 138
Common Indian Monitor (Varanus bengalensis) 109, 150, 153, 159, 168
Common Kingfisher (Alceo atthis) 114, 150, 168

Common Krait 36, 147
Common Langur alt. Hanuman Monkey (Presbytis entellus) 25, 28, 33, 53, 74, 80, 81, 97, 105, 106, 113, 137, 147, 150, 153, 157
Common Mongoose 124
Common Otter 121
Common Palm Civet (Paradoxurus hermaphroditus) 79, 150, 153
Common Peafowl see Peacock
Common Pochard 37, 92, 93, 124
Common Teal 37, 124
Coppersmith 75, 133
Cormorant (Phalacrocorax carbo) 48, 155
Cotton Teal 32
Crested Eagle 48
Crested Goshawk 56, 84, 84
Crested Hawk 92, 97
Crested Hawk Eagle 153
Crested Serpent Eagle (Spilornis cheela) 33, 37, 75, 92, 93, 97, 109, 114, 133, 138, 153
Crested Swift 133
Crimson Tragopan 25
Crossbill 44
Crow Pheasant 138
Darter (Snakebird) Anhinga rufa) 143
Desert Cat (Felis libyca) 130
Desert Fox 105
Dhole see Indian Wild Dog
dragonfly (Trithemis avrora) 95
Dugong alt. Sea Cow 117, 127, 128
Dusky Horned Owl 37
Dusky Leaf Warbler 64
Eastern Golden Plover 59
Emerald Dove

(Chalocophaps indica) 61, 61, 64
Estuarine Crocodile (Crocodilus porosus) 119, 121, 138
Fairy Bluebird 84, 138
Falcated Teal 124
Fantail Flycatcher 97
Fiddler Crab 120
Fish Owl 133
Fishing Cat (Prionailurus viverrinus) 36, 42, 42, 44, 49, 59, 90, 96, 112, 121
Fishing Eagle 48, 112
Five-striped Palm Squirrel (Funambulus pennanti) 138, 139
Flying Fox (Fruit Bat) (Pteropus gigantus) 144, 144
Flying Lizard (Draco dussumeeri) 138, 160, 160
Flying Snake 138, 160
Flying Squirrel 42, 147, 159
Forest Eagle Owl 37
Freshwater Turtle (Pelochelys cantorii) 120
Gadwall (Asas strepera) 124, 125
Gangetic Dolphin 121, 124, 168
Garganey 111
Gaur alt. Indian Bison (Bos gaurus) 21, 48, 54, 56, 60, 61, 62, 63, 64, 66, 67, 74, 79, 82, 83, 85, 89, 90, 137, 145, 149, 150, 151, 157, 159, 165, 168
Gharial Crocodile (Garialis gangeticus) 32, 168
Giant Squirrel 147, 151
Glossy Ibis 112
Golden Cat 44
Golden Eagle 25
Golden Jackal 124
Golden Langur (Presbytis geei) 43, 44, 45
Golden Pochard 121

Golden-backed Woodpecker 114
Goliath Heron 121
Goral 165
Grey 21
Gray Teal 124
Great Crested Grebe (Podiceps cristatus) 123, 125
Great Indian Bustard 105
Great Indian Hornbill 44, 60
Great Indian Horned Owl 37, 109, 114
Great Indian One-horned Rhinoceros (Rhinoceros uni-cornis) 36, 44, 47, 47, 61, 62, 63, 64, 165, 167, 168
Great Stone Plover (Esacus magnirostris) 143, 144
Great White Pelican 123
Green Avadavat 84
Green Bee-eater 97
Green Pigeon 64
Green Pit Viper 138, 170
Green Turtle 127
Grey Drongo 133
Grey Heron (Ardea cinerea) 44, 123, 124, 143, 155, 160
Grey Junglefowl 150
Grey Partridge 37, 64, 109, 114, 133, 150
Grey Pelican 123, 155
Grey Tit 97
Grey-headed Fishing Eagle 60, 168
Greylag Goose 99
Hair-crested Drongo 54, 60, 64
Hangul alt. Kashmir Stag 12, 23, 24, 23, 24, 25
Hanuman Monkey see Common Langur
Hen Harrier 33, 37
Hill Myna 48, 60, 70
Himalayan Black Bear 25, 28, 33, 170
Himalayan Brown Bear 24, 25, 25, 28

Himalayan Civet 49
Himalayan Marmot **24**, 25
Himalayan Palm Civet 168
Himalayan Pit Viper 170
Himalayan Roller 42, 64
Himalayan Tahr 21, 28
Hispid Hare 36, 44
Hoary-bellied Squirrel 42
Hog (*Axis porcinus*) 33, 35, 36, 48, 64
Hog Deer 137, 138, 168
Honey Badger *alt.* Ratel 12, 33, **36**, 97, 138, 163
Honey Buzzard 37, 92, 97
Hoolock (White-browed) Gibbon (*Hylobates hoolock*) 13, **42**, 49, 53, 56
hornbill 42, 150
Houbara Bustard 130
House Swift 75
Ibex 28
Imperial Pigeon 61
Indian Cheetah 73
Indian Chevrotain *alt.* Mouse Deer (*Tragulus meminna*) 13, 49, **49**, 138, 147, 150, 153, 159
Indian Common Toad (*Buto melanostictus*) **62**
Indian Elephant (*Elephas maximus*) 13, **17**, 21, **32**, 36, 42, 44, 47, **48**, 56, **58**, 59, 60, 61, 63, 64, **70**, 96, **97**, 137, **146**, **148**, 149, 150, 151, 153, 157, 159, 165, 168
Indian Flapshell Turtle 125
Indian Giant Squirrel (*Ratufa indica*) **150**, 153, 163
Indian Grey Hornbill **84**, 160
Indian Hare 97
Indian Jungle Nightjar 124

Indian Lorikeet 44, 48, 60
Indian Monocled (Spectacled) Cobra 36, 54, 168
Indian Moorhen 112, 168
Indian Pangolin (Scaly Anteater) (*Manis crassicaudata*) 60, 137, 138
Indian Pied Hornbill 60, 61, 70
Indian Pitta 33
Indian Porcupine (*Hystrix indica*) 33, **153**
Indian Rock Python (*Python molurus*) 33, 54, 60, **112**, 159
Indian Roller (*Coracias bengalensis*) **63**, **132**, 133
Indian Roofed Shell Turtle 86
Indian Shag (*Phalacrocorax fusci collis*) **112**, 143, 155
Indian Softshell Turtle 86
Indian Tiger (*Panthera tigris*) 11, **12**, **16**, **32**, 33, 36, 42, 44, 49, 53, 56, 59, 64, 70, **74**, 79, **83**, 86, 90, **91**, **96**, 100, 101, **102–103**, 105, **108**, 108–109, 113, 120, **121**, 131, 132, 138, 153, 157, 163, 167
Indian Wild Boar **25**, 44, 49, 53, 60, 61, **64**, 70, 74, 79, 80, 90, 97, 105, 112, 113, 120, 132, 147, 150, 153, 159, 163
Indian Wild Buffalo 44
Indian Wild Dog *alt.* Dhole (*Cuon alpinus*) 53, 74, 79, 83, **90**, 90, 97, 100, 109, 138, 147, 150, **152**, 153, 159, 163
Indian Wolf (*Canis lupus*) 12, **70**
Irrawaddy Dolphin 121, 124

Isibill 59
Jacana 79
Jackal 25, 36, 49, 60, 61, 79, 91, 97, 105, 109, 113, 132, 147, 150, 153, 163
Jerdon's Baza 56
Jungle Cat (*Felis chaus*) 32, 36, 42, 29, 53, 59, 90, 96, 105, **107**, 109, 113, 124, 132, 138, 147
Jungle Crow (*Corvus macrorhynchos*) **74**, 75, 100
Kalij Pheasant 28, 33, 44
Kashmir Black Redstart 25
Kashmir House Sparrow 25
Kashmir White-browed Rose Finch 25
King Cobra (*Ophiophagus hannah*) 33, 54, 60, 138, **139**, 159, 168
King Vulture 112
Koklass Pheasant 25, 28
Lapwing 75, 150
Large Egret (*Ardea alba*) 121, 123, 168
Large Green Barbet 75
Large Indian Civet 138
Large Whistling Teal 124
Laughing Thrush 55
Leatherback Turtle 127
Leopard *alt.* Panther (*Panthera pardus*) 23, 25, 28, 32, 36, 44, 49, 53, 56, 62, 64, 70, 74, **79**, 90, 96, 100, 105, 109, 112, 113, 132, 138, 147, 159, 168
Leopard Cat (*Felis bengalensis*) 32, 36, 42, 44, 49, 59, **60**, 61, 90, 96, 137, 147
Lesser Adjutant Stork 97
Lesser Florican *alt.* Leekh 36, 39, 168

Lesser Kestrel 92, 97
Lesser Owl 79
Lesser Whistling Teal 32, 44, 48, 92, **93**, 97, 100
Lesser-tailed Drongo 64
Limbless Skink 125
Lion-tailed Macaque 141, 157, 159
Little Cormorant 143, 155
Little Egret 150, 168
Little Grey Bee-eater 150
Little Indian Porpoise 121
Little Scops Owl 153
Little Spider-hunter 54
Long-billed Vulture (*Gyps indicus*) 57, 92
Lynx 12
Magpie Robin 60, 92
Mahratta Wood-pecker 75
Malabar Giant Squirrel 141, 159
Malabar Great Black Woodpecker 153
Malabar Grey Hornbill 153
Malabar Hornbill 138
Malabar Pied Hornbill 92, 97
Malabar Squirrel 138
Malabar Trogon 153
Malayan Giant Squirrel 60, 62, 168
Malayan Squirrel 42
Marbled Teal 42, 44, 111, 124, 137
Markhor 12, 21, 25
Maroon Oriole 61
Marsh (Muggar) Crocodile (*Croco-dilus palustris*) 32, 36, 79, **80**, 86, 99, **101**, 109, 114, 132, 144, 147
Marsh Harrier 33, 112
Meadow Pipit 64
Median Egret (*Egretta intermedia*) 80, 121, 168
Merganser 48, 59, 61
Mistle's Thrush 33
Monal Pheasant (*Lophorus imperjan-ius*) 25, 28, 44, 171

mongoose 74, 109, 147
Monitor Lizard 36, 54, 147
Mrs Gould's Sunbird 42, 54, 60
Mudskipper (*Periothalmus barbarus*) **120**
Muntjac *alt.* Barking Deer (*Muntiacus muntjac*) 28, 28, 33, 36, 42, 53, 56, 60, 61, 62, 64, 74, 79, 85, **86**, 97, 138, 146, 147, 150, 153, 159, 163, 168, 170
Musk Deer (*Moschus moschiferus*) 12, 25, **28**, 28, 170, 171
Nepal Kalij 171
Night Heron 143, 155
Nilgai *alt.* Blue Bull (*Boselaphus tragocamelus*) 12, 13, 74, **80**, **85**, 97, 100, 109, 112, 113, 130, 132, 163
Nilgiri Langur 141, 157, 159
Nilgir Tahr 141, **157**, 159
Niltava 42
Northern Pintail 124
Olive Ridley Turtle 121, 124, **125**, 125, 127
Open-billed Stork 112, 143, 155
Orange Flycatcher 171
Orange-bellied Blue Magpie 44
Orange-billed Chough 171
Ornamental Snake (*Chrysopelea ornata*) 138, **159**
Osprey 112
Painted Partridge 109
Painted Sandgrouse 133
Painted Stork 100, 109, **110**, 112, 143
Pale Blue Flycatcher 54
Pale Harrier 37, 60, 112

Pallas's Fishing Eagle 121, 123
Pallas's Leaf Warbler 54
Palm Civet 112, 124, 138, 147, 150
Palm Swift 75
Pangolin 49, 168
Paradise Flycatcher 25, 33, 97, 109, 133
parrotbill 60
Peacock *alt.* Peafowl (*Pavo cristatus*) 33, 37, **37**, 60, 61, **67**, **75**, **98**, **100**, **109**, **114**, 115, 149, 150, 168
Peregrine Falcon 112
Pheasant-tailed Jacana 109, 112, 123
Pied Bush Chat 124
Pied Indian Hornbill 54
Pied Kingfisher 168
Pied Wagtail 48, 100
Pied Woodpecker 133
Pig-tailed Macaque (*Macaca nemestrina*) 56, **57**
Pintail Duck 37
Plumbeous Dolphin 121
Plumbeous Redstart 33
Pond Heron 143, 155
Pratincole 123
Prinia 42
Purple Moorhen 79
Pygmy Hog (*Sus salvinius*) 44, **44**, 45
Racket-tailed Drongo 54, 60, 92, 153, 160
Rat Snake 147, 168
Red Fox 36
Red Giant Flying Squirrel 153
Red Jungle Fowl (*Gallus gallus*) **33**, **37**, **64**, 70, 75, 100, 168
Red Lace-wing Butterfly (*Cethosia biblis*) **21**
Red Panda *alt.* Cat Bear (*Ailurus fulgens*) 12, 39, 42, 44, **45**, 165, **169**, 170
Red Spurfowl 109

Red Wattled Lapwing 100, 124
Red-breasted Falconet 42
Red-breasted Flycatcher 25, 54
Red-breasted Parakeet 48, 61, 64, 168
Red-chested Pochard 37, **93**, 111, 124
Red-headed Merlin 33, 42
Redshank 124
Rhesus Macaque (*Macaca mulatta*) 28, 33, 53, 64, 74, 97, 113, **115**, 121
Rhino-horned Beetle (*Lucanus cervus*) **105**
River Tern (*Sterna ausantia*) 121, 143, **144**
Robin Accentor 171
Rock Bush Quail 133
Rock Pigeon 150
Rock Python 36, 138, 147
Rose Finch 70
Rose-ringed Parakeet 75, 98, **112**, 168
Rosy Flamingo 123
Rosy Pelican 123
Rubycheek 44
Ruddy Shelduck (*Tadorna ferruginea*) 61, 97, **101**, **124**
Rufous Flycatcher 75
Rufous-bellied Eagle 56
Rufous-bellied Nitava 44
Russell's Viper 138, 147
Rusty Spotted Cat 96, 147
Sambhar 33, 36, 42, 48, 53, 60, 61, 62, 64, 70, 74, 80, 83, 90, 91, 97, 100, **109** 112, 113, 132, 138, 146, 147, 150, 153, 157, 159, 163, 168
Sand Boa (*Eryse conicus*) 91, 138
Sarus Crane (*Grus antigone*) **110**
Satyr Tragopan (*Tragopan satyra*) **16**, 171
Saw-scaled Viper 138

Scarlet Minivet 84
Scavenger Vulture 33, 75, 92, 100
Scops Owl 37
Serow (goat antelope) 21, 53, **60**, 165
Shaheen Falcon 133
Shama 60, 61
Shikra 92, 168
Shoveller 111, 124
Siberian Crane (*Grus leucogeranus*) **110**, 111
Sidewinder Snake 105
Sikra 97, 138
Slender Loris (*Loris tardigradus*) 137, **139**, 141, 147
Sloth Bear (*Melursus ursinus*) **12**, 13, 21, 33, 36, **49**, 60, 64, 74, 84, 105, 109, 138, 147, 150, 153, 167, 168
Slow Loris (*Nycticebus coucang*) 42, 53, **54**, 56
Small Indian Civet 79, 124, 138, 147, 153
Small Indian Mongoose 138
Small Minivet 75
Small-clawed Otter **64**
Smooth-coated Indian Otter (*Lutra perspicillata*) 54, **120**, 138, 147
Snow Leopard (*Panthera uncia*) 25, 42, **41**, 165, 170
Spangled Drongo (*Dicrurus hottentottus*) 77
Sparrow Hawk 37, 92
Spoonbill (*Platalea leucorodia*) 112, 143, **155**
Spot-billed Duck 150
Spot-billed Pelican (*Pelicanus philippensis*) 123
Spotted Dove 150
Spotted Eagle 37
Spotted Forktail 48, 54
Spotted Longtail Wren 54
Spotted Munia 97
Spotted Owl 37
Spotted Owlet 124

Spotted-bill Duck 111
Stone Curlew 121
Stork-billed Kingfisher 168
Streaked Warbler 64
Striated Thrush 42
Striped Hyena (*Hyaena hyaena*) 12, 74, 109, 113, **115**, 124, 132, **132**, 138, 150, 153
Stump-tailed Macaque 53
Sultan Tit 48
Swamp Partridge 37
Tailor Bird 75
Tawny Eagle 112
Thamin (Brow-antlered) Deer (*Cervus eldi eldi*) 51, **51**
Thick-billed Pigeon 61, 64
Three-striped Palm Squirrel 138
Tiny-eared Owl 153
Travancore Tortoise 159
Tree-pie 109, 114
Tree-pie Crow 100
Tufted Duck 111, 124
Varditar Flycatcher 97
Vine Snake 138, 168
Western Tragopan 28
Western Yellow-billed Blue Magpie 25
Whimbrel 121
Whiskered Tern 121
Whistling Teal **93**
White Ibis 112, 143, 155
White Stork (*Ciconia ciconia*) **144**
White Tiger 96
White-backed Vulture 100
White-bellied Fishing Eagle 121
White-bellied Sea Eagle 128
White-breasted Kingfisher (*Halcyon smyrnensis*) 74, **75**, 75, 114, 150, 168
White-browed Flycatcher 97
White-browed Ground Thrush 124

White-capped Redstart 33, 48
White-cheeked Bulbul 25
White-crested Thrush 33, 42
White-eyed Buzzard 84
White-eyed Buzzard Eagle 138
White-eyed Pochard 37
White-necked Stork 97, 109, 112, 133
White-rumped Shama (*Copsychus malabaricus*) **59**
White-throated Kingfisher (*Halcyon smyrnensis*) **168**
White-winged Wood Duck 42
Wigeon (*Anas penelope*) 32, 124, **125**
Wolf Snake 138, 147
Wood Owl 79
Yak (*Bos grunniens*) 170, **170**, 171
Yellow Bittern 44
Yellow Varanas **109**
Yellow Wagtail 48
Yellow-backed Sunbird 42, 54, 60
Yellow-bellied Flycatcher 75
Yellow-faced Leaf Warbler 54
Yellow-legged Pigeon 61, 64
Yellow-throated Marten 170

PHOTO CREDITS

Copyright rests with the photographers and/or agencies listed below.
Key to placement of pictures: b = bottom; bl = bottom left; br = bottom right; c = centre; cl = centre left; cr = centre right; i = inset; sfb = second from bottom; sft = second from top; sfl = second from left; sfr = second from right; t = top; tl = top left; tr = top right

BCC = Bruce Coleman Collection; NEWS = Nature Environment & Wildlife Society; Di = Dinodia; Ec = Ecoscene; FN = Foto Natura; FLPA = Frank Lane Picture Agency; GC = Gerald Cubitt; GI/TS = Gallo Images/Tony Stone; HA = Heather Angel; IE = Ibex Expeditions; NV = Natural Visions; PH = Paul Harris; SE/AB = Seeing Eye/Anders Blomqvist; TS = Toby Sinclair; TI = Travel Ink; WF = Wilderfile

1 GI/TS
2—3 GC
4—5 TS
6—7 GC
8–9 NEWS
10 GC
11 t, b TS
12 t Di/Pramod Mistry
　sft FN/Martin Harvey
　sfb TS
　b FLPA/Terry Whittaker
13 HA
14 tl, tr TS
15 t NEWS
　b GC
16 t FLPA/Terry Whittaker
　b NEWS
17 t FN/Jan Vermeer
　b FLPA/David Hosking
20 GC
21 GC
22 GC
23 GC
24 t, c, bl GC
25 tl, tr GC
　b FLPA/E. & D. Hosking
26 GC
27 GC
28 i GC
　l GC
　r FLPA/Mark Newman
29 GC
30 GC
31 GC
32 i FLPA/Mark Newman
　c FLPA/M. Ranjit
　b GC
33 t, b GC
34 GC
35 GC
36 t FLPA/Gerard Lacz
　b FLPA/Terry Whittaker
37 t GC
　b Ec/Neeraj Mishra
38 GC
39 GC
40 PH
41 FLPA/Terry Whittaker
42 t WF/G. B. Mukherji
　bl, br GC
43 WF
44 tl Ec/Neeraj Mishra
　tr GC
　b GC
45 t GC
　b FLPA/Ron Austing
46 t TS
　b WF/V. Muthuraman
47 FLPA/David Hosking
48 tl, tr TS

b GC
49 t TS
　bl FLPA/Frank Lane
　br FLPA/Mark Newman
50 GC
51 GC
52 NEWS
53 FLPA/Terry Whittaker
54 GC
55 HA
56 FLPA/Terry Whittaker
57 tl FLPA/Terry Whittaker
　tr GC
　c FLPA/David Hosking
　b HA
58 SE/AB
59 FLPA/David Hosking
60 t NEWS
　c FLPA/Gerard Lacz
　b GC
61 FLPA/Terry Whittaker
62 tl FLPA/Martin Withers
　bl NEWS
　tr Di/Isaac Kehimkar
　br FLPA/Tony Wharton
63 FLPA/William Clark
64 bl FLPA/Robin
　　Chittenden
　tr FLPA/Tony Whittaker
　br FLPA/J. & C. Johns
65 TI/David Forman
66 NEWS
67 GC
68 NEWS
69 GC
70 tl NEWS
　tr GC
71 WF/Vivek Sinha
72 NEWS
73 WF/E. Hanumantha Rao
74 t FLPA/David Hosking
　b NEWS
75 t Di
　b FLPA/Michael Gore
76 FLPA/Robin Chittenden
77 FLPA/T. & P. Gardner
78 t IE
　bl NEWS
　br HA
79 FN/Fritz Polking
80 bl FLPA/Winfried
　　Wisniewski
　tr Di/S Nagaraj
　br HA
81 Ec/Alan Towse
82 FLPA/Philip Perry
83 Ec/S. K. Tiwari
84 i FLPA/John Holmes
　tr WF/Vivek Sinha
　c, br FLPA/

E. & D. Hosking
85 FLPA/Winfried
　　Wisniewski
86 tl NV/Geoffrey Kinns
87 WF/Vivek Sinha
88 GC
89 GC
90 t FLPA/Robin Chittenden
　i FLPA/Terry Whittaker
90–91 GC
91 i FLPA/Chris Mattison
　r GC
92 TS
93 tl FLPA/E. & D. Hosking
　tr FLPA/T. & P. Gardner
　cl FLPA/H. D. Brandl
　cr FLPA/Roger
　　Wilmshurst
　b HA
　i FLPA/W. S. Clark
94 GC
95 GC
96 tl Di
　tr TS
　b GC
97 i Di/Isaac Kehimkar
　tr, b GC
98 t Di
　b GC
99 FLPA/FN
100 NEWS
101 t NEWS
　c, b IE
102–103 FN/Martin Harvey
104 GC
105 FN/René Krekels
106 tl FLPA/David Hosking
　bl GC
　r FLPA/Martin Withers
107 GC
108 i HA
　b GC
　br FLPA/Terry
　　Whittaker
　c TS
109 i WF/S. Karthikeyan
　br FLPA/
　　E. & D. Hosking
110 t GC
　bl FLPA/Winfried
　　Wisniewski
　br FLPA/John Bastable
111 FLPA/Winfried
Wisniewski
112 t TS
　i, tr, bl GC
　br NEWS
113 Di/Buraj N. Sharma
114 t Di/A Shvin Memta
　i Di/Isaac Kehimkar

115 tl, tr, bl, br GC
　c FN/Fred Hazelhoff
116 GI/TS/Philip Reeve
117 GC
118 t TS
　bl, c, br GC
119 FLPA/T. & P. Gardner
120 c FLPA/Terry Whittaker
　bl, br GC
　sfl Di/V. I. Thayil
　sfr FN/Jan Vermeer
121 t NEWS
　b GC
122 GC
123 FLPA/Jurgen Sohns
124 tl FLPA/Jurgen Sohns
　tc, tr Ec/M. Gore
124–125 Di/Anil. A
125 tl FLPA/Roger
　　Wilmshurst
　tc FLPA/C Brown
　tr FLPA/Martin Withers
　c Ec/Robert Baldwin
126 NEWS
127 Geoff Spiby
128 t NEWS
　c BCC/Alain Compost
　cr GI/Stefania Lamberti
129 FN
130 t TS
　b GC
131 TS
132 i TS
　bl FLPA/M. Ranjit
　br FLPA/Terry
　　Whittaker
133 t Di
　b GC
134–135 Di
136 GC
137 GC
138 tl GC
　tr FN/Nick Bergkesrel
　i WF/R. Saravanakumar
139 cl GC
　tr Ec/Neeraj Mishra
　cr FLPA/Mark Newman
　br FLPA/M Ranjit
140 GC
141 GC
142 t Di/M. Amirtham
　b WF/V. Muthuraman
143 FLPA/David Hosking
　i FLPA/Roger Tidman
144 cl FLPA/David Hosking
　tr FLPA/Pratap Surana
　sft FLPA/
　　E. & D. Hosking
　cl FLPA/W. S. Clark
　cr FLPA/Winfried

Wisniewski
　br GC
　i FLPA/Roger Tidman
145 Di
146 t TS
　b HA
147 t GC
　b GC
148 WF/R. Sukumar
149 GC
150 i GC
　tr Di/Isaac Kehimka
　br FLPA/Eichhorn
　　Zingel
151 GC
152 t WF/E. Hanumantha
　　Rao
　bl, br GC
153 t Di/V. I. Thayil
　i GC
154 Di/David Hosking
155 FLPA/John Holmes
156 WF/R. Saravanakumar
157 TS
158 PH
159 WF/S. Karthikeyan
160 tl WF/
　　R. Saravanakumar
　i FLPA/T. S. V. de Zylva
　b Di/V. I. Thayil
161 GC
162 GC
163 IE
164 NEWS
165 SE/AB
166 GC
167 GC
168 tl NEWS
　tr Carol Pollich
　b Carol Pollich
169 GC
170 tl PH
　bl, br Gouvault Haston
　cr FN/M. Boulton
171 SE/AB
176 FLPA/David Hosking